Knowledge Is Power—
and the Key to Detecting Bargains

Soon you'll know…

❖ how to judge the age of a garment from the care label
❖ what the rolled edge of a scarf reveals about its quality
❖ what to wear when shopping at a thrift store—or any shop without a dressing room
❖ which hats you should never pass up
❖ the do's and don'ts of buying at auctions
❖ how to measure waistbands—with your fingers!
❖ the pitfalls of "diffusion lines"—similar name, different quality
❖ how to buy resale in London, Paris, Amsterdam, Geneva—and more!

No Matter Where You Buy, Get the Best!

Secondhand Chic

Secondhand Chic

Finding Fabulous Fashion
at Consignment, Vintage,
and Thrift Stores

Christa Weil

ILLUSTRATIONS BY CHLOË MARCH

POCKET BOOKS
New York London Toronto Sydney Tokyo Singapore

An *Original* Publication of POCKET BOOKS

POCKET BOOKS, a division of Simon & Schuster Inc.
1230 Avenue of the Americas, New York, NY 10020

Library of Congress Cataloging-in-Publication Data

Weil, Christa.
Secondhand chic : finding fabulous fashion at consignment, vintage, and thrift stores / Christa Weil ; illustrations by Chloë March.
p. cm.
ISBN: 0-671-02713-1
1. Shopping Guidebooks. 2. Used clothing industry Guidebooks. I. Title.
TX335.W36 1999
380.1'45—dc21 99-30443

First Pocket Books trade paperback printing July 1999

10 9 8 7 6 5 4 3 2 1

POCKET and colophon are registered trademarks of Simon & Schuster Inc.

Interior illustrations by Chloë March
Cover design by Jeanne M. Lee, front cover illustration by Chloë March
Book design by Laura Lindgren and Celia Fuller

Printed in the U.S.A.

RRDH/

To Mom and Dad

Contents

PART 3

Tender Loving Clothes Care

PART 4

Getting the Most out of Secondhand Stores

Introduction

*I*f you've ever shopped at a consignment, vintage, or thrift store, you know that with good judgment, patience, and a little luck, you can get incredible value for your money. Why? The prices—even for brand-new, top-quality pieces—are oftentimes shockingly low. The sale of secondhand clothing is a "secondary market," like the one for used cars. But unlike the used-car market, clothing resale has no points of reference like the *Blue Book* (which lists dollar figures for specific vehicle models and years). No two people will agree on how much a secondhand garment should cost. In a consignment or a vintage store (defined on pages 16–18), prices are based on the owner's "feel" for the market. In thrift stores, prices are often set by rote. What this means is that a two-year-old Donna Karan jacket that originally retailed for $450 might show up at the consignment store around the corner for $300, the one across town at $150, and the thrift store in between at $25, just like every other jacket on the rack. Crazy? You bet. For shoppers who know how to spot value, this translates into incredible deals.

THE NAME OF THE GAME

Getting good value is the key to winning the secondhand shopping game. What's important to keep in mind is that value, like a coin, has two sides. A garment is valuable in one sense because it's beautifully made, using fine materials. In another, a garment is valuable because it's perfect for your figure, personal style, budget, and current wardrobe. One of the biggest problems with resale shopping is that we sometimes lose sight of the second side of the coin. After all, who could resist a barely worn Jones New York suit going for $50? A pair of Calvin Klein jeans marked down to $15? New Nine West pumps priced at $20? So heady are the opportunities to get great deals the temptation is to run wild—to bolster our wardrobes, or to get the rush that comes with beating the system. But, as with a lot of rushes, a crash is liable to follow. Once you get home and try on that Jones suit, you realize the mustard-yellow color makes you look like a zombie. Or the so-called Calvin Klein jeans are, on closer inspection, Calvin Krein jeans, and judging by the state of the seams, barely worth 50 cents. Or those beautiful pumps, so pristine, so stylish, are also so narrow you can barely stand walking across the room. All these incredible bargains are practically worthless because you can't wear them at all.

PICKING WINNERS

But don't a few mistakes come with the territory? Doesn't the nature of secondhand shopping, with its huge variety of merchandise, unregulated sizing, inconsistent standards, and again, crazy prices, lend itself to occasional bad judgment? Of course it does. But I'm convinced it is possible to minimize mistakes. It comes down to that simple concept, value. Resale shoppers who can spot the two kinds of value—the kind based on quality and the kind based on personal needs—have made themselves *connoisseurs* of all-around excellence in clothing. These women are well on their way to having a world-class wardrobe—or at the very least, the best on the block.

What Exactly Is a Connoisseur? *Webster's Third International Dictionary* defines a connoisseur as "one who understands the details, technique, or principles of an art and is competent to act as a critical judge." Connoisseurs aren't only found in the Picasso and Monet aisles of the fine arts world. In fact, you probably know a few already—the friend who gets down on her knees at tag sales, not to give thanks for her finds, but to check the underside of an old sofa, knowing that the ratty upholstery might be disguising an antique treasure. Or maybe your kid, the computer-games whiz, who knows Lara Croft better than her programmers. Or your aunt in the kitchen with her prize-winning deep-dish apple pie. These people are all connoisseurs; maybe you are too, but just never thought about it that way. Possibly because expertise came so easily. Connoisseurship is nothing more than passionate interest backed by understanding gained from good books, teachers, or experience. The kind of study that gets you connoisseurship is usually painless and most often a joy, because your driving interest makes learning fun. Let's go back to your buddy at the tag sale. What's she looking for? Signs, indicators, clues—these help her peg the value of the piece. What kind of wood did the maker use? Is it neatly varnished even where it's out of direct sight? What kind of joins hold it together? Is it glued, nailed, or dovetailed? How about the decorative elements—is that scrollwork hand-carved? Is there any evidence of repairs? This is connoisseurship. It's exactly the kind of expertise we should all be using to find the best values at resale. Only for us it translates into questions like: how good or unusual is this fabric? Is the buttonhole hand-sewn? How are the seams finished? Where are the flaws?

Why Connois-
seurship Helps
You Shop
Secondhand

Connoisseurship is important for a couple of reasons. Every experienced consignment, vintage, or thrift-store shopper has the same gripe: resale shopping takes an awful lot of time. At the thrift stores, you have to weed through racks and racks of no-gos to find a few pieces worth a second look. At consignment and often at vintage, the quality is prescreened, but still there are no guarantees. *Here is where connoisseurship comes in.* Once you have strengthened your expertise, you will be able to move down a rack at speed. Your fingertips will be sensitized to top-quality fabrics. Your eyes will latch onto the properly set-in shoulder, the expensive button, the extraordinary tweed. In this way, you go straight to the best goods, leaving the other stuff behind for less choosy shoppers. The early chapters of

Secondhand Chic are dedicated to developing these abilities. Some of the topics covered in Chapters 3 through 6 include:

- how to use your senses of sight, touch, and, yes, even smell to determine the relative quality of a fabric
- how to build your expertise in materials and workmanship
- how to recognize the details that spell deluxe manufacture, as well as the shortcuts that indicate cheaper goods
- what to look for in individual items of clothing, such as skirts, pants, jackets, etc.
- how to decode labels

GETTING TO KNOW VALUE AT THE SOURCE

Connoisseurship doesn't exist in a vacuum. Some secondhand queens swear they never set foot in department stores or boutiques. While I understand their pride, I still think they're out of their minds. In Chapter 4, I'll explain why you should nurture your connoisseurship in the most exclusive shops you can find. These offer what amounts to a Grade-A education in quality. As long as you handle finer goods with respect (after all, real craftspeople made them), there's no reason not to take advantage of looking, touching, trying on. What's more, doing fieldwork in retail is the only way to get a realistic sense of prices, which will only make you feel better when you find a resale steal.

Why You Can't Count on Labels

At this point, you might be thinking: "Who needs all this work? I can peg value by looking at the label." My argument is that *labels can be very misleading.* Here's why:

The rise of diffusion lines. Spot quiz—rank these labels according to price point/quality: Emporio Armani, Armani A/X, Mani, Giorgio Armani Collezione. If this posed no problem, I tip my fedora. Are you as good with Donna Karan's diffusion lines, or MaxMara's? Even department store private labels have gone multilayer. Unless you have a photographic memory for the relative rankings, labels may only confuse the issue. Your ability to detect quality operates independently.

Some top-name pieces may be made specifically for outlet stores. Naturally these items are cheaper than their haute-couture counterparts. And it's only logical that the quality follows suit. Here's where relying on labels gets dangerous. Say you snap up a brand-new Brand X dress at your local consignment store, thinking it's a great value at $80. Everything's rosy until the following weekend, when you run into the same dress at the outlet village—ticketed at $75. Consignment-store owners can be as easily swayed by labels as the rest of us. This is why I go into such detail about construction, which can tell a fascinating story about a garment's place in the hierarchy.

Quality fluctuates from year to year. How many times have you walked through a department store or major chain and said, "There's nothing here this year; it's gone totally downhill." This probably isn't your imagination. Myriad factors go into the manufacture of proprietary lines, and all can affect the end result. For example, the new style director over at the mall store we'll call Ashbot's might have very peculiar ideas about the colors women want. Or, more drastically, the company's stock has taken a swan dive, and cost efficiencies have been made across the board, translating directly into the quality you see on the racks. Or, more positively, the company has sourced a great new supplier who provides heavyweight worsteds to rival Armani's. The point is, you can't judge a garment solely by its label, and shouldn't, because there are so many other factors to look for.

You're not going to recognize every label. Unless you're a global shopper in all price points, in which case you could teach me a thousand things or two. But say you aren't, and say you come across a label reading St. Michael. Who the heck is St. Michael? It sounds suspicious, like the name on the stuff that falls off trucks. So you pass it by. But it turns out this is the house brand of the Marks & Spencer chain in England, which happens to make fine quality midpriced clothing. One way around the foreign label problem is to memorize the list provided in Chapter 4. But over the long run, it's actually easier to supercharge your ability to spot value. This is especially true if you shop at vintage-clothing stores, which feature long-gone labels from decades past, or if you shop overseas, where a high percentage will be unfamiliar. (International resale is discussed, by the way, in Chapter 17.)

Counterfeiters are getting rich thanks to our love of labels. In resale and even in off-priced retail, counterfeit clothing is known to crop up. I spotted a piece the other day at one of my local thrifts, a wool skirt labeled Philippe Adec, a very classy French brand. Very unclassily, it had no lining and a snap closure. No way, I thought, and moved right along. It's not just the criminals who are passing along counterfeit goods—good guys are too, in the form of Arizona customs agents, who have turned bogus brands they've confiscated over to local charities, with the go-ahead of the trademark holders.

Crooked resellers like the label game too. In a recent troll of thrifts in New York City, I came across Yves Saint Laurent labels that had been snipped out of the original pieces and sewn into inferior garments. The stitching was a dead giveaway—à la Frankenstein—but when the crooks wise up, this may not always be true.

All this is by way of saying that you can't trust a tag—or, more accurately, what you think you know about a tag—to accurately peg the quality of clothing. Funnily enough, as little as 50 years ago, we would have known better anyway. Why? Because dressmaking and tailoring would have been one of our skills. We could finger the difference between good fabric and the shoddy stuff. We could evaluate the merits of different closures, because the money to buy them came direct from our purse. Today, when most of us wouldn't dream of making our own clothing, the ability to discern quality has also largely been lost.

How to Make Value Work for You

Along with the ability to spot the best, I believe we've lost another skill. Remember that value has two parts? Besides objective value, there's value based on how well a garment works for you. One of the most important elements of this is fit. Many of us have a real problem here. Why? I suspect it's because finding clothes that look tailor-made requires looking at our bodies exactly *as they are*—without loathing, but also without mercy. If the thought gives you shivers, think about all the Hollywood stars of the 1940s and 1950s. They always looked great, not because they weighed 110 pounds, but because their clothing fit beautifully and flattered the best elements of their figures. Sadly, none of us has arch-costumer Edith Head at our disposal, but we can learn from her tricks—things like how garments should fall across the shoulders; which hemline best suits our legs; the cuts and styles that work best with our figures; the silhouettes that will always be classics; and how to alter an outfit so it looks like it was sewn on. All this being said, consignment, vintage, and thrift stores can be especially challenging when it comes to finding the right fit. What's more, the trying-on situation in your standard thrift isn't much better than somebody's attic. However, armed with the tips provided in Chapters 7 and 8, you'll have a dramatically improved sense of what works and doesn't work for you.

I Love It; I'm Not Going to Buy It

Other aspects of personal value include knowing how a piece will work with what you already own, and making an informed buying decision on that basis. At the risk of your chucking this book out the window: most of us have too many clothes. Someone once estimated that we wear 30 percent of our wardrobe 70 percent of the time. It may be unscientific, but it sounds about right. It means an awful lot of clothing is just sitting there, crowding up the closet, arguably adding to the jumble in our minds. If you have a king-size closet (or a king-size mind) then this isn't a problem, but if yours are like mine, the crunch factor quickly gets critical. As resale shoppers, our problems are even worse, for we tend to buy piece by spontaneous piece. Carried too far, this can result in a mishmash of colors, shapes, and styles. This is why, in Chapter 8, I set out a plan for rationalizing your wardrobe: putting together a style template of basic pieces, and establishing a system for filling in gaps.

Maintaining Value after Purchase

One of the best things about secondhand is that if you buy a piece of extremely high quality, and you care for it properly, it will wear well for years, long past the point at which retail trendwear gives up the ghost. Proper care is extremely important. In Chapters 11 and 12, I'll describe the best methods for cleaning, mending, and storing clothes of all kinds.

Once you've read the chapters dealing with personal value, you'll have a much clearer idea of what you need in order to always look great. The areas covered will include:

❖ what pieces not to buy, under any circumstances
❖ which flaws aren't all that bad
❖ how to ensure good fit, especially under the often difficult trying-on situation of thrift stores
❖ how to peg your best styles, colors, and proportions
❖ how to ensure the long life of your clothes

Gaining Value after Purchase

A few pages ago, I called the consignment, vintage, and thrift realms a "secondary market" for clothing. But that's not telling the whole story. Increasingly, clothes, particularly at the very high end, are being sold and resold three, four, and five times. Their quality and the good name of their makers have made these items a "commodity." In a few rare cases, as with a couture suit of a particular vintage, it is possible to buy at resale for $1,500, wear it for a few years, then sell it again at a higher price. That's right. Some fortunate few women actually make a profit recycling their wardrobes. The rest of us connoisseurs are satisfied to regain a portion of our initial investment. In Chapter 16, I'll show you how.

THE BIG WRAP-UP

This book offers no magic formula. Learning the principles and applying them effectively takes time and practice. Never mind the often-hyped formula of self-improvement in five minutes or less. We all know that real change takes longer. It takes commitment and discipline to do anything well, and that includes becoming a resale connoisseur. That being said, if you don't have the time or the avid interest, you don't have to read this book cover to cover. Dip in here and there, and apply the strategies where you can. Even a few tips should pay off big, making you a better resale—and all-around—shopper.

PART 1

The Secondhand Fashion Fundamentals

Chapter One

———— ✧ ————

All About
the Secondhand Market

"Secondhand clothes have gone uptown. Cities such as Boston,
Los Angeles and Washington D.C. now have used apparel stores
that resemble upscale boutiques in everything but their pricetags."

—*Money*, June 1996

"It's fascinating to see how this thrifty pastime has changed
into a fashion phenomenon."

—*Time Out*, January 1998

"Mimicking some of their uptown retail cousins, many used-
clothing retailers are offering quality merchandise, attractive
displays and comfortable spaces that make them look like any
other store. Used-clothing companies have also ditched the
'thrift-store' moniker and call themselves resale shops or
vintage stores. Call them what you will, but the trend is clear:
Americans are spending more money on used stuff."

—ABCNEWS.com, October 1998

It seems you can't open a maga-
zine or turn on the TV lately without getting word about the rise of
secondhand clothes. The consignment, vintage, and thrift modes of
shopping—indeed, the resale of everything from sporting goods to
computers—is losing its air of down and out, and attracting a grow-

ing middle-class market. According to the National Association of Resale and Thrift Stores (NARTS), there are over 15,000 resale shops in the U.S. The association itself currently has over 1,000 members. Receiving about 200 inquiries per month, it is growing at 15 percent per year.

While the wide-scale interest is a relatively new phenomenon, the business itself is not. It's a good bet that the first used-clothing transaction took place in a cave. Since then, the resale business has had a long, successful, and extremely colorful history. Take a peek at a Victorian London market, through the eyes of a 19th-century reporter:

"THIRTY CLAMS?...WITH **THIS** TEAR?....I WANT A MAMMOTH REDUCTION"

Petticoat Lane is essentially the old clothes district. Embracing the street and alleys adjacent to Petticoat Lane and including the rows of old boots and shoes on the ground, there is perhaps two or three miles of old clothes...gowns of every shade and pattern are hanging up. Dress coats, frock coats, great coats, livery and game keepers coats, paletots, tunics, trousers, knee breeches, waistcoats, capes, pilot coats, working jackets, plaids, hats, dressing gowns, skirts, Guernsey frocks, are all displayed.

Odds are this is where Dickens's Oliver Twist would have come to fill out his wardrobe (and here too his master Fagin would send boys to sell their nicked wares). The market was a rowdy place. The reporter went on to explain that "clothes first come through the Old Clothes Exchange. The Exchange had been so noisy that the East India Company, who had warehouses nearby, complained; sometimes it took 200 constables to keep order." Just imagine what it was like during sales.

If Petticoat Lane is a bit too reminiscent of the nasty old clichés about resale, why don't we look back even further, to the royal courts of France, where exacting rituals of dress and decorum reigned. *Culture of Clothing,* a sociological history of clothing in that country, notes that the tax records of the mid-18th century list approximately 1,700 resellers of clothing in Paris. At the high end was the so-called *revendeuse à la toilette* (a reseller who visited during the noblewomen's lengthy, gossipy get-up sessions before they appeared in court). Revendeuses bought and sold old fabrics, lace, jewels, and other items from the rich and resold them to equally upper-class customers. They can be seen in engravings of the period acting as "both confidantes and merchants at the morning toilets of the ladies."

Just like it was in the past, today's secondhand business is stratified, with different stores aimed at different segments of society. What's different now is the crossover—the well-heeled are haunting the dingiest of thrifts, and the hard-pressed for cash are shopping at the snootiest of consignment stores. Moreover, today we're seeing a rise in specialty resale stores, such as Transfer in New York City's Soho, which features garments (mostly sizes 4, 6, and 8) straight from the catwalk and magazine feature shoots.

FIRST THINGS FIRST: A FEW DEFINITIONS

Consignment   This is a place where women who want to dispose of certain wardrobe items can resell them, with the store acting as middleman. Here's how it works. Our consignor, let's call her Mrs. Pink, recently lost 20 pounds and can no longer wear her lovely wool skirt, from the mall store called Ashbot's, purchased a year ago for $100. When she brings the skirt in, the store owner or manager will take a hard look, making sure it is clean (a must), free of damage and obvious signs of wear, of a recent season (though this is not always necessary), and suitable for the store's clientele. If they accept it, the store could tag the skirt at anything from $5 to $500, but most likely somewhere in the range of $30 to $90. If the garment sells, most stores will pay Mrs. Pink 40 to 60 percent of the selling price. The store will display the piece for an average of 60 to 90 days. If it doesn't sell at the original price after a set period, it may be marked down. If it still hasn't sold within an agreed-upon period (often another six to eight weeks), Mrs. Pink must reclaim it. If it does sell, she collects a check.

Many consignment stores stand in sequined reproach to the bad old reputation of resale—they can be as exquisite as the best boutiques in town. And guess who is in the back office, agreeing on prices for last season's castoffs? The cream of local society, my dear—but the good stores properly keep this mum. In fact, Carole Selig, owner of Encore on New York's Madison Avenue, said to be the oldest consignment store in the country, would only confirm that Jackie Onassis had been a frequent consignor because the story had already been published. The identities of her other consignors? She diplomatically refuses to say. This is not to imply that all consignment stores carry *only* haute-couture goods; quite the opposite. Most, like Buy Popular Demand in Chicago, stock Ann Taylor and Gap along with high-end gowns, maximizing their appeal to a wide range of clients.

Advantages of Shopping at Consignment Stores
Time savings—the items have been prescreened by the management.
Rational display—usually the clothing is sized, and sometimes arranged by color. Sale goods are often on a special rack.
Consistency of goods—the owner's taste prescreens the merchandise—either you like it or you don't.
Condition of clothing—most stores accept only dry-cleaned clothes, on hangers, with little sign of wear.
Real dressing rooms—you'll have privacy and good lighting.
Markdown policy—pricing can range anywhere from 25 percent (for brand new, current season items) to 75 percent off the retail cost. Extreme bargains to be found if store holds clearance sales.
Service—frequent customers get preferential treatment.

Disadvantages of Shopping at Consignment Stores
High $$$—reflecting original cost of garments.
Attitude—while the vast majority of stores offer a warm welcome, some can be snobby.

Vintage Vintage (or "retro") clothing stores specialize in older and antique fashions. Here the merchandise may range from Huckapoo polyester shirts to Lily Pulitzer golf shorts to Balenciaga ballgowns, depending on the tastes of the owner and her clientele. In larger cities, vintage stores may specialize in certain fashion eras. Store owners generally purchase their stock from vintage-clothes wholesalers, from individuals like you and me who have been clearing out the attic, or from thrift stores.

Advantages of Shopping at Vintage-Clothes Stores
Distinctiveness—most of the items are truly one-of-a-kind.
Volume—if you love Victorian lace, you'll find it in quantity if you find the right store.

Craftsmanship—the better clothing of the past has construction to
   die for.
Research opportunities—vintage stores are like style museums. You
   can learn even if you don't care to buy.

Disadvantages of Shopping at Vintage-Clothes Stores
Possible high $$$—reflecting rarity of the garments.
Fragility—many of the clothes are too delicate for everyday wear.
Condition—not always impeccable.
Sizes—can be very tricky to get right.

Thrift The majority of giant thrift-store chains, including those run by the
Salvation Army, Goodwill, and the Junior League, are not-for-profit
operations, offering acres of goods, including housewares, furniture,
and books, at very reasonable (and often astonishing) prices. The
merchandise is obtained mainly through individual donations, but
sometimes also by special arrangements with retail stores and/or
manufacturers. Single-store thrifts may be nonprofit (usually run by
local charitable organizations), or for-profit. Fairly new to the thrift-
store scene are charity-affiliated for-profit thrift chains, such as
TVI/Value Village, and so-called "resale" stores, like Buffalo Exchange,
which buys garments directly from the public and resells at a profit.
Traditionally, thrift-store shopping has demanded hard-core connois-
seurship (and stamina), yet in many parts of the country stores are
increasingly catering to middle-class customers. Many stores now
feature "designer racks" and pricing policies that demonstrate a new
awareness about the value of their wares.

Advantages of Shopping at Thrift Stores
Bargains—the best are found here.
Atmosphere—for-profit thrifts often feature retail-like environments
   and organization of merchandise.
Variety—new merchandise is constantly coming in.
New clothes available—thanks to manufacturers and others donating
   unsold goods.

Comprehensive—most thrifts sell everything, making it possible to
put together an outfit, right down to scarf and shoes, in one place.

"Designer racks"—featured in many thrifts, helps hone search down.

Charitable—you're supporting a worthy cause by buying there.

Disadvantages of Shopping at Thrift Stores

Atmosphere—not-for-profit thrifts may be run down.

Time requirements—lots of time needed to shop stores fully.

Condition of clothes—there is no guarantee that clothes are clean,
much less in good condition.

Lack of rationale in display—clothes often unsized, and haphazardly
arranged.

Fitting rooms—in some nonprofits, it's a case of "What fitting rooms?"

OTHER KEY STUFF ABOUT SECONDHAND:
WHO, WHERE, AND WHY

*Who Are the
People Who
Shop Resale?*

As a rule, the people who shop in consignment stores are indistinguishable from those in your standard mall store—except, perhaps,
that they aspire to a better class of clothing. In vintage and thrift
stores, the shoppers tend to be more colorful. Let's start off with
some stereotypes, shall we?

The Bargain Queen: Wild-eyed, she charges in from the
parking lot, hugging the rack so you have to go around,
trying on everything from raccoon coats to motorcycle
helmets, buying up sacks and sacks of *schmatte* that will
sit untouched in her closet until it all gets dumped off at the
next thrift down the pike. She's there for the thrill of the chase.

The Dotty Grande Dame: Wearing enough gold to set off a metal
detector, she glares at the customers who dare glance at her.
Gets into yanking matches with other rich old gals for some
scuffed-up handbag that she "saw first."

Bizarrely Coiffed Anarchists: Making a transgressive statement by mixing plaid with fake ponyskin. Multiply pierced. Known to try on clothing over what's already on, buy it, and wear it out the door.

The Ill-washed: Unerringly, they detect your kind heart and want to be your best friend.

Irony-mongers: They hold up any item dating to the 1970s and, in very loud tones, make knowing references to TV shows that didn't merit viewers the first time round, never mind eternal life on cable. May be discussing your outfit behind your back.

Yes, on any given day, there will probably be a few of these types trolling the racks. They are part of the ambiance, and frankly, are a heck of a lot more entertaining than the crowd over at the White Oaks Mall. Oddly enough, the one kind of person you rarely see at thrift stores is the aggressively obnoxious. Thrift-store staffers, many of whom may have come up from hardship, have little patience for somebody who is blatantly disturbing the peace.

And then there are the rest of the shoppers. Many are so-called "creatives"—singers, dancers, actors, artists, musicians, writers, and the like—people who are working in fields notorious for being "gratifying" while paying jack. Others may be employed in subsistence-wage fields, such as nonprofit, publishing, or social services. Still others may be students, or those in the pre-bucks, trainee stages of their jobs, like medical interns and apprentice tradespeople. Others are traditional working people of all kinds—from attorneys to zookeepers—who want a solid work and leisure wardrobe but are offended by the prices these command at retail. Then there are mothers saving for a mortgage or the kids' education, but need—as we all do now and again—to spend a few dollars on themselves. The list goes on. That skinny girl over at the shoe rack wearing the killer leather jeans? She's a freelance stylist working for a top fashion magazine, hunting down a pair of pumps to counterbalance the luxe of a couture ballgown. That big guy with the little helper running ahead, tossing back garments for inspection? He's Gianfranco Ferré—he designed the ballgown.

Where Do I Find Stores? Check the Yellow Pages (see *Charitable Organizations; Consignment; Resale; Thrift Stores; Women's Apparel, used*). If you have access to the Internet, look up Thrift, Consignment, and Resale on a good search engine to find page upon page of listings. In England, look in the Yellow Pages under *Ladies' Clothing, Charity Shops*. In France, look in the Yellow Pages or have someone check the Minitel for *Dépot-Ventes* and *Vête- ments—Griffes*. Perhaps one of the best methods of all is to talk to your fellow resale shoppers. Like all good hobbyists, they're apt to happily share information and lore.

How Do I Convince My Sister that There's Nothing Tawdry about Resale? She still needs convincing? How behind the times. Why don't we start by picking apart her arguments:

Those clothes are dirty. Well, sometimes, if acquired from thrift, resale, or certain vintage stores, they may be. But you should remind her that garments aren't necessarily spick-and-span in retail stores, either, especially toward the end of the season, by which time hundreds of people may have tried a blouse on, smeared it with Chapstick, stepped on it, borrowed it for a night out, etc. Another good argument if she goes to a gym: she'll pick up a lot more cooties off an aerobics mat or weight machine than she'll ever encounter at a thrift store. The capper? If she's paying $15 instead of $80 for a garment, she can get it dry-cleaned three times over and still have money left for shoes. If she remains squeamish, you can point her toward consignment stores, whose policies demand that merchandise be professionally cleaned.

Those stores are depressing. Here again, everything's relative. I can think of nothing more depressing than going into Ashbot's at the tail end of a Saturday to find a bedlam of garments tossed here and there, items missized, dressing rooms filled with other people's no-gos, and salespeople nursing the career option of mass murderer. All this and I'm still paying full price? Nuh-uh. I'd rather shop in a comparably squalorous thrift store, knowing that lovely pieces are probably wildly underpriced, particularly labels that are unfamiliar. Again, if this argument doesn't work, you can point your sister toward consignment stores and those thrifts that make a point of presenting a pleasant atmosphere.

Aren't thrift stores supposed to be for poor people? Those experiencing hard times do shop at thrift stores, it only makes sense. But the stores are not intended for any one kind of customer. The reason thrift stores are in existence is not to provide shopping opportunities for the disadvantaged, it is to gain revenue for their programs. Goodwill Industries, for example, made half of their total revenue in 1998 from their chain of thrift stores. This money is in turn refunneled into their community projects. The more people making purchases, the better off the organization is, so there is no reason to feel guilty spending money there.

I've been in one of those places and the prices weren't that much better than retail. Odds are, the place was a high-end consignment or vintage-clothing store, which can and will sell garments for prices miles beyond those found at middle-market retailers. Your sister should bear in mind that a beautiful blouse that costs $200 new is, for some, still a bargain at $75. She should keep looking. There are plenty of stores out there for every pocketbook.

There's so much to weed through! Yes. But tell her she'll be getting an education as she goes, especially if she uses guidance from this book. Once she's worked her way through a couple hundred white T-shirts, she will never again settle for any old T-shirt anywhere, because the potential variations—in cotton weight, color, stitching, seams, cut—will be obvious even in a garment this minimal. By becoming familiar with the possibilities, by using her eyes, fingertips, and know-how, she'll learn *what she requires of a piece of clothing,* becoming a more efficient, smarter shopper in the long run.

It takes too much time to find pieces I can wear. This is the downside of shopping resale. In thrift stores, the garments may not be arranged by size, and tags may be missing. She could hunt for hours and still come up empty-handed. However, this book will help both you and your sister learn to find high-quality clothing by the systematic use of sight and touch, and then make realistic judgments about how well those clothes work, given your individual styles. With time it's possible to become a faster, more efficient, and more effective shopper. What's more, all the lessons here can and should be carried over to retail, where, in case she's forgotten, it also takes too long to find wearable pieces.

I don't like to shop that way; I can afford to buy new. This means she can also afford to pay for things like the retailer's overhead (the slacker sales help), advertising (employment opportunities for supermodels), and business decisions made up the line (executive buying trips to Paris, all expenses paid). Sure, she can afford it. But does she really want to?

She's Still Not Convinced.   What else can I tell her about the benefits of secondhand?

Lower cost. This is the obvious one, the biggie. Never mind $2,000 couture suits popping up at Goodwill for $50 or less. Sadly, this doesn't happen every week. What does happen is major retailers like JCPenney supply overstock and irregular goods through surplus merchandising programs, resulting in amazing savings on everyday items. Read between the lines, and we come to the next point.

Often, the garments up for resale are brand new. Apart from retailers looking to get tax or other benefits from unsold merchandise, there are some crazy shoppers out there, people who regularly flood the secondhand market with new goods. You probably know one. Maybe you are one. I'm talking about women who love shopping so much, they buy simply because they were born to. Once they've purchased that adorable black dinner bag, it instantly loses all allure. So off it goes to resale, labels intact. Compulsive shoppers are ladies I'm very thankful for. Others contributing to the new-merchandise flow include:

- women who have recently lost or gained weight, or who buy clothing as a futile incentive to do so
- disfavored boyfriends and ex-husbands, whose gifts of clothing will never—*ever*—be worn
- garment-industry insiders who are a legitimate source of sample merchandise
- people like us who make mistakes, especially when it comes to shoes

You can build a humongous wardrobe shopping secondhand. Though I advise against this in Chapter 8, many of you die-hards will merrily ignore it. For you, resale is a way to have wardrobe abondanza for minimal investment. How good you look is another thing altogether—again, see Chapter 8.

Resale can help you determine your best style option. A thrift, vintage, or consignment store can stock a wider variety of styles, colors, and makes than a standard store could ever possibly afford. Granted, they're not all your size, but secondhand nonetheless offers the chance to try on countless different styles—not to buy, necessarily, but to learn which looks best flatter you. This is especially true when conventional stores are all beaming down the same three gimmicks from the designer universe, i.e., ankle-length skirts, midriff tops, and acid green.

If you're an experienced secondhand shopper, you can pull a complete outfit together more easily than in a retail store. Department and chain stores do have resale beat in terms of coordinating tops to bottoms in a single line, but if you know your stuff you can work wonders in a resale store, because most stock not only clothing, but shoes, scarves, bags, and jewelry, all within an easy walk of each other.

Personalized service. If you are a steady customer at an on-the-ball con-signment store, you can expect a level of service akin to that offered by personal shoppers at places like Bloomingdale's and Nordstrom. The store owner will call you when pieces arrive in your size and style, and act as a partner in helping build your wardrobe. Even if you are a first-time customer, a good consignment store should offer the kind of warmth and attention that is hard to come by at the mall.

You'll get honest opinions from sales staff and other customers. As Veronica Lytle, owner of My Secret in Orange, CT, told me: "It does me no good to tell a customer something looks great when it doesn't. If she goes to a party and tells her friends where she bought the dress, I want everybody thinking she looks wonderful." These words were echoed by every consignment-store owner I've spoken to. They have a big stake in making clients look good. In thrift stores, you can also get honest opinions, especially from your fellow shoppers, some of whom live to give opinions.

It's a social experience unlike any other. Thrift and consignment stores are some of the few places I know where people of completely differ-ent backgrounds can have instant, mutually gratifying conversations about their one common interest. The inclination is natural for peo-ple to go girlfriend: chitchat, swap advice, offer opinions. Back in the 1850s, when the first department stores opened in Paris, they were an instant hit, historians say, because they offered price tags (previously, people had to ask), a wide range of stock, and the opportunity to browse. The fact that many other women were there doing the same thing only made it more enjoyable. Today, while retail stores can be oddly alienating places, at resale, some of the old magic still holds.

It's a chance to use your wits. Cunning is a vastly underrated quality when it comes to the shopping experience. At retail, it takes no brains at all to assemble an outfit the magazines say is hot, plop it down at the reg-ister, and go. But at resale, you have to be on your toes. At a very basic level, it's firing up the old hunt-and-gather instincts. But it holds the possibility of another ancient skill as well: negotiation. (How, when, and where to negotiate is discussed in Chapters 13, 15, and 16.)

You can get better long-term value for your money at resale. Given the quality of the fabric, workmanship, and trimmings, a previously owned jacket made to superior standards will look better and wear longer than new garments made to inferior standards. This is why an Yves Saint Laurent couture piece ends its life in a fashion museum, while a lesser imitator ends up in a landfill.

Speaking of which: resale is good for the environment. We've all heard about the waste stream, the overconsumption of resources, the ecological and even psychological damage that accompanies the apparel-manufacturing process, most notably in the Third World. Where our grandparents would have mended, altered, and handed down garments until they fell apart, we have become accustomed to the idea of disposable goods. Of the household waste generated per family in the U.S., about 3 to 5 percent consists of textiles. In addition to this clogging of landfills, we need to account for the environmental cost of making the textiles in the first place. Huge volumes of waste water are generated in their manufacture, water that may contain heavy metals from the dyeing process, as well as runoff dyes themselves. Growing cotton efficiently requires pesticides and fertilizer, and oil is consumed in the manufacture of synthetic fibers. By making the decision to purchase secondhand clothing, you are helping to prolong the useful life of a garment, reducing waste, and amortizing the cost of its manufacture upon the environment.

By shopping at thrift stores, you are supporting the efforts of vital charities. Nonprofit thrift stores not only help pay for charitable programs that are increasingly necessary as government funding diminishes, they also provide jobs for the people who work there.

Shopping secondhand helps local business. Megaretailing is a fact of modern life, with every mall in every city across the country featuring the usual round of identikit stores. The rise of mall culture has taken a toll on small business owners, particularly in downtown areas, because these operations are not able to compete when it comes to buying power and price-cutting policies. Yet one kind of business has flourished in the face of monster retailing—that's right, resale. The people running these places are your neighbors, part of your community in a way that Sam Walton will never be. Shopping secondhand doesn't just keep good clothing going, it keeps good people going too.

OK? But before your sister guns the Fiesta, ready to beeline off to Goodwill, settle her down and tell her to spend some time looking through the rest of this book. It will pay off. What with the money she saves and the value she adds as a clothing connoisseur, she might even share some of her best finds with you.

Chapter Two

◈

The Wonders That We Weave: Fabrics and How They Got That Way

$f$abric never forgets where it came from. Even after it's sheared, combed, carded, spun, and knitted into a pullover sweater, wool acts largely like it did back when it was on the back of a sheep. The same is true for all fibers, from linen—arguably the oldest one woven by man—to the latest synthetic wonder from the textile lab.

Getting to know fabrics is the foundation of clothing connoisseurship. Understanding specific fibers—their advantages and peculiarities and downsides—is the first step to becoming an expert about quality. In this chapter, we'll take a quick look at how fabrics are made, then go up close and personal with the most popular natural and artificial fibers. This sets the stage for Chapter 3, which is devoted to training your eyes and hands to hone in on exactly what you're looking for. You will be amazed at how even a little extra knowledge pays off. After reading this chapter and the next, you'll find it a lot easier to zero in on the fabric you love best, be it Sea Island cotton or doubleknit polyester. With your new savvy, you'll also set higher personal standards, limiting your search to silk of a certain quality and weight, or comfortwear with a high percentage of spandex. Finally, once you've found these wonderful pieces, you'll know exactly what to expect in terms of performance, and whether their wearing qualities work with your lifestyle.

"NICE THREADS!"

Groovy as it may be, the expression is also accurate. Clothes *are* threads, woven or knitted or even pounded together to make fabric. Let's take a closer look to see how. Imagine a simple cotton-poly T-shirt. Unravel the knit, and you get threads. Untwist the threads, and you're down to the absolute basic element, the fibers. *Fiber* is the catchall term used to describe the wisps of cotton and strands of polyester that are blended together in this particular T-shirt. But experts often make a further distinction. They'll say yes, cotton is a fiber, but technically speaking, polyester is a *filament.* The main difference between the two is their length. Fibers are on the short side. Filaments go on and on and on. Silk is the only natural filament—unspool a silk cocoon and you get a single strand that averages a mile long. All the other kinds of filament are synthetically made, and theoretically could unreel forever.

Since they're so short, fibers must be *spun* in order to make yarn or thread. In basic terms, spinning is similar to what happens when you pull some fluff off the end of a cotton swab and roll it between your fingers, forming a long, tight mass. Whether the fibers originate from cotton plants or camels, the choicest ones are usually the longest, because when spun they form the tightest, hardest, smoothest threads, resulting in the most elegant fabric. Shorter fibers make a fuzzier thread or yarn (all those stubby ends sticking out), resulting in a bulkier, more rough-hewn look and feel.

For their part, filaments are also usually spun. Why? Certainly they're long enough to make a usable thread, but very often their diameter (thickness) is so fine you can barely see them, much less weave or knit them, until a bunch are twisted together. (For simplicity's sake, I'll call both fibers and filaments "fibers" from now on.)

As we'll see, the *length* and *diameter* of the fibers play a key role in determining how a fabric looks and feels. Other qualities are important too, such as the *crimp* (kinkiness), *absorbency, smoothness, stretchiness,* and *resilience* (ability to bounce back). Is this starting to sound like a shampoo ad? It's no coincidence. Even synthetic fibers have a lot in common with human hair. In the textile-lab equivalent of a Texas beauty parlor, straight-as-a-stick acrylic gets dyed, dried, and curlified to make it look more woolly and natural.

WHAT TEXTILE MILLS DO

Once you've got thread or yarn, you've got to make the strands hold together. Despite some technical upgrades, nobody's really improved on the two methods used since time immemorial: *weaving* and *knitting.* You can probably already tell one from the other, but knowing exactly how and why they're different is the mark of a woman who really knows clothes.

Woven fabric is made on a loom. On this contraption, long rows of up-and-down, or *warp,* threads are stretched tight like piano wires—creating a framework for a *filling thread* to pass over and

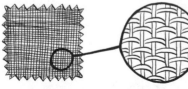

under, like the baskets some of us wove underwater in college. The simplest and most common type of weave is the *plain weave,* where the filling thread goes over * under * over * under. Another popular weave is *twill,* where the filling thread goes something like over * under * under * over * under * under, and then, when it moves up a row, keeps the same rhythm but shifts one thread over. This makes a diagonal pat-

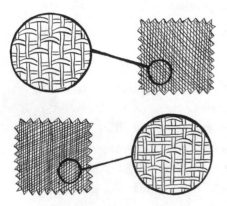

tern—one you may be able to spot in your jeans, which are nearly always twill fabric. The last major kind is the *satin weave.* A lot of people think satin is a specific type of fiber, like silk. It's not. Satin can be made with cotton, wool, silk, or polyester, as long as the weave goes something like over * under * under * under * over * over * over * under * over * over—you get the picture. Here the filling threads "float" for long stretches across the top of the weave. Their unbroken length helps give satin its distinctive gleam.

Knit fabrics are different. Some are easy to spot, like fuzzy mohair mufflers. Others are trickier, possibly because they're not made of wool (knits don't have to be), possibly because the interlock is so teeny the fabric looks woven until you get really really close. (Diane von Furstenberg's silk wrap dresses are a good example.) Whether they're made with a pair of needles or a turbocharged knit-

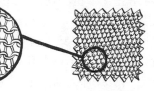

ting machine, all knits have one thing in common: they're made up of *interlocking loops* rather than criss-crossed threads or yarn. In a side-by-side comparison, wovens tend to be stronger than knits, and knits tend to be stretchier than wovens.

Stretch also comes into play in both woven and knit fabrics as a result of the manufacturing process. Once finished, fabric has distinct *grains* running crosswise and up and down. Crosswise, the fabric usually has a bit of stretch. Meanwhile, the up-and-down grain drapes softly but doesn't have a great deal of give. Clothing manufacturers consciously use these qualities when piecing together fabric to ensure that the garment fits and hangs well.

Mostly, though, the amount of stretch depends on the material that makes up the fabric. Which brings us to the fibers themselves. You thought your closet was jammed with clothes? Brace yourself. Thanks to 10,000 years of fabric history, it's also loaded with ancient rites, swashbuckling exploration, and scientific genius.

CAN I BORROW YOUR COAT?
A ROUNDUP OF NATURAL FIBERS

Wool   Once upon a time in Spain, the merino sheep was so highly prized that anyone caught smuggling one out of the country was sentenced to death. While it sounds harsh, it's not surprising—those woolly wonders made Spain so much money the taxes alone financed Columbus's trip to America. Today, merino is still the king of the wool-producing breeds. Why? Its fibers are white (easy to dye) and very fine, about the same diameter as a human hair, which makes for a delightfully soft yarn or thread.

All wool is obtained by shearing, usually in the spring, when it's warm enough for the sheep to go without its heavy coat of fleece. After a long winter, the fleece is completely mucked up by mud, twigs, and everything else a sheep will stray into (these animals are not famous for their smarts). So the first order of business after the fleece is collected is to immerse it in a hot bath, which gets out the grunge and the natural grease. Then, the wool is "carded" to get all the fibers running in the same direction. Next it's combed, separating out all fibers of two inches or less. These shorter hairs will be used to make *woolen,* or fuzzy fabrics, such as bulky knits and tweeds. The longer fibers will be used to make fine sweaters and suiting fabric, known in the business as *worsteds.*

Wool has many appealing characteristics. First, its natural crimp helps it trap pockets of air, which keep the sheep (and you) toasty no matter how nasty the weather. Also, wool sheds water droplets (ask any Scottish fisherman), but absorbs water vapor, meaning it can pull perspiration right off your body. Finally, wool springs back when crushed or stretched—even up to a third of its length—meaning it packs without wrinkles.

If you come across a label reading Virgin Wool, don't think for a minute the sheep hasn't been around. What it really means is that the fiber is fresh, rather than recycled from old fabric (in the U.S., reused wool must be clearly labeled as such). Lambswool on the label is something else altogether. It means the source was under seven months old, so the fleece is finer, lighter, and softer, which translates directly into the quality of the sweater.

Despite all these fine qualities, wool has a downside. With heat, moisture, and pressure (I'm talking the washing machine), the tiny scales running along the fibers' surface intersnag and coil, causing wool fabric to shrink. (If you pound it too, the fabric will mat completely, forming felt.) This is why you always gently hand-wash wool items, or send them out to the dry cleaners.

Wool's Advantages
Warmth
Highly absorbent, draws away perspiration
Natural resilience makes it crease-resistant
Water-repellent

Wool's Disadvantages
Woolens can pill
Requires careful hand-washing or dry cleaning
Moths find it tasty

Specialty Animal Fibers When it comes to telling the sheep from the goats, our own Federal Trade Commission (FTC) doesn't make fine distinctions. According to the FTC, the fleece from both these animals can be labeled as wool, as can that from camels, rabbits, and alpacas. But fabric manufacturers know how alluring specialty fibers are to consumers. Usually they list the exact source on the contents label. As you're moving along the rack, if your hand feels something softer, finer, more appealing than other garments, pull it out and take a look at the contents. It could be you've found something special.

Alpaca: A South American cousin of the goat, the alpaca lives high in the Andes mountain range, and evolved a lightweight, lustrous soft wool with lots of crimp to keep warm in the chilly climate. Alpaca used to be an extremely common fabric fiber (even one that wasn't considered very special) but is now usually seen only in finer pieces of clothing.

Angora fur: Not to be confused with the Angora goat, which yields mohair (see below). Angora fur comes from a special breed of domesticated rabbits, whose coat is clipped or combed every three to four months. Angora is the ultimate sweater-girl material: with its soft, longish fibers, it's extraordinarily touchable.

Camel hair: It gets mighty chilly in Outer Mongolia. That's why the two-humped Bactrian camel develops a fuzzy underlayer of hair as insulation. This doesn't mean the camel's humping a lot of extra weight: some people claim a 22-ounce camel-hair fabric is as warm as a 32-ounce garment made of wool. A lovely tan color, the hair is usually left undyed in the finished fabric, which is often blended with wool into coats.

Cashmere: Semiwild goats living in the mountainous Kashmir region of India provided the world its first samples of cashmere. Now China has taken over, along with Australia, New Zealand, and Scotland. So what's the big deal about this fiber? Once you feel it, or better yet, wear it, you'll never ask again. With its tiny diameter and buoyant crimp, it makes for a garment that is supersoft, snuggly warm, yet light as air. Cashmere woven with the finest fibers (sometimes called *pashmina*) is so delicate they say you can pass a shawl through a wedding band. But there is one problem with all of it: the price. The goat's delightful undercoat is intermingled with less delightful thick guard hairs. The strands must be separated by hand, making for a labor-intensive process.

Mohair: Made from the fleece of Angora goats, which are thought to originate in the Himalayas. Almost two million of these animals are now being raised in Texas. Mohair is praised for its resilience and lustrous sheen. In knit form, it is the hairiest of the specialty fibers, making for sweaters that look like the people in Edward Koren's *New Yorker* cartoons. However, when woven, mohair is indistinguishable from fine sheep's wool.

Cashgora: You may occasionally run into this name on a label; it refers to the fleece from an animal that's a cross between cashmere goat and an angora.

Cotton   In 1350, the English explorer Sir John Mandeville came back from India hopping with news: "There is a wonderful tree which bore tiny lambs on the ends of its branches." These days, we'd gently draw him aside and tell him he'd found a cotton plant. Thanks to the world's love of

✳ Comfort Factor ✳

Clothing manufacturers love to talk about the comfort factor of their fabrics, but what does all the jargon mean? At the most basic level, if a fabric is loosely knitted or woven (like gauze), air passes easily from one side to the other, making for high *breathability.* Another factor is a fabric's *conductivity:* how well the fibers transfer heat from inside to out. Low-conductivity fabrics like acrylic and silk help keep heat close to the body. High-conductivity fabrics like cotton and linen allow heat to pass through. Still another aspect is *absorbency.* On an average moderate-stress day, our three million sweat glands give off a pint of perspiration. If it sits on the skin unabsorbed, we're going to feel clammy (if it's cold), or sweaty (if it's warm). All natural fibers absorb sweat. Synthetic fibers don't, which in the past lent them a bad reputation. But today, manufacturers are able to engineer these fibers with tiny grooves running along their surfaces. This adds a quality you may have heard about in connection with sports clothes: *wickability,* where moisture passes off the skin onto the garment, where it quickly dries.

blue jeans, cotton is the most used fiber of all, holding 65 percent share of the total apparel market. It all starts four to six weeks after planting, when cotton flowers fall to reveal the tiny boll. This spends a few weeks ripening. When it can't get any fatter, it splits, revealing the white, fluffy interior fiber that protects the seeds. After the fiber has dried in the sun, the cotton is picked. After it is deseeded, the fiber goes to a mill where it is drawn, combed, and spun into yarn or thread. As with wool, the length and fineness of the fibers determine their end use. The longest, choicest fibers, traditionally from the *Sea Island* and *Egyptian* species (and the Egyptian subspecies *pima*) are used to make the fine, tight threads that go into the best cotton shirt fabric. Most everyday cotton clothes are made from average-length fibers.

As you might expect from a fiber that flourishes in the South's hot sun and pelting rains, cotton easily withstands the rigors of the washing machine, even at boiling-hot temperatures. It is also highly absorbent, making it comfortable to wear in humid conditions. Cotton's downside is that it wrinkles easily, which is why it's often blended with polyester, which doesn't wrinkle at all, or is treated with special coatings to help it stay crisp.

Cotton's Advantages
Hard-wearing
Absorbs moisture, good for summer
Machine-washable

Cotton's Disadvantages
Tends to crease
May shrink when washed
Mildew can develop

Silk   Legend has it that silk was discovered by a Chinese princess, Si-ling, in 2640 B.C., when she accidentally dropped a silkworm cocoon into hot water and saw big potential when it began to unravel. For thousands of years, the Chinese jealously guarded the manufacturing process, and the trading route into that country, known as the Silk Road, was well trodden by traders who made a fortune selling the material to the courts of Europe. Now, after 4,500 years of intense cultivation, silk moths have become so domesticated they can't fly. (Note to ethical vegetarians: silk is not an animal-friendly fiber.) Once the moths have laid their eggs, the eggs are collected and put into cold storage until the leaves of the white mulberry tree start to bud in the spring. Once hatched, the silkworm (actually a caterpillar) spends the next four to five weeks feasting on the fresh leaves, which are replenished every two to three hours. When it can't take another bite, the caterpillar latches on to a twig and starts to spin its cocoon. The cocoon material is silk. The animal maneuvers the filament over and around itself for two to three days. Once finished, it's curtains for the worm. The cocoons are gathered and baked to kill the animals inside. They're then placed in tanks of warm water to loosen the silk's gummy coating and reveal the end of the filaments, which are carefully unspooled. Any broken fibers are used to make *spun silk,* which is of lesser quality. *Raw silk* is spun silk that has been brushed to give it a cottony effect. *Wild silk* is from worms fed a less exquisite diet, usually oak leaves, which is reflected in the rougher quality of the finished fabric. *Shantung* (also called *duppioni*) *silk* is high-quality fabric distinguished by its slubs, or irregularly nubby threads. In the silk business, professionals measure the fabric in units called momme: lesser-quality washable and other types of silk range from 6 to 12 momme; heavier, better-quality silks such as crepe de chine average from 14 to 18 or even higher momme; and silks used in suiting fabric are the heaviest at up to 22 momme.

> *Whenas in silks my Julia goes,*
> *Then, then (methinks) how sweetly flows*
> *That liquefaction of her clothes.*
> —Robert Herrick, English poet, 1591–1674

In the Roman Empire, silk sold for its weight in gold, which is hardly surprising given its characteristics. The filament is extremely fine—the finest of all natural fibers—extremely smooth, and shaped like a prism. These qualities give it a luster that can only be matched by artificial fabrics. Another quality of silk is tremendous strength despite extremely light weight—nature made it this way to protect the developing animal from the elements and to keep the cocoon firmly attached to its twig, no matter how hard the wind would blow. Also, because the cocooned worm must develop at a consistently warm temperature, silk does not readily let heat escape. This low conductivity makes it somewhat like the insulation that wraps a house, and is why the fabric is warm to wear despite its light weight. But because silk is so labor-intensive, it is an expensive fiber; all the more so because it's always imported. Despite a lot of people's best efforts, silkworms have never thrived in the States.

Silk's Advantages
Luxurious feel
Strength despite light weight
Natural luster
Dyes brilliantly—lush colors possible
Low conductivity = warmth
With good, heavy silk, wrinkles fall out easily in steam from the shower

Silk's Disadvantages
Requires hand-washing or dry cleaning
Reacts to perspiration and may stain
Expensive

Linen and Ramie

Said to be the oldest fiber, linen was also the world's most important until cotton took over at the end of the 18th century. Linen is made from the inner bark of the long stems of the flax plant, which is cultivated in temperate and subtropical regions around the world. To this day, flax fibers are prepared for spinning using an efficient age-old process: the stems are cut near the roots and are thrown into a pond or tank for a few days, where the natural rotting action of bacteria eats away at the unusable inner core. The fibers are then cleaned, straightened, and spun. The natural waxes present in flax are what gives linen its luster.

Any material that keeps a four-foot-tall plant standing upright has to be extremely strong. This strength carries over to the finished fabric. And talk about long-wearing—linen is the fiber ancient Egyptians used to wrap mummies for their voyage to the afterworld. I once saw a piece of mummy fabric up close in the textile department of the Cooper-Hewitt Museum in New York. Apart from some mysterious stains, it looked exactly like one of my grandmother's old table runners. (Come to think of it, the runner had stains too, but I'm pretty sure that was tea.) Anyway, linen's strength is why so many antique bedclothes turn up at flea markets; with proper care, it lasts and lasts. But there's also a downside that's important to remember. Flax fibers are designed by nature to point in a single direction: up toward the sun. If linen gets bent out of shape, it tends to stay that way, wrinkling easily in fabric form. If creased sharply enough in the same place over a long period, linen fibers may even fray and snap, which is why the fabric should never be too crisply ironed, and why heirloom cloth should be refolded every so often. Back on the plus side, linen is an excellent conductor of heat, explaining its popularity as a cool summer fabric.

Ramie is a natural fiber resembling linen, but originating from the stem of the ramie shrub, which grows in the U.S. and the Far East. The difficulty in processing ramie has limited its use, but it is an extremely strong fiber, and it will occasionally turn up in summer garments.

Linen and Ramie's Advantages
Strength
High conductivity = transfers heat away from the body
Hard-wearing
Dries quickly
Naturally smooth surface sheds dirt
Natural luster

Linen and Ramie's Disadvantages
Pure fiber will wrinkle wickedly
Constant creasing in the same spots may cause threads to fray or
    break
If lined, will require dry cleaning

PULP IT UP: THE ROSTER OF MAN-MADE FIBERS

Many people don't realize there are two kinds of artificial fibers: *man-made* and *synthetic*. The difference between them is a big one. The three man-mades—rayon, acetate, and triacetate—may sound test-tubey, but are actually more plant than plastic. In fact, the main ingredient in all three is plant material, finagled in the laboratory to create filaments with unique appearance and wear characteristics. It may help to think of man-made fibers as the Pringles potato snacks of the fabric world.

Rayon and
Lyocell
Rayon was the very first man-made fiber. It was patented in 1855 by the Swiss George Audemars, who figured that if a lowly caterpillar could produce a beautiful, hard-wearing filament, heck, so could he. Through much of the 19th and early 20th centuries, rayon was extremely popular as a hosiery fiber—it lent the look of silk stockings at an affordable price. This material got its name because, like silk, it brightly reflects rays of light.

The basic recipe for rayon is much the same since the time Audemars whipped up the first batch. Wood pulp, usually from pine trees, is purified and chemically treated so that it forms a thick, gluey material. This is forced through a device known as a *spinneret,* which looks something like a showerhead. The emerging identical strands harden upon contact with an acid bath. Further chemical treatment makes them even tougher; then they're spun into thread. *Viscose* and *cupro* are two specific kinds of rayon.

Because it originates in the plant kingdom, rayon behaves a lot like its cousin cotton—it is absorbent, drapes well, and feels very nice against the body. Formerly, it had a bad reputation for spotting in the rain and going to pieces if accidentally machine-washed. Today, it is usually coated to prevent spotting, and is also made in a machine-washable form (called *lyocell,* which you may see marketed under the tradename Tencel). Since certain kinds of rayon remain dry-clean only, it's very important to check (and pay attention to!) the care label.

Rayon's Advantages
Looks like silk but less expensive
Absorbent and dries quickly
Drapes well

Rayon's Disadvantages
May require dry cleaning
May be damaged by heat, dryness, moisture
Frays more easily than many other fabrics

Acetate and
Triacetate

Also made from wood, or possibly cotton fibers that are too short to spin, acetate is manufactured in a process similar to rayon. Chemically, acetate is akin to airplane glue; in the manufacturing process it hardens upon contact with air. This chemical connection makes acetate a bit high-strung as fibers go—it melts upon contact with heat and is liable to dissolve under the influence of alcohol, or for that matter, acetone-based nail polish remover. But its shimmering beauty makes all forgivable. You probably know acetate best as a lining for coats and jackets; it's a favorite here because it won't pill even under the constant abrasion of sliding sleeves. But lately, the fiber has come out of its shell, and is being worn as an outer fabric in its own right. While acetate is dry-clean only, *triacetate* is a washable variant.

Acetate's Advantages
Looks like silk but is cheaper
Drapes nicely
Resilient, resists wrinkling
Doesn't pill

Acetate's Disadvantages
Weak compared with other fibers
Very heat-sensitive
May dissolve upon contact with nail polish remover and fresh perfume
Most acetate needs to be dry-cleaned

PARLEZ-VOUS POLYESTER?
THE WONDERFUL WORLD OF SYNTHETICS

Acrylic, polyester, nylon, spandex—let's give the chemists a big hand. Somehow they figured out how to make the molecules of coal tar, water, petroleum, and air—ordinarily as bumbling as a junior-high marching band—link up like the drill team from West Point. This was the first step toward making plastic, and the plastic fibers we call synthetics. How they managed this is very complicated to explain (meaning I don't get most of it). Suffice it to say that just because synthetics are all borne of a spinneret doesn't mean they all act alike. In fact, the individual qualities of the various synthetics makes it possible to instill unprecedented variety in fashion fabrics.

Acrylic   This fiber wants to pull the wool over your eyes. Even though it starts out as coal, water, petroleum, and limestone, acrylic's ultimate warmth, fluffiness, and softness does an excellent imitation of sheep fuzz. This has as much to do with the *way* it's made as with the chemicals involved. As a first step, prefabricated acrylic chips are melted, then forced through a spinneret to make fine filaments. These are then crimped (to mimic the kinkiness of wool), chopped (to mimic the short fibers of wool), and spun, creating an end-product that—surprise, surprise—looks and acts a lot like wool yarn. But unlike wool, acrylic is machine-washable, and moths hate the taste. Also, acrylic is relatively inexpensive to process, which is why it often turns up in lower-priced garments. One problem with acrylic— indeed with most knitted fibers but especially knit synthetics—is that it tends to pill. You know pills, those annoying little balls of fluff that accumulate where the material gets wear and tear. There's little you can do to prevent pilling, but they can be razored or very carefully scissored off for a (temporary) freshening-up of the garment.

✳ Microfibers ✳

These are artificial fibers finer than any found in nature. Microfibers can be polyester, nylon, acrylic, or rayon, or a blend. When first introduced in 1989, only polyester was used, which is why you may find an older garment labeled simply "100% microfiber." Today manufacturers must specify which kind or kinds went into the fabric. Microfibers' tiny diameter means they have a silky feel and can be woven very tight, making them resistant to rain, cold, and wind. For this reason, they're often used to make outerwear.

Acrylic's Advantages
Durable, soft to the touch
Machine-washable
Relatively inexpensive

Acrylic's Disadvantages
Heat-sensitive
Tends to pill
Accumulates static (cling alert)

Polyester   Introduced in 1953 by DuPont, polyester is the synthetic fiber most often used in the U.S. A while back it gained a poor reputation, based mainly on its poor breathability. (Links with leisure suits and booty-shaking did nothing to improve poly's image.) But today the tide has turned, thanks in large part to the roll-up-the-sleeves attitude of the polyester lobby, fronted by the Polyester Fashion Council. In 1984, they put on a splashy fashion show featuring all-poly garments. Designed by Calvin Klein, Oscar de la Renta, and other stars, the clothes helped play up the long-hidden glamour of the fiber. Also contributing to polyester's new image was the rise of microfibers. Since the filaments can be made even finer than silk, the resulting hand, or feel, of microfiber fabric is delightful. Additional laboratory tinkering made it possible for polyester to wick moisture away from the body, instead of just letting it sit there and get clammy.

Despite all the changes, polyester still retains its most impressive quality—ease of care. Poly easily holds its own against the washing machine and dryer, doesn't shrink, and is the most wrinkle-resistant fiber known. This is why it's often blended with cotton and other fabrics that tend to lose their shape, or helps bolster other synthetics that could suffer a breakdown if forced to go it alone in the washing machine. On the downside, polyester doesn't always let oily stains go. This could be a family thing—the fiber is made with petroleum.

Polyester's Advantages
Easy wash and dry care
Doesn't shrink at low temperatures
Will hold its pleats come hell or high water
Very strong
Relatively inexpensive
Stretchy and soft

Polyester's Disadvantages
Builds up static (cling alert)
May pill
Older fabric doesn't absorb sweat, will get clammy

Nylon   If you're looking for strength, look no further than nylon—it's the
(Polyamide) strongest fiber known to man. Nylon carried parachuting soldiers
through the skies in World War II. Nylon is used to make rip-stop
luggage. Nylon is used to make bulletproof vests. Nylon is used to
make panty hose—go figure. In an extremely complicated series of
chemical steps, nylon is made from air, water, and coal, then is
extruded into filaments, of which fishing line is a relatively thick
example. (Why a fiber able to haul in fifteen feet worth of fighting
marlin can't withstand the pressure of my pinky toe has to be one of
the biggest mysteries going, and I would love to have an explanation
from the panty-hose companies. In the meantime, we'll take it on
faith the fiber is not to blame.) Nylon is used on its own and in countless blends to give strength and durability to weaker materials.
Because it is light, the fiber doesn't add bulk, which is particularly
helpful in active outerwear. Chemically speaking, nylon is a member
of the *polyamide* family, and you'll often see it labeled as such in European content labels.

Nylon's Advantages
Easy care
Resists wrinkles
Dries quickly

Relatively inexpensive
Strong

Nylon's Disadvantages
Static (cling alert)
Tends to pill
Melts at high temperatures

✳ Blended Fibers ✳

Blending fibers allows manufacturers to maximize the best qualities of each component, and, since some fibers are more expensive than others, to lower the cost of the finished product. Most of the time, fabrics are blended at the spinning stage. Though all kinds of blends are possible, the following artificial fibers are frequently added to achieve certain specific qualities:

nylon: lends strength and durability
polyester: improves washability and wrinkle resistance, allows permanent creases to be set in springy fabrics like wool
acrylic: creates bulk without weight
rayon: adds to the natural feel of a garment

Fiber blends also allow for the creation of fabrics unlike any ever seen before. One of my funkiest buys ever was a top made of 60 percent polyurethane, 23 percent polyester, and 17 percent polyamide. Though it's cut like a standard tailored blouse, the fabric looks and feels like the stuff used to make extra-thick garbage bags. Hot as a sauna to wear, but fun.

Spandex (Elastane, Lycra) During World War II, scientists worked feverishly to create a chemical substance that could act as a substitute for rubber. While critical to the war effort, rubber was a huge pain to get hold of, since it came from tropical trees just a hop, skip, and dive from Japan's kamikaze pilots. The scientists persevered, and spandex was the spectacular

result. An elastomeric (stretchy) fiber, it can be drawn out to 500 percent of its original length and snapped back exactly the same as
before. Moreover, spandex can do this again and again and again,
which is why it easily keeps the pace in exercise class long after your
thighs have given up.

Spandex is never used on its own. It's invariably a small percentage of the total fiber makeup of a fabric. Moreover, it's expensive to
incorporate, so budget-minded manufacturers strive to keep it to a
minimum. The more spandex present (especially over 10 percent),
the more stubbornly the garment will hold its shape—and you,
because it acts like a very comfortable corset. But even as little as 2
percent goes a long way in preventing baggy knees and saggy bottoms in hard-wearing, mostly cotton pieces.

I Can't
Believe It's
Not Leather: A
Couple More
Synthetics

Ultrasuede
Made of polyester and polyurethane, ultrasuede is made in Japan in a
top-secret, hush-hush process. The fabric looks and feels like suede,
but is washable.

Polyvinyl Chloride (PVC)
Typically used in jackets and pants, PVC looks like leather but is in
fact plastic. It does not breathe so can get very warm to wear, but it
wipes clean, is excellent in the rain, takes a lot of abuse, and looks
cool.

Fibers of the
Future

Right now, fashion is on the brink of a second synthetics revolution
(the first taking place in the 1950s–70s, when many of the artificials
mentioned above were introduced). To give just a few examples: fiber
made from glass is now used to reinforce boat hulls and cars; fairly
soon it will be commonplace in clothing. British designer Warren
Griffiths makes garments incorporating cassette tape and paper. The
blouses in Prada's Spring '98 collection featured panels of latex (that's
right, the stuff used to make condoms). But it's not only new synthetics that are hitting the runways. The stinging nettle plant, long considered to be a pesky roadside weed, is now being harvested in

Nepal, its fibers used to produce beautifully draping, subtly colored woven fabrics.

The incredible variety of fiber and blend possibilities—a variety that multiplies with every new discovery—is a godsend to the fashion industry. Even a genius designer can only cut a skirt so many ways. But innovative fabrics and blends lend fresh excitement to even the most mundane pieces. And while these innovations may seem cutting-edge today, it won't be too long before they're filtering into resale stores. Keep a sharp lookout—before you know it, some polyvinyl chloride–blend pants may be calling your name.

CLOSET SAFARI

Back at the beginning of the chapter, I indicated that many of the fibers profiled here could be found hanging around in your own closet. Now that you've read up on the fundamentals, it's time to see what you've got. As soon as you can spare a solid half-hour, clear off the bed, throw open the closet and dresser drawers, and go on a safari through your wardrobe. Pull the pieces out and take a look at the contents label, which is most often found on the collar, or sometimes up the inner side seam. (By law, all clothes sold in the United States must indicate what kinds of fibers are present, down to the percentages.) As you're looking, flip back to the specific fiber profiles to refresh your memory. If fibers haven't played a role in your shopping radar before, big surprises may be in store. If you have a solid sense of touch, you may discover that cashmere or high-percentage spandex already exists in your wardrobe. Or you may be shocked to find that your favorite suit contains nylon. As you work your way through the pieces, spend some time closing your eyes and *really feeling* the differences between the fibers and blends—how slippery acetate lining is, how spongy polyester. If you love the feeling of a particular piece, try to commit that feeling to memory. Then open your eyes again and look very carefully at how cleaning has affected the garments, and which fibers show the most signs of wear. If you have two pieces with identical fiber content, notice how manufacturers can make the same material look and feel slightly different, depending on the weight and manufacturing technique. And don't limit the safari to your own closet—if you have a partner or kids, get into their clothes come laundry time. (But don't go through their drawers. You're sure to find something you weren't expecting, and I'm not talking polyamide blend.) Really get to know your fibers in the privacy of your home. Next, we'll be hitting the road.

Chapter Three

⬥

Getting the Handle of Fine Fabrics

*Y*our doctor and I think you should be getting more fiber. She's talking about Bran Buds. I'm talking about hands-on experience with wool and linen and triacetate. At this point, it may seem like we're spending an awful lot of time on textiles and their characteristics, but the in-depth immersion will prove worthwhile. This is why:

Rule #1 of Resale: The quality of the fabric used in a garment is the best tip-off to quality overall.

Or to put it more bluntly: shoddy fabric equals shoddy clothes. Find the outstanding cloth in a heap of merchandise and you've found the outstanding pieces of clothing. You're not sure how? Don't worry. None of us were born with this skill. It has to be nurtured through focused effort, and will come to life as soon as you start paying attention to the characteristics of fabric. In fact, the learning process is very natural, especially if you love to browse. It all comes down to developing your senses—sight, sound, and, most especially, touch.

PLEASE DO TOUCH THE MERCHANDISE

Does it seem strange that in that list of the senses, touch is the one at the top? If you're like most people, when you're moving down a resale rack you rely on your eyes, zeroing in on colors and cuts that look like they suit you. This is certainly the best way to shop in retail stores, where the styles are arranged logically and there's a bounty of sizes to choose from. But in the resale environment, eyes-only shopping can end in frustration. See if this sounds familiar. Relying only on sight, you go down the row, picking out the colors that catch your attention. Unfortunately, on closer examination, none of the picks work. This jacket's cheap shoulder pads have NFL aspirations. That blouse's seams look like crinkle-cut fries. So, frustrated, you go *back* down the same rack, painstakingly examining every piece. Am I right? No wonder resale shopping takes forever!

But if you put faith in your sense of touch and get your hands working hard the first time around, you'll also pull out the pieces that *feel* terrific. This instantly enlarges your pool of potential winners, and cuts the time wasted on duds. Packing expertise into your fingertips will supercharge your ability to detect value. Resale shopping is a lot more efficient once you've got the touch. (Don't follow the advice of one otherwise excellent resale guide and wear gloves. You might as well put on a blindfold too. Gloves only make sense when handling delicate antique fabrics that might be endangered by the hand's natural oils.)

I'VE NEVER FELT THIS WAY BEFORE

Strange, isn't it, how society caters to every one of our senses but touch. We have art museums to delight the eyes, the top-twenty countdown for our ears, Häagen-Dazs sample spoons for taste, perfume counters for smell. But touch has no dedicated feeder at all. Certainly we can pay to *be* touched, legally or otherwise, but the flip side—arrays of sensations to delight the fingertips—seem to be absent from the pleasure sector. Or are they? I think we all fill the gap in a semiconscious way every time we hit the stores. Why else bother browsing when there's no money to spend? Touching fabrics feels good, and it makes us feel better to do it.

In her wonderful book *A Natural History of the Senses*, Diane Ackerman mentions a study in which premature babies wrapped in fleecy blankets gained weight faster than those who were not—the babies thrived because they were being bombarded by pleasing tactile sensations. Maybe that's why so many of us unwind after a bad day by detouring through a good clothing store—to touch, hold, examine. They don't call it "retail therapy" for nothing; it's like an hour with a shrink, or at a spa. Somehow the simple act of exercising the senses wipes all the stresses away.

After all, we're born to touch, to grasp, to hold. What are the first words most kids learn? *Don't touch!* But we do. We can't help it. Cats have whiskers, dogs have a keen sense of smell, we have fingers and a highly mobile thumb to help us find our way through the world. Nature made touching such an easy thing to do. Our fingertips are ridged—not to help the FBI track us down, but to snag items more easily, like the dots on the fingertips of rubber gloves. They also help us detect minute changes in texture.

But it's not the ridges themselves that do the feeling—that happens one skin layer down. If nerve endings were any closer to the surface, exfoliation would be torture. Here, little bulbs called *Meissner corpuscles* sit at the end of sensory nerves. Where they're the densest, for instance in our fingertips, there can be as many as 9,000 per square inch. Each bulb has a bunch of bedspring-like sensors within. If one of them detects gentle pressure, it shoots a nerve impulse up the arm to the spinal cord, then on to the cerebral cortex in the brain, which figures out what's being felt.

The attention span of sense receptors is famously short. Just as you can't smell coffee after your nose has been over the pot for more than a few seconds, your touch receptors will stop firing after a very brief period of time. This is why we stroke fabric instead of simply putting down a fingertip. We not only get more information, we get more *different* information—tiny variations in surface texture—which gives us a fuller picture of the touched object. How sensitive are our hands to different surface qualities? Consider this list of adjectives from *Roget's Thesaurus:*

Rough, coarse, grainy, granulated, gritty, gravelly, nappy, pily, shaggy, hairy, nubby, bumpy, lumpy, studded, knobbed, pocked, pitted, smooth, fine, delicate, dainty, finespun, gauzy, filmy, gossamer, downy, fluffy, velvety, fuzzy, satiny, silky…

You can imagine the differences among them, can't you? Plus the hundreds more words describing other kinds of feels and textures.

I WANNA HOLD YOUR HAND

When a professional such as a fashion designer considers a textile for use in a clothing line, one of the key elements of the appraisal is how that fabric feels. In fact, the pros use a specific word to describe that feeling—the fabric's *hand*. (Saying that a fabric has a "silky hand" seems backwards somehow, but wine experts do the same thing when they talk about "the blackberry nose" of a fine Bordeaux.) *Fairchild's Dictionary of Textiles* defines hand this way: "A quality or characteristic of fabrics perceived by the sense of touch, e.g. softness, firmness, drapeability, fineness, resilience—in other words, its tactile quality."

Weaving, knitting, and chemical treatment play a huge role in how a fiber feels—even like fibers can feel unrelated depending on their manufacturing origins. By the same token, entirely different fibers can be made to feel remarkably similar. Among the fashion must-haves of Spring '98 were little sweaters with a "dry" hand— knits that felt ever-so-slightly crisp and scratchy to the touch. Though made from a variety of different fibers, they all had that same kind of fashionable scrunchiness.

Evaluating fabrics like an expert is not rocket science. With a little training, we're all capable of distinguishing the great from the not-so-hot. It all comes down to feeling—really feeling—the sensations provided by fabrics from all ends of the scale and working them into our memory banks. In this way, we create so-called "sense memories" that can be referred to again and again. Sense memories of high-quality fabrics are like gold in the bank, because they:

✿ help us home in on the top pieces
✿ help us shop faster (especially under jammed-rack conditions)
✿ give us the jump on other shoppers (who are still relying mostly on their eyes)

The quality that most distinguishes the work of the best designers is their immediate and total response to the feel of the fabric.
—Frances Kennett, *Secrets of the Couturiers*

BUILDING A DATABANK OF SENSE MEMORIES

Is your sense memory bank a big empty vault where quality fabrics are concerned? Don't worry. You can start making deposits right away. And in a couple of months, you'll begin reaping interest—especially from pals who are stunned and amazed at your new ability to find hidden treasures. The general plan for building sense memories works as follows:

1. Introduce your hands to as many fine fabrics as possible.
2. Spend time feeling, examining, and comparing them.
3. With any given fabric, decide which qualities stand out (heaviness, smooth drape, fuzzy surface, scratchiness—or, if you're the poetic type, liquidity, oomph, spooky resemblance to sister's perm, etc.).
4. Write your impressions down.

The note-taking part may sound suspiciously like work, but honestly, you'll be glad you did it. Memory alone is only good for so many discoveries. Writing a quick description of, say, three-ply cashmere, forces you to think hard about what you're feeling, which more or less beats the sense memory into your brain. For some reason, the physical effort of writing also makes memories more meaningful. Finally, senile dementia may be right around the corner, but your notes will serve you forever.

Since you're not a textile production manager or fashion journalist, you don't have to use the experts' vocabulary. Everybody describes sensations their own unique way. Where your sister might find that doubleknit polyester feels springy, resistant to the skin, and pliable, you might say it feels like a day-old pancake. Both ways are fine, as long as they stick in your mind.

WHERE OH WHERE ARE THOSE WASCALLY FABWICKS?

There are two ways to go about building your sense memories. One is the *easy-does-it technique.* Whenever you shop, no matter what kind of clothes store, pay special attention to the contents labels and try to jot down a quick note of your tactile impressions. If you haven't written descriptively since high school, don't worry; the notes are for you alone. I suggest keeping an inexpensive little notebook especially for such purposes—slim enough to fit in your handbag, pretty enough so you won't mind pulling it out in public. You'll find it a lot easier to refer to earlier insights if they're all gathered in one convenient place. To give you a better idea of what to look out for, some of my own notes appear over the next few pages. Try to pay special attention to the kinds of expensive fabrics you'd like to add to your wardrobe. Eventually, you'll become more and more familiar with the different feels, to the point where you can guess what a fiber is even before looking at the contents label.

The other way to build sense memories is the *crash program.* This takes a couple of weeks and is very intense, but the effort will swiftly enhance your resale shopping skills. Again, it involves doing fieldwork, but this time in a focused way. You will be examining specific fabrics ranging from the mediocre to tip-top, within square footage that can be covered without raising blisters. Your destination: a department store, the best one within 50 miles. Radical fringe secondhanders will mutter darkly, but the fact is you can learn more about clothes in a good (and I stress good) department store than just about anywhere else. If it helps, consider it a temple of learning, like a library, and be sure to leave the credit cards at home. Also be aware that for the purpose of this exercise, we're largely staying clear of the women's departments, the better to focus on cloth.

Once on site, you'll be spending time in various departments in order to familiarize yourself with specific fabrics (the exact locations are described in the Fabric Finder section on pages 156–59). Fortunately, like fabrics tend to be grouped in the same area, so getting a sense of, say, excellent woven cotton shouldn't involve traveling more than a few yards. Once you've decided which fabric you'll focus on, the basic procedure is as follows:

Step 1: To build sense memories of, say, fine cotton, consult the Fabric Finder, which will direct you to the men's dress shirt department. Once there, take a quick look around, establishing the whereabouts of the least-expensive brands, all the way up to the priciest. (In the finer clothing departments, the price is a reliable rough indicator of quality—the higher the price, the better the fabric is likely to be. Bear in mind, though, that in casual wear, price is often a less accurate guide.)

Step 2: Pick out about three to four sample shirts covering a range of prices. Always check the contents labels or tags so you're sure you have 100 percent cotton (or whatever) in hand.

Step 3: If you're having trouble finding a representative range, consider enlisting the help of the sales staff. Service-oriented salespeople should be delighted to point you to good examples. If you prefer to browse on your own, remember you have the right to do so undisturbed.

Step 4: Once you have identified your samples, give them all your attention, noting the tactile qualities (with eyes closed), then eyeballing up close to check the fineness of the fibers and tightness of the weave. Rub the fabric between your fingertips and listen to the sound. Heft the shirts to feel any difference in weight. In other words, get to know the best stuff so well you'll recognize it label-less and wrinkled at resale. Likewise, spend some time examining the less distinguished garments, the better to know what to avoid. After you've communed with the fabric, take some notes.

Finally, please don't try to cover more than two or three fibers at a time. If you don't pass out, you'll burn out, and feel negative about the whole idea of connoisseurship. Instead, space the sessions out over a number of trips, and in the meantime, use every opportunity to informally feel different fabrics.

DEPARTMENT STORE FABRIC FINDER

Wools   The *men's suit department* is the #1 location for fine worsted wools—the kind that the top designers also use in their upmarket women's lines. This is the place to see how beautifully wool drapes, and how it springs back into place when it's crunched. Be sure to check the hangtags—worsteds labeled "superfine" or "super100s" are the finest examples out there, and worth getting to know very well. Another place to find good woven wools is in the *men's scarf* department, where challis, cashmere, and other examples will be on hand in the winter months.

For excellence in wool knits, your next stop is *men's sweaters*. Seek out the lambswool, merino, and cashmere (obviously, there will be more on hand during the cooler months). Compare these woolens with each other, and against the lowest-priced pure wool knit on offer.

Super-100 wools feel lighter and more refined than lesser-quality counterparts, like you could wear them in summertime without baking. Also, when you hold this finer fabric up close, you don't see as much superficial fuzz.

Feel the differences in softness and weight, and have a good look at the curly fibers themselves.

Cashmere fibers are so small you can barely make them out, one of the reasons this fiber feels so soft. Also, compared with other knitted sweaters of the same approximate size, the cashmere one feels like it weighs much less.

Silks   The *women's scarf department* is the best place to learn about different kinds of silks. Hermès, one of the most expensive brands on the planet, is famous for the heavyweight silk they use in their scarves. Ferragamo, Gucci, and other top labels will offer similarly luxurious silk weights. Since scarves of this quality are usually kept under the counter, you'll have to ask for assistance to see them. In this case, stash the notebook until after you've had a good chance to feel, compare, and formulate your sense memories. Be sure to bring over a bargain-priced silk scarf to compare with the high-ticket items. If the store has a *bridal department,* continue your silk research up there—the most expensive dresses will be made of shantung (the nubbly silk made when twin cocoons are unspooled together) or heavy silk satin. One more place to get a good sense of the heaviness and intense, vibrant color possible with fine silk is in *designer ties.*

To me, the finer silks feel remarkably like skin, while the cheapies more like tissue paper. Lighter weights crinkle like crazy, heavier ones don't. The surface of lesser-quality spun silks often looks chalky. A notable quality of raw silk — it often has a highly distinctive sweetish smell..

Cottons   If you want to learn about cotton knits, off you go to *men's underwear.* Like the guys wearing it, specimens will range from wimpy to beefy. Have fun. One easy way to gauge the thickness of white cotton knits is to look at your fingertips through the fabric—if you see a lot of flesh color, the knit is very skimpy.

Better-quality knit cotton is a lot heavier than the cheap stuff.

The best woven cottons will be found in the *men's dress shirt* department. Try to hunt

Notice how pure cotton holds a crease mark you make with your finger, while polyester blends pop creases right out. Also, notice how poly-cotton blends feel less silky than pure cotton.

down Sea Island or Egyptian samples, and use these as the model all the other shirts must live up to. While you're there, find a cotton-poly blend and carefully examine the difference between this and the pure fiber. Another place to see fine cottons is in the *bedding* department, especially if the store stocks high-end sheets. Here too you can get a better sense of the differences between pure cottons and blends.

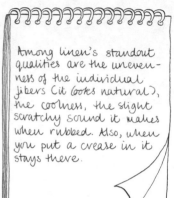

Among linen's standout qualities are the unevenness of the individual fibers (it looks natural), the coolness, the slight scratchy sound it makes when rubbed. Also, when you put a crease in it stays there.

Linen   While you're in *bedding,* see if they stock linen sheets. While the linen used in bedding tends to be finer than that used in clothing fabric, you'll be able to note many of this fiber's hallmark characteristics. Note how pure linen holds a wrinkle, and how linen-poly, if they have it, does not. *Tableware* (cloths and napkins) is another place to seek out fine linen.

✳ How the Experts Do It ✳

Sometimes, even fashion professionals can't identify what fibers are present in a cloth sample. So, when confronted with a mystery fabric, what do these highly trained, exquisitely sensitive individuals do? They set it on fire. The "burn test" is one of the most effective ways to determine content, because different fibers burn in different ways. For example, linen takes longer to light than cotton, and once it's blown out, the fabric closest to the ash is very brittle. Acetate's flickering flame smells like burning wood chips. Polyester burns with a black smoke that smells sweet.

Obligatory caution: Clearly, flame tests are a dumb thing to try at home. And heaven (and high-priced legal aid) help you if you try it anywhere else.

Rayon Your best bet for high-volume rayon is the *junior dress department*—start out there, then make a quick dash into *women's better dresses* to get a sense of the top-quality material. Rayon is a chameleon fiber par excellence. Note how many guises it can appear in—from gauzy India import-style fabric to viscose that looks like the finest silk.

Viscose and cupro, a kind of rayon, may look like silk, but feel slightly warmer to the touch.

Acrylic does a great imitation of cashmere, but will often have a telltale sheen.

Synthetics and Microfibers As a true connoisseur, you need to know a cheesy synthetic the instant you feel it. In a very good department store these may be harder to find, but *children's activewear* usually does not disappoint. Finding excellent examples of microfibers is easier—simply head to the *rainwear* department.

ADVANCED TOUCHY-FEELY

Department stores aren't the only places to check out fine fabrics. There are countless other opportunities everywhere you look.

- ⟡ *Furniture* and other *home stores* will have books full of samples. Sit down and have a thumb through the next time you're in.
- ⟡ *Hobby stores* carry fabrics, especially strange synthetics that could well show up on the catwalk next season.
- ⟡ If you're flying international, *airport duty-free* areas are Aladdin's caves of impeccable fabrics, especially silks.
- ⟡ On a less sublime level, *bedding superstores* hold enough cotton to blanket a small town, with little sample squares conveniently placed for the feeling.
- ⟡ And if you're in a downmarket *discount store,* don't miss the opportunity to browse the $5.99 rounder, to lock in your sense memories of the absolutely nots.

There's one more location that is highly recommended, much like a grad school for sense memories. If you're motivated enough, get thee to a great *fabric store*. There you'll find a veritable archive of fabrics, their relative prices clearly marked on dangling tags. This is the place to do cross-fiber comparisons—to quickly feel the differences between woven cotton and wool, rayon and silk, linen-rayon and linen-poly. But be sure your target store is the best in the region—those carrying a few pawed-over bolts of cotton and poly will be a waste of your time. In good stores the sales help may be particularly informative, and pleased to share their expertise. They may even let you take some swatches for the road.

—✦—

Chapter Four

The Telltale Indicators of Top-Quality Clothes

Here's a resale riddle:

The gods of secondhand have smiled down upon your faithful visits to the Second Time Around consignment shop and sent blessings in the form of two marvelous pantsuits. Both of them fit, both of them flatter, and both of them are priced at a low $75. The bad news is, that's exactly the amount you're able to spend, and you're torn over which pantsuit to buy.

What do you do? *What do you do??*

If your answer is "check out the labels and go for the hottest name!" you have committed a serious offense against the resale gods. The punishment is to read the rest of this chapter.

Labels don't point the way to smart buying decisions. Smartness does: being able to distinguish the great from the so-so by using your powers of observation. By now, you should be becoming adept at detecting fine fabric, the single biggest part of the quality equation. But fabric isn't the only indicator—lots of others factor in. You're probably aware of some of them already, and take them into account when it comes time to buy. The next step toward clothes connoisseurship is assessing these indicators consistently, rationally, and systematically, every time a piece catches your eye.

Doing so will help minimize buying mistakes and save precious time. Women who are savvy about the telltale indicators can lock onto a fabulous button at twenty paces, and know it's a tip-off to a great piece. The quickest flash of a splendid lining has the same effect. On the flip side, connoisseurs know that fraying seams equal schlocky merchandise, no matter whose name is on the label, and won't waste their time trying the garment on. By putting construction details before labels to tell them what's what, these women are independent thinkers in a world largely brainwashed by the forces of marketing. When faced with a riddle like the one above, they live by:

Rule #2 of Resale: A garment's true value lies not in its label, but in its workmanship.

CLOTHING STRIPPED NAKED

Peel off fashion's flashy ads, model shenanigans, designer hype, and hoopla, and what's left are a few fundamentals. First, there's the quality of the clothing's design—the aesthetic "vision" of the creator—a rather fuzzy topic that gets a great deal of attention in the fashion press. And then there are two more fundamentals—these quite concrete—that the glossy magazines, for their own mysterious reasons, rarely go into. They are: (1) quality of materials (the fabric and trimmings), and (2) quality of assembly (the workmanship used to put it together).

When you get right down to it, materials and assembly are the main reasons that a haute couture skirt costs $3,500, while its Bargain Barn counterpart is $35. The couture piece is made from the finest materials available and is entirely hand-sewn to ensure perfect fit. Meanwhile, the Bargain Barn skirt is put together with low-cost fabric and lightning-fast assembly, so that it can be sold at the lowest possible price point. It's as though these garments exist in alternate universes of materials and workmanship. In the couture universe, a big black hole sucks down the dollars in the name of perfection. In the bargain universe, the production budget's so tight even an asteroid belt is out of the question.

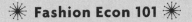

✳ Fashion Econ 101 ✳

In retail stores, cheaper garments are almost always of lower quality than their more expensive counterparts. That's because the maker must minimize the outlay on materials and assembly in order to insure profit on a low-priced piece.

Obvious, right? But wait, there's more, and this is where it gets unpredictable:

✿ Companies producing huge volumes of clothing can and sometimes do provide better-than-average materials and assembly given the retail price, due to the enormous scale they deal in and the clout they have with their suppliers.

✿ Certain manufacturers are so utterly confident of the appeal of their brands they will cut corners on quality while maintaining high price, assured that their customers won't notice the difference.

✿ Ongoing automation in garment manufacturing enables speedy and low-cost assembly of smaller and smaller production runs, resulting in greater variety for the consumer. Improved quality may also be built in, depending on the manufacturer's goals.

The economic mechanisms of the fashion business can be as complex as a Commes des Garçons cut-and-fold dress. But as long as you understand that materials and assembly are the two most obvious benchmarks of quality, you know enough to cut through the malarkey and get to the true value of clothes. It really couldn't be simpler. *The better the materials and more painstaking the assembly, the higher the inherent value of the piece.* When you see these aspects for what they are, unswayed by ad hype and fashion's other smoke-and-mirrors tricks, you will be a true connoisseur.

Again, the telltale indicators are the key. Some of you are familiar with them already, perhaps because you sew, perhaps because you're very observant. Or perhaps you were blessed with a mother, grandmother, aunt, or some other wise elder who really knew their stuff about clothes, who whisked you off to the local department store, turned merchandise inside out, and made little speeches about things like seams. If you missed this experience, or if your teenage psyche blocked it through sheer public embarrassment, here's another chance at those lessons. The checkpoints described below apply to all kinds of clothing, from shirts to shorts to evening gowns. While our recent efforts focused on training your hands, the quality indicators test your powers of observation. Judging them accurately means carefully examining a garment, inside and out, and applying basic knowledge, provided here, on how clothes are put together. Naturally this means spending more time considering your potential purchase before dashing off to the register. But once you make this kind of inspection a habit, untold brilliant finds can be yours.

THE TELLTALE INDICATORS

Let's return to those two pantsuits from a couple of pages back, reexamining them for the quality indicators. A true connoisseur would take about a minute to decide that one of the outfits shows superior materials and workmanship. The manufacturer's aim to go top-of-the-line is evident all over the garment. If resale pricing were rational, this pantsuit would cost twice as much as the other one. But, as we know, resale pricing and rationality don't always go hand in hand.

Fabric   Do you recall Rule #1 of Resale? *The quality of the fabric used in a garment is the best tip-off to quality overall.* Here's where we put it to the test. Checking the contents labels of the two pantsuits, we see that both are made of 100 percent wool. But the first, the one designed by Biff Spiffing, is lighter in weight and finer to the touch. It's also softer, whereas the rival pantsuit, by Jacques LaSchlaque, feels slightly coarse and scratchy. Why is there such a big difference when both are made of the same stuff? Most likely because the former was woven with high-quality worsted wool, whose longer, tighter-spun fibers make a finer thread, resulting in a better grade of cloth.

If we hold the fabric up close and take a good look, more evidence comes to light. There's more fuzz visible atop LaSchlaque's fabric, reinforcing the notion that it was made with shorter, less desirable fibers. We can't be sure of the wool's background, of course, but it really doesn't matter. The important point is this: which fabric would you rather have next to your skin? Spiffing wins the touch test hands down.

Fine cloth is never out of fashion.
—Thomas Fuller, 1654–1734

Pattern
Matching

Making our evaluation easier is the fact that both pantsuits are fashionably pin-striped. On the Spiffing outfit, the stripes link up cleanly across most seams, darts, and breaks. On the LaSchlaque, the stripes wobble so badly the fashion police ought to give it a Breathalyzer.

In superb clothing, stripes, checks, plaids, and other bold motifs are carefully aligned across breaks in the fabric, creating an illusion of seamlessness. A splendid example from the past is one of Yves Saint Laurent's 1985 haute-couture ensembles, a Chinese-inspired silk evening pantsuit. Here sinuous black peonies climb uninterrupted across a pink field, *not only* across the armhole seams, *not only* across the front fastening of the tunic jacket, *but across the spatial divide from jacket to trousers*—not a stem or delicate petal broken. The outfit is breathtaking—and so, no surprise, is its price.

On a less sublime level, manufacturers have production costs to consider, and perfect pattern matching is expensive. For one thing, an unusual amount of fabric will go wasted when this kind of pattern is cut. For another, the sewer requires time—a lot more time—to carefully align the pattern's pieces. For these reasons, the manufacturer may be inclined to cut corners. (Computer automation in pattern design is streamlining the pattern-matching process, but it hasn't yet perfected it.) Given these issues, it's unreasonable to expect premium pattern matching in budget-priced clothing. Even midpriced pieces are, alas, not always perfectly matched. Still, when you check a garment over, you should see evidence of *honest effort* to get the motifs coming together as cleanly as possible. If the job is truly sloppy, you can be sure that the rest of the construction will be of the same standard, and the garment is worth no more of your time.

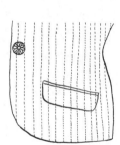

In order of importance, here's where pattern matches come to the test:

1. Patterns (especially plaids and other horizontal motifs) should connect cleanly across any front fastening.
2. Vertical motifs (such as stripes and plaids) should appear to connect from collar to back.
3. Motifs on lapels and pockets should appear to be symmetrical on the two sides (in other words, mirror each other).
4. Vertical motifs should drop evenly alongside side seams (without a lot of wavering in and out).
5. The main lines of patterns should continue straight through any pockets.
6. Motifs should link gracefully across darts.

More pattern notes:

✿ Due to complicated technicalities involving curves and fabric grain, the pattern will rarely match perfectly over the shoulder when the sleeves are "set-in" (the normal kind of sleeve, with a seam at the armhole).
✿ In certain high-quality pieces, buttons or other fastenings are hidden, so as to emphasize the pattern.

attachments hidden to show off great pattern matching

✧ Keep pattern matching in mind in your search for quality clothes. If you spot a garment with a bold pattern, run your eyes quickly over its seams. If the matches are dead on, this is a superior piece.

Interior Finish Constructing a garment is a lot like carpentry. It's all about measuring, cutting, joining, and sealing so the finished product looks great and won't fall apart. As we all know, there are good carpenters and naughty carpenters. The good ones show up on time, work efficiently, and don't leave a mess. Most important, they leave you with cabinets that look as nice on the inside as they do on the outside. Then there are the naughty carpenters. The guys who show up late, tramp mud all over, take endless coffee breaks, and leave you with cabinets that look fine on the outside, but the inside reveals a wreckage of pencil marks, splintered wood, sloppy painting, and a couple of dented beer cans. The naughty carpenter may be a lot cheaper, he may be the spitting image of Harrison Ford, but every time you open that cabinet you want to cry.

Carpentry is a lot like clothing manufacture, with one big exception. With a garment, we can give the interior a good checking over before we lay down a red cent. Funnily enough, a lot of us don't. From now on it ought to be a firm habit. What we're looking for is tidy interior workmanship, especially at the seams—the joinery of the pieces of fabric that altogether make up the whole garment.

Whenever a seam is sewn, two raw fabric edges remain behind. If left unfinished, they will fray, which looks lousy, and even the chintziest garment maker wouldn't dare leave them this way. Instead, the industry has a number of different techniques to control the raw edges. The most traditional seam-finishing technique is tucking the edges under and sewing them in place. This can either be done simply or with tricky folds and overlapping—the choice depends on the weight and/or type of fabric, the location of the seam, and the desired finished look of the piece. The following are some of the most widely used seam finishes—the ones every connoisseur should know. (Don't worry, this is about as technical as

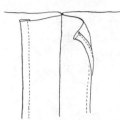

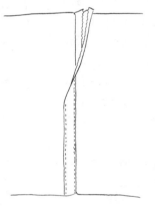

we're going to get.) If you're interested in learning about other kinds of seam finishes, have a look at a good sewing guide.

Clean-finished: One of the simplest of finishes. Here the raw edges of fabric are pressed flat, like a butterfly's wings, down along either side of the seam on the interior of the garment, with the edges turned under and stitched closed.

clean-finished seam

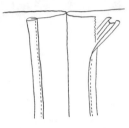

Bound: Like the clean-finished seam, the raw edges are pressed flat, butterfly-style, but in this case the edges are then bound, or wrapped, with thin strips of matching fabric. Finishing a seam this way takes a lot of work, so bound seams are most often found on high-quality pieces, especially so-called "unconstructed" clothing without a lining.

bound seam

Flat-fell: Here the seam is sewn so that the raw edges appear on the exterior of the garment. They are then tucked under and stitched flat from the top (topstitching), creating the kind of seam you see running down the legs of blue jeans. What with all the folding, tucking, and double-stitching, this one is incredibly strong. It is widely used in sports, casual, and active wear.

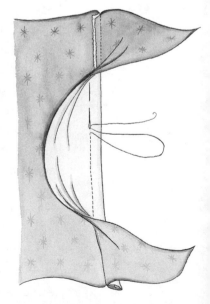

French: With this seam, all you see is a crease on the exterior and a narrow flap of fabric on the interior. A highly refined finish, this is often used to assemble fine blouses and other clothes made of delicate, sheer, or very lightweight woven fabric.

flat-fell seam

These seams are all made with the traditional sewing machine. But the manufacturer has another technique for finishing raw edges. He can *overlock* them with a spe-

French seam

cial machine called a serger. Never heard of it? That's no surprise. This unglamorous workhorse of garment assembly is never going to get a centerfold in *Vogue* magazine. But it's a good bet that a high percentage of the pieces in your wardrobe features one of three telltale overlock finishes.

Of all the seam-finishing options, overlocking is the fastest and most efficient. The serger is able to trim the fabric, sew the seam, and bind the raw edges all in a single operation. In manufacturing, fastest tends to be cheapest, and the five-thread overlock is the method of choice in lower- to midpriced clothes.

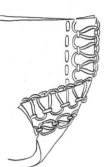

ive-thread overlock

While overlocking is cost effective, you shouldn't disdain it, for with certain fabrics it's the only way to go. Due to the tendency of the raw edges to curl, *knits are almost always overlocked with a three- or four-thread method,* whether they're from Chanel or Bargain Barn. (The difference is, Chanel will use the same yarn to overlock as was used to knit the garment, while Bargain Barn may employ a cheaper substitute.) Very flimsy, hard-to-sew fabrics like chiffon are also often made up on the overlock machine, because this formidable beast, with its multiple thrashing knives and needles, can grip the fabric much better than can the standard sewing machine. Linens and brocades may be overlocked as a means to cut down on fraying. And finally, an overlocked seam may, for various reasons, be an aesthetic choice rather than one based on budget.

All this being said, it *is* a plus when a more time-consuming and refined seam-finishing technique (like those mentioned earlier) is used with woven fabrics. The manufacturer willing to bind raw edges or use French seams is likely to strive for exquisite quality all around. If we turn back to the Spiffing and LaSchlaque, a quick look at one of the leg seams of the latter reveals overlocking used to stitch the fabric together. Again, this is common

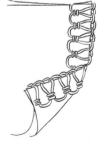

three-thread overlock   four-thread overlock

in a midpriced outfit, and it's increasingly clear that this suit never had pretensions to greatness. What is bad—very bad—are the thread chains (the tail ends of the overlock threads) still evident on the interior. This is sloppy and worth big points off, the equivalent of loose threads left by a sewing machine.

After you've checked out the seams on the interior, have a look at the exterior seamlines as well. Bumps, bulges, and ripples here are sometimes intentionally sewn in for a rough-hewn effect. Most of the time, though, they're unintentional. We've got to live with bumps and ripples when they show up on our thighs—thankfully, this isn't the case with crinkly clothes.

thread chain

Button, Button There's something undeniably magical about buttons. In my favorite vintage store a while back, the owner spilled her sackful of repair buttons onto the counter, getting ready to do some mending. At the sound of the clatter all shopping stopped, and everybody came over to have a look, even though they weren't for sale.

Why do we love buttons? Probably something basic about human nature—even animal nature: like magpies, we find it hard to resist stuff that's small, bright, and shiny. A great button is a joy unto itself, but for connoisseurs, it's more than that. It's also a prime marker of a great piece of clothing. If you spy, barely visible in the racks, a button gleaming like the sun on the silk route to Samarkand, zoom in for a closer look. Odds are, the garment it adorns is also a treasure.

Even though they have the entire button world at their beck and call, high-end designers often use rigorously plain (and quite inexpensive) nylon or polyester buttons in order to maintain a clean-lined look. So, *a boring button does not indicate inferior quality.* But the flip side can be stated with enough assurance that it becomes:

Rule #3 of Resale: *An extraordinary button points to an extraordinary garment.*

Here's the sort of thing to look out for:

Real brass: Since synthetics are cheaper to mold and stamp, they are frequently used as substitutes for real metal. If you spy a metallic-looking button and aren't sure if it's authentic, weigh it in your hand. Imposter buttons feel oddly light. They're also oddly warm, and if you flick them with a fingertip they click, where you might get a little tone off metal. (To boost your expertise, consider spending some time in a great button emporium checking out different kinds and price points). A synthetic button may also carry telltale scratches. It is generally made of an acetate core coated with copper, followed by a gold or silver metal-look finish.

✳ A Brief History of Buttons ✳

According to Joyce Whittemore's wonderful *The Book of Buttons,* these closures have been around for ages. Ancient Greeks used buttons and loops to fasten their linen *kitons* at the shoulder for that classically fashionable drapey look. Early Persians buttoned their boots closed. Thirteenth-century Crusaders returning from the Holy Land brought back the notion of the buttonhole, and thereafter in Europe garments became more form-fitting. The nobility decked itself out with gold, silver, copper, ivory, and jeweled buttons, while the less exalted wore buttons made of base metal or fabric. Francis I of France had one outfit that bore 13,600 of them. As the centuries wore on, materials and techniques became even wilder. Eighteenth-century examples bore amazingly detailed scenes painted in enamel, decorations made with grass, flowers, and shells, and even insects mounted beneath glass. Back then, exquisite buttons were taken off the garment every time it was washed (though in olden times that wasn't very often). In this century, the rise of easy-care clothing helped bring about the rise of mass-produced buttons of plastic, nylon, and polyester. While usually workaday in appearance, these materials can be made into little bits of perfection by a great button designer.

If the coating is damaged, you sometimes see the greenish color of the copper or the white of the core showing through, which would not be the case with real brass.

Pearl: Pearl buttons aren't made from real pearls; they're drilled from the inner lining (mother-of-pearl) of harvested shells. Back in the days of seafaring trade, the shells usually came from Australia, India, China, and Japan, loaded in the hulls to act as ballast for the trip home. Real mother-of-pearl buttons tend to be cool to the touch, irregular or rough on the back, and fleetingly iridescent (pinpoints of shine, as in silk). Molded synthetic imitations are warm, entirely smooth, and any iridescence will have fake-looking uniformity, like frosted nail polish.

Horn: These are cut from the horns and hoofs of cattle. They were the original "plastic" buttons, as this material softens when heated and can be pressed into various shapes. Horn buttons may appear as rough-edged chips (favored especially on Alpine-style loden coats), finely polished dress buttons (seen on all kinds of elegant garments), or horn tips (sporty duffel coats and pea jackets). While the beautiful, irregular grain of horn is hard to capture in synthetics, it's still often impossible to distinguish the fake from the real thing.

> *One William Niles of Jersey City, NJ,*
> *gained a patent in 1879 for the*
> *"manufacture of ornamental buttons*
> *made from blood and other materials."*

Couturier buttons: Also known as *passementerie* buttons, these handmade beauties are often used in haute couture. They are made from a silken cord wrapped again and again around a button form in an attractive and intricate decorative pattern, then tied off with a central knot.

"House" buttons: Many design houses use distinctive buttons bearing a special motif such as Versace's medusas or Chanel's crossed *C*s and

lion's heads. (Coco Chanel was a Leo. Chanel's button motifs change with the seasons, and are avidly tracked by connoisseurs.) Otherwise, the house's name may appear on the buttons (even some midlevel makers now do this).

Eccentric buttons: Buttons don't have to be "jewely" to be wonderful. In 1938, the Parisian couturier Elsa Schiaparelli made a jacket with buttons in the form of molded plastic locusts—insects otherwise known for their starring role in biblical plagues. Needless to say, all of Paris swooned at the wit. Also needless to say, her local button man didn't have the plastic pests in stock; they had to be custom designed. This is important to keep in mind when you see a button that has a peculiar shape, an unusual size, or some outlandish detail. Odds are it was specially commissioned for the garment, and as such is a great tip-off to quality.

A button has a silent partner that is equally important in the closure role—the hole. If you've never given buttonholes a second thought, you'd be surprised at the kinds of stories they tell:

Machine-worked: This is the most common type of buttonhole, and will be found on 99 percent of the garments in your closet. It feels rough inside and out, and usually sports a couple of dangly threads, because the stitching is done first, *then* the slit is cut. Some buttonholes are stitched tighter than others—tight is good, because it's neater. Machine-stitched buttonholes may have a slight keyhole shape. This is a detail adopted from the world of men's tailoring. The wider part is meant to accommodate the back loop of a shank button.

Bound: Here the edges of the slit are bound with strips of matching fabric, creating an opening that resembles a mail slot on a front door. It looks a lot neater than an ordinary buttonhole, and it takes quite a bit more effort to make up. If you spot a bound buttonhole, pay extra attention—-somebody's added serious value to the piece.

Handstitched: If you find one of these babies, pounce—the garment may be haute couture, or at least lovingly handmade. Here, the slit is cut *before* the stitching takes place, so there are no dangly threads. Also, the stitching around the hole is smooth on the outside, rough on the inside. One more reason that haute couture costs the sun, moon, and stars—the time needed to finish just one hand-sewn buttonhole is four hours.

The pantsuits are getting lonely without us so let's check back in. For once, the LaSchlaque comes out trumps—the buttons on the jacket and waistband are of wire filigree, quite a bit prettier than the Spiffing's utilitarian black nylon. But, as mentioned earlier, a run-of-the-mill button is highly forgivable, as long as other factors shine out. (Be sure to give every button, even the plainest, a close look. On a brand-new, ultrafashionable $2,000 suit, I once saw a nylon button that had been unmolded incorrectly, leaving behind a very shoddy-looking plastic ruff.)

Lining Notes Coats, jackets, dresses, skirts, and pants are many-layered things—apart from the visible outermost fabric, there may be up to three more layers between your skin and the outside world. The garment's hidden *interlinings* are critical to its final appearance. With high-end clothing, different kinds of material are used in different spots, creating varying degrees of stiffness, flex, and roll. When a garment "fits like a second skin," interlinings often deserve the thanks, because they literally help mold the fabric to the shape of the body. Poor-quality or poorly selected interlinings do just the opposite, causing such flaws as crinkly waistbands, jackets that collapse through the button area, collars that wrinkle and distort, and areas that refuse to iron back into shape.

Equally important, and easier to evaluate, is the *innermost lining,* visible on the inside of the garment. It has four specific roles: covering up raw seams and any intervening layers, maintaining the shape of the outer fabric, making the garment easier to take on and pull off, and making it more comfortable against the skin.

We talk about slipping into and out of pieces of clothing. This would be very tricky indeed if the lining wasn't slightly oversize, to allow give, and wasn't made of a slippery fabric. In earlier times, cotton or silk did the job. Now lining material is usually acetate, acetate/rayon, or rayon. Like every other part of a garment, a lining can be run-of-the-mill or extraordinary. An extraordinary lining heralds a special piece. Some examples of shining linings:

Jacquarded lining: Here a name or logo is woven right into the lining fabric to make a subtle pattern, which naturally costs the manufacturer more. Many high-end manufacturers add this nicety, but just as many don't, so it's not a demerit if you don't see it.

Lining of extraordinary color: If the lining deliberately doesn't match the outer fabric—say it's apple-green acetate in a black jacket—the maker is showing off. They want you to look closer. By all means do so; this is probably a winning piece.

Lining of an unusual material: Here's where your hand-development efforts come into play. If the lining doesn't feel like acetate, rayon, or a blend of the two, you may have hit the jackpot (which the contents label can confirm). Silk linings frequently adorn deluxe ready-to-wear, and are used in nearly all haute-couture pieces.

Intricately constructed lining: All linings start out life as pieces of a pattern, but some are more intricately put together than others. Most decent-quality jacket linings have a pleat down the center of the back, for more give. In more tailored jackets and coats, the linings conform more closely, possibly with two extra darts in the back panel.

No lining at all, but beautifully finished interior seams: In summer-weight and unconstructed pieces, the lining may be partial or left out altogether. Doing so actually costs the manufacturer more, because it means all the interior seams must be impeccably finished. In this case, a manufacturer is hoping to win your admiration for workmanship that is beautiful inside and out.

Unfortunately, LaSchlaque wasn't trying to win anything but a couple more pennies per unit—the pants are unlined altogether. The absence of lining in a jacket, pair of pants, or a skirt is not always a boo, as the previous paragraph makes clear. In winter-weight woven wool, however, it's inexcusable. Whatever the piece is, let it go. *You will always be able to find a comparable one* with *a lining.* Money's too precious to waste on clothes that will cling and make you scratch.

In the Pocket   Pockets can either be useful (usually found below the waist) or decorative (usually found above). Either way, they are made from extra pieces of material and require additional sewing time; therefore, they add to the production cost. Some kinds are more expensive to incorporate than others. Here's a pocket summary:

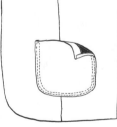

patch pocket

Patch pockets: These are applied to the outside of the garment. While ordinarily square or rectangular, they can take any shape, and may be embellished with flaps, welts, or special stitching. In quality garments, a patch pocket is lined with the same material that lines the interior. On less-well-made pieces, such as LaSchlaque's jacket, the seam that attaches the pocket to the outer fabric is left raw and thready inside (the notion being that budget-minded buyers won't check here). Meanwhile, Spiffing's joins are worthy of a Beverly Hills plastic surgeon—the stitchwork is practically invisible.

A flap positioned just above the pocket adds one more piece of fabric to the total, and is itself worthy of close examination. A fine flap is also lined on the inside, and this lining is invisible when the flap is down in place. As with pockets, the juncture of flap and the garment should be impeccably clean rather than raw-edged.

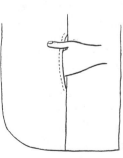

inside pocket

Inside pockets: These consist of an opening along a seamline with a fabric sack inside, the sack usually made of the lining material or cotton. Again, the juncture of the main fabric and the sack material should be as clean and unthready as possible.

shed pocket with welting

Slashed pockets: Appearing to float on the front or back of a garment, this is considered the most difficult pocket to construct properly. As difficulty generally equals expense, its presence indicates that the item is worth your attention. Slashed pockets may have a flap or be welted (the opening has fabric "lips"). Welting further adds to the complication, especially if it's very narrow, so be on the lookout for this fine point.

General pocket notes:

⬧ Curved or rounded patch pockets are more trouble to sew on perfectly than those with straight edges (and so are more expensive to produce). If you see them, take special note.

⬧ When looking at the interior of a high-end unlined garment, any visible pocket sacks should bring to mind origami—absolutely beautiful in their own right. They should also be attached prettily to the interior, so as not to be flapping free.

⬧ In haute couture, where one of the aims is to hide figure flaws, designers will actually build in pocket optical illusions to trick the eye, such as making the one on the left breast a shade narrower than the one on the right, to disguise, say, a slightly hunched shoulder. Obviously, with lopsided ready-to-wear pockets, such excuses don't fly.

⬧ Speaking of which, always eyeball pockets carefully to make sure they're hanging at the same level.

⬧ Pocket openings are sewn closed in new clothes because the natural urge before a try-on mirror is to strike a pose, namely jam hands in pockets and look cool. If you come across a jacket where the pockets are still sewn, it's possible that the piece is brand new (though some people never unsnip their pockets, preferring to keep the lines clean).

⬧ Fashion historians rely heavily on the size/proportion/placement of pockets to determine the exact period of a garment.

Buttons don't have a lock on the closure of clothing. Other gizmos that have made their inventors wealthy (or embittered) over the years include zippers, snaps, hooks, frogs, and more. On our two pantsuits, the zippers themselves are practically identical, but the one sewn on the Spiffing trousers somehow appears neater. Looking more closely, the reason becomes clear: Spiffing painstakingly matched the zipper tape (the fabric just around the teeth) to the color of the surrounding wool. The tape used by LaSchlaque is a couple of shades lighter. Now, this isn't a valid reason to drop the pants and run screaming, but it is one more example of how budget manufacture can fall short of perfect.

Thanks to countless overheated letters to men's magazines, the zipper is often associated with easy access to X-rated parts. The funny thing is, it was originally sold as an aid to modesty. Before the 1920s, ladies' garments closed with buttons or hooks. Gaps frequently opened up between these fastenings, especially when the fabric was stressed. The zipper, originally known as the "slide fastener" (later, the "hookless hooker" and the "Hookless #2," until finally the name "zipper" was adopted), was introduced as a means of preventing this dread "gap-osis." Today's zippers are made of either plastic or metal. There are three basic types: the *open-ended,* which is used to close coats and jackets; the *standard,* which is sealed at the bottom, and seen most often in casual pants, and the *invisible,* which disappears into a seam and cannot be seen from outside. Whatever type of zipper is used:

- ❖ the raw edge of its tape should either be hidden under a seam or sufficiently neatened so that the eye doesn't come to rest on thready edges.
- ❖ the teeth should not come in contact with bare skin. A fabric "zip guard" is provided on all but the cheapest of skirts and pants. With dresses, the fabric to either side of the zip should be plumped, to hold the teeth away from the skin. Note, though, that even some high-end designers are guilty of overexposed zippers (especially on lightweight slip dresses).

✥ the weight of a zipper should correspond to the fabric—zips that are too heavy cause garments to pucker or drape poorly and downgrade the overall look.

If you ever find yourself in Vienna's Kunsthistorisches Museum, consider taking a connoisseur's look at the *Court Jester of Ferrara,* painted by the French artist Jean Fouquet in 1445. In that painting is the first-ever depiction of ye olde *hook and eye,* looking just as ugly on the jester's collar as it does on modern-day clothing. Some high-end designers are so attuned to aesthetics they will actually wrap this hardware with matching thread. It's also often possible to substitute a button for a hook and eye, usually a more pleasing alternative.

Self-belts are often of ghastly quality. A plastic belt trying to pass as leather is a dead giveaway of low-end merchandise. But if the belt, and especially the hardware, is neatly covered with matching fabric or silk cord, you can be assured that decent quality was a goal.

Uncommon closures, as always with the unusual, can be a tip-off to the extraordinary. *Snap closures* on a highly tailored suit are audacious, and they must be impeccably applied in order to work, as they do on Claude Montana's ultrasharp Spring '98 suits. In the same vein are the invisible *magnets* that ingeniously close some of Alberta Ferretti's jackets of the same season. Beautiful silk cord *frog closures* have been around for millennia in the Far East, but they still have a visual impact that counts.

Label Lore   The earlier advice to ignore the name on the label doesn't mean you should disregard the whole tag, for labels are an important quality indicator. That's because they are *constructed,* just like the garment is. How well that label is put together—the quality and care of its materials and workmanship—is an accurate mirror of the garment as a whole. A budget manufacturer would no sooner put an exquisite (and expensive) jacquarded label into a $5.99 T-shirt than a high-end maker would use a cheapo printed tag. Let's take a closer look at this usually overlooked element of fashion.

*The type of label and its cost are closely
related to the type of garment and the level
of the market in which it is selling.*
—Harold Carr and Barbara Latham,
The Technology of Clothing Manufacture

The finest labels are *woven* in a slightly raised pattern on a fabric backing. The more colors used, the costlier the label is, but some very classy designers deliberately go for the simplicity of just two hues. On a fine label, the edges of any lettering and logos will appear smooth and crisp rather than "stairstepped," and there will not be a loose-strand "hairiness" on the reverse side. Indeed, in the best clothing the labels tend to be sewn down on four sides, although this may not be done if the stitching will mar the outside of the item, as in knitwear.

Meanwhile, in the cheaper regions of the label world, tags are *printed* (which leaves no design evident on the reverse side). What's more, with certain kinds of printing techniques, long strips bearing the name over and over are cut apart with a hot knife, leaving sharp edges that bug the heck out of you once you're wearing the garment.

Examining the labels on our two pantsuits, we see another way in which standout labels can differ from those that are not so hot. LaSchlaque splurged for a woven brand label, the one with his name on it, but ran out of steam with those bearing the size, content, and care instructions, which are all printed. With Spiffing, every label except the care instructions is woven. Even that last one is printed on a thicker, more substantial tag. (European manufacturers, no matter what their stature, seem to have largely adopted a printed contents/care label).

*The Little
Extras*

These are the things that you don't always expect to find inside a garment, but when you do, it gives you the warm and fuzzy feeling that the manufacturer has your best interests at heart.

Hidden pockets: This is a biggie, especially in coats, jackets, and smooth-front trousers. While men take hidden pockets for granted, in women's wear they're practically nonexistent, except at the highest end—for example the delightful pieces of Richard Tyler, whose signature motif is an interior pocket with a zigzag edge.

Hanger aides: These are the satiny loops or straps sewn into better garments to keep them hanging steady in the closet. Another variant is the interior neck loop along the collar in jackets and coats—or, even better, a loop of metal chain.

Interior weights: Found only at the highest end of the fashion world, these sewn-in metal slugs or chains help the garment hang more beautifully (a flat gold chain sewn around the interior is one of the signatures of a contemporary Chanel jacket).

✳ Why Quality Counts ✳

All this quality talk might send some into a funk. Isn't fashion supposed to be *fun?* Who cares about boring old quality? Well, *you* should, at least a little. Even if your fashion passion is 1960s hotpants, you owe it to yourself to find the best-made short-shorts on the rack. The better-made pieces are always the better buy. Why? They will:

- look better
- last longer
- transcend passing fashion trends more gracefully (though no guarantees made for hotpants)
- be a more accurate reflection of your amazing taste and judgment (as above)
- possibly be reconsignable after a few years, as long as they're properly cared for

But a girl's gotta have some fun. Go ahead and ignore quality if the piece is:
dirt cheap + adorable + fits like a glove
If any of these ingredients are missing, odds are you'll end up with just another *schmatte* (garment-speak for "rag") adding to the clutter in your closet.

Spare buttons: Their presence in a sleeve or pants leg not only indicates a certain level of quality, it hints that the garment is fairly new.

Shoulder pads in jackets, dresses, and tops: High-quality shoulder pads are either hidden or detachable, are covered in the same fabric as that used on the exterior (or a reasonably nice equivalent), and are made from padded fabric rather than foam. Bunched up, wandering, and/or unusually large pads are negatives on the quality roster.

While the Spiffing didn't have any little pluses, the LaSchlaque revealed yet another little minus, a missing button. And with this, we thank our two pantsuits for helping out with the program and bid the two of them adieu.

Before closing out the chapter, there is one more important point to be made—important enough to be:

Rule #4 of Resale: *Your quality check must be thorough.*

Relying solely on a button or some overlocking to tell the garment's whole story is almost as bad as buying on the basis of a designer name. These factors are simply elements of the whole. Odds are, some of the indicators will be great, and others not so hot—it's the sum total that should sway your decisions. And if, after all this, you still take home the occasional LaSchlaque, that's fine, as long as you know that's what you're getting.

Chapter Five

Garment Insider

As we saw in the last chapter, certain aspects of superior workmanship, like a well-finished seam, are shared by all kinds of fine clothing. In this chapter, we'll see how varying types of garments—such as skirts, blouses, and pants—also have their own particular hallmarks. In fine clothing, there are myriad ways a manufacturer can build in quality. Given the huge variety of cuts, styles, and functions—even within a category as narrow as T-shirts—it would be folly to try to list every last one. Those provided here are intended as a starting point, meant to get you looking at and thinking about the kinds of details that count. Once this becomes habit, you'll start evaluating independently, and expanding your personal checklist of quality lore.

Experience isn't interesting until it begins to repeat itself—
in fact, until it does that, it hardly is experience.
—Elizabeth Bowen, *The Death of the Heart*

FIELD RESEARCH

Before we get to the hallmarks themselves, a few more words about building that checklist. The best way to go about it is by having frequent encounter sessions with exquisite clothes—new ones—in better boutiques and department stores. Such a deal: examining and trying on collection-caliber pieces doesn't cost a cent, but does give you a Ph.D.-level understanding of materials and workmanship. Naturally, there is a frustration factor in getting so close to pieces you can't yet afford, but look on the bright side. Later on, when similar pieces show up at half or even one-fiftieth the price at resale, you'll instantly recognize them and snap them up, getting the jump on less knowledgeable shoppers.

Fear Not
the Designer
Floors

If you're anything like I once was, you feel intimidated in the glitzier stores, thinking the salespeople will peg you as an impostor. Deep down, you believe that unless you can buy, you have no right to try on such beautiful clothes. Now I know how wrongheaded this is. Salespeople themselves would be the first to agree. For one thing, who's to know that you won't hit the Powerball tomorrow? For another, if your body is clean, your makeup smudgeproof, and your attitude pleasant, you're already much more welcome than that little Ms. Moneybags who flings stuff around, climbs into it with her shoes on, and treats the sales staff like dirt. Finally, if you can discuss workmanship seriously, a saleswoman is likely to go out of her way to help, because so few customers actually care. To otherwise ensure good service:

✧ If your style is generally easygoing in comfy outfits and shoes, sharpen up a bit for visits to high-end emporiums. You'll feel more invincible and you'll automatically get more respect in return. Another trick—take along the glitziest shopping bag (in decent shape) that you own. Who's to know that it holds your lunch or some old walking shoes? Salespeople will take you more seriously if they think you've been spending big elsewhere.

✧ It's perfectly acceptable to take garments off the hangers to check the insides. Just be sure to hang them back like you found them, draping them evenly with the pleats aligned. The saleswoman may rush to do it herself, but your efforts will be appreciated.

✧ Don't ever bad-mouth the merchandise, even if the price/quality equation is appalling. These garments are the saleswoman's livelihood, and she won't appreciate hearing how crummily they're made.

✧ Serious examination is best done in the dressing room. Be sure to take in as many items as are allowed in your size, so you can check hang and fit as well as assembly.

✧ If there are other customers around who look like they need help, don't monopolize the salesperson's time.

In your search-and-try-on program, don't limit your efforts to the classy emporiums. Now and again it's a good idea to buzz through the mass merchandisers as well. Why? One reason is that the quality might surprise you. Many of these organizations (and their suppliers) are working hard to improve the appeal of their goods. The rise of so-called "quality assurance" programs means flawed merchandise is weeded out before it ever reaches the stores. What's more, many stores now recognize their customers' hunger for high fashion. Megaretailer Sears, Roebuck sends product development staff to the runway shows in Paris, London, and Milan in order to quickly adopt the most fashionable styles and silhouettes.

Another reason to check out budget-priced stores is that those that take quality less seriously provide a reality check of the kinds of materials and assembly you want to avoid. The clothes will teach you countless lessons about poor workmanship, unappealing fabric, and who-cares assembly. By keeping your eyes and hands trained to detect both the top and the bottom of the clothing ranks, you'll vastly improve your ability to home in on treasures at resale.

HOME STUDY

Stores aren't the only places to check quality. Yet again, you'll be amazed at how much info lurks in your own closet. Get in there and see what you've got, just as you did earlier with fabrics. Enlist tolerant girlfriends and relatives and do the same with their clothes—they'll be fascinated by what you can tell them. If there's a man about the house, look at his clothing, and get ready to weep at its superior tailoring.

A few final words: once you know what you're looking for, quality hallmarks will leap out every time you go over a piece. As with the last chapter's indicators, it's the overall impression that counts. If a skirt or a top falls short in one area, it may shine in another. Like people, garments are rarely perfect.

Blouse
- ❖ The tinier the stitches used to assemble the blouse, the better. Sixteen stitches per inch is the sign of a very high standard.
- ❖ French cuffs (buttonless cuffs with holes on either side) are more complicated to construct than regular barrel cuffs, and they require cufflinks. As a result, such blouses are limited to the highest quality rank. If you see French cuffs (and don't mind a bit of extra ironing), pounce. Classic, attractive links can be found at the jewelry counters of many thrift stores.
- ❖ If the buttons are otherwise basic, four holes are preferable to two (they stay on longer).
- ❖ A gauntlet button (on the sleeve placket above the wrist) is a nice extra touch. Fashion historians say this button either (1) helped doctors keep their sleeves up during medical procedures, or (2) allowed the wearer to raise hands over the head without the sleeves drooping down.
- ❖ Buttons at the cuff and collar points should be smaller than those running down the front placket.
- ❖ Look for pleats at the juncture of sleeve and cuff. If you don't see any, beware, the sleeve may fit awkwardly once on.
- ❖ Raw edges inside pockets are a huge demerit.
- ❖ Pockets should hang evenly when blouse is buttoned.
- ❖ Long tails (and generous use of fabric overall) is a sign of a generous manufacturer.
- ❖ The placket upon which the front buttonholes sit should be folded double and/or should be firm enough not to sag under the weight of the buttons.
- ❖ Recent advertisements and style guides make a big deal of a "split" yoke (the piece of fabric that sits above the shoulder blades). But according to one shirtmaking expert, the only one who benefits is the maker, who can cut the two parts out of smaller pieces of fabric, cutting down on waste. The ideal yoke should, however, be *doubled,* that is, made from two layers of fabric.
- ❖ In back, the collar should cover its own seam.
- ❖ Borrowing from menswear tailoring, ultra high-quality blouses may have a bottom hem that is rolled rather than pressed flat.

BLOUSE

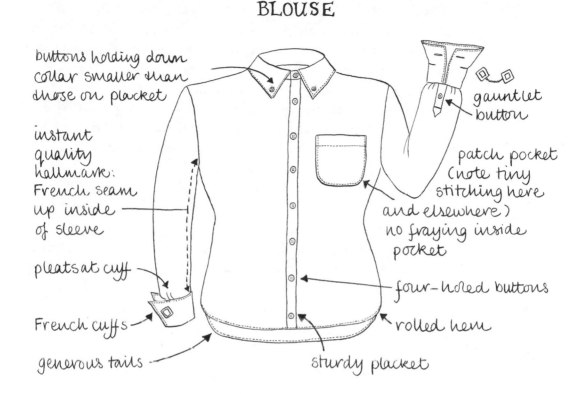

buttons holding down collar smaller than those on placket

gauntlet button

instant quality hallmark: French seam up inside of sleeve

patch pocket (note tiny stitching here and elsewhere) no fraying inside pocket

pleats at cuff

four-holed buttons

French cuffs

rolled hem

generous tails

sturdy placket

Instant quality hallmark: French seam up inside of arm (see Chapter 4).

T-shirt ✧ With T-shirts, fabric quality is paramount. Whether it's cotton, cotton-poly, or some other material, make sure the weight is what you want. Use the fingertip test (how much flesh color can you see through the fabric?) as a quick indicator.

✧ Don't let a T-shirt's apparent simplicity fool you into thinking you don't have to try it on. A well-cut tee is less common than you might think. Especially trouble-prone is the area where the arms attach to the main body, where the fabric can bind or sag. Likewise, neck openings can sit bizarrely and fabric can ride up your midriff. *Always* try it on.

- Another hard-to-detect problem with tees is fabric cut off the grain, which causes the shirt to twist on the body. This defect will only show up after the first washing, and could be the reason the tee landed in resale. *Always* try it on.
- Tees cut to contour the body are a sign of value.
- "T"-shaped garments (where sleeves stick straight out) will probably not fit as nicely as those whose sleeves fall closer to the body.
- Be sure to check the contents label and washing instructions. Some rayon blends must be hand-washed.
- Carefully inspect the quality of any embroidery or screenprinting. Note that counterfeiters sometimes do a better job than the original makers.
- Seams will be overlocked. Be on the lookout for thread chains, and loose or sloppy stitching—as with blouses, finer stitching indicates greater quality.
- The color should be crisp and not faded.
- A great deal of surface fuzz indicates an older garment.
- The neckline and sleeve cuffs should retain elasticity.
- Seek out collar and/or shoulder seams that have been reinforced on the interior with tape or fabric strips.
- An unusually shaped neck (wide, scoop) is a mark of quality.
- A little bit of spandex gives a lot of shape.
- The depth of the hems at the sleeves and bottom is part of the design equation. Unusually deep hems means that the maker was going for a distinctive look, rather than run-of-the-mill.
- A printed label indicates lesser quality. A cheap label bearing a tip-top name points to a counterfeit garment.

The US Army's 1955 military specification for cotton
quarter-sleeve undershirts . . . ran to 8 pages
of detailed instruction on constructing the perfect t!
—The T-shirt Book,
John Gordon and Alice Hiller

Instant quality hallmark: Woven label.

T-SHIRT

instant quality hallmark: woven label

no sagging at neckline or cuffs

sleeves carefully cut and attached to reduce binding

contoured for better fit

fabric doesn't twist on body

deep hem

Dresses & Dresses show their age worse than any other garment. If it looks tired on the hanger, it's not likely to look better on your back.

& Very expensive day dresses (worn by ladies who lunch) have an armorlike quality, due to the substantiality of the fabric and lining (summerwear, too—the air is just *frigid* in that dining room, dahling).

& With a superior dress, even if the color or pattern is relatively muted, the quality of the dyes and printing give it an unmistakable visual "pop."

& Look carefully at the construction of the lining. If it closely follows that of the dress, this is quality manufacture.

& The lining should be attached to the dress at the armhole, waist, and hips.

& The lining should cover the stitching at the hem, but should not drop below the hemline.

& Ensure that the lining is not distorted away from the dress shape by inferior workmanship or incorrect cleaning.

- In cheap dresses, the inner waistband often looks raw and messy.
- With a quality dress, the ends of any straps should be trapped between two layers of fabric rather than simply tacked down.
- In ultra-quality dresses, beads and sequins are individually sewn on.
- If the arms are of sheer fabric, the armhole seam should be neatened as prettily as possible.
- Bias-cut dresses look like unfilled sausage skins on the hanger (because the stretchy fabric, cut on an angle, doesn't drape well until it has a body as support). Don't dismiss it until you've tried it on. With bias-cut dresses, look inside for hanger loops, which will prevent any distortion from hanging.
- With knit dresses, make sure collars and cuffs maintain shape and the backside hasn't bagged (tape reinforcement sewn onto inner seams is a good sign).
- Coat-dress styles should have an interior button to hold the innermost side securely in place.
- The popularity of unlined slip dresses has encouraged the idea that it's OK to have raw-edged zipper tape exposed in a garment. It's not OK, it's sloppy—no matter which bigshot designer does it.
- Make sure longer dresses have a slit or fabric fullness around the legs, otherwise you'll hate the thing for hobbling you.
- Cheap shoulder pads are covered in sort-of-matching nylon fabric. Better-quality pads are covered in the same material as the dress. They're also removable, or invisible altogether under the lining.

Instant quality hallmark: A concealed zipper running along the side of the torso to the waist. This manufacturer was willing to spend in order to ensure an unbroken expanse front and back.

You can say what you like about long dresses,
but they cover a multitude of shins.
—Mae West, *Peel Me a Grape*

DRESS

instant quality
hallmark:
concealed zipper
running along
the side of the
torso to the waist

deep facings
at collar
and
armholes

lining
attached at
armhole,
waist and hips

fabric cut
generously
enough to
prevent
hobbling

lining should
cover stitching
at hem

Skirt ✥ If the skirt is made of wool or other fabric that might cling, it should be lined.

✥ With a basic straight skirt, look for a generous hem. Hems will be less deep on full/flared/circular skirts.

✥ Check the interior lower edge of the waistband. Is it concealed in the lining (best), bound with satin (good), or overlocked (OK)?

✥ A zipper flap ought to be positioned between teeth and your skin, or the lining around the zipper should be slightly raised, to prevent chafing.

✥ The lining may either be attached to the outer fabric or loose. If it hangs loose, a short thread chain holding it in place at the hem is a nice touch.

- ❦ Carefully check the top of slit openings for splits or tears. An arrowhead-shaped sewn reinforcement on a kick pleat is an elegant means of strengthening the fabric at this weak spot.
- ❦ If there is a slit, mitered corners sharpen the look of the adjacent fabric.
- ❦ A dual-button closure above the zipper is generally more secure and comfortable than a hook and eye.

Instant quality hallmark: Front "tulip" closure or other curvy hemline (note: these styles are difficult to alter).

SKIRT

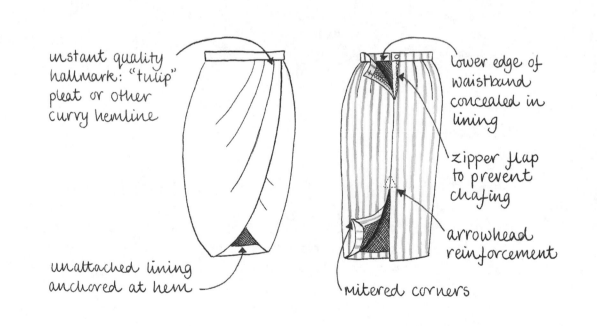

instant quality hallmark: "tulip" pleat or other curvy hemline

unattached lining anchored at hem

lower edge of waistband concealed in lining

zipper flap to prevent chafing

arrowhead reinforcement

mitered corners

Pants ✤ All wool and/or potentially clingy trousers should be lined, at least to the knee.

✤ Linings should be attached to the trousers at the knee, crotch, and ankle.

✤ Check the interior lower edge of the waistband. Is it concealed in lining (best), bound with satin ribbon (good), or overlocked (OK)?

✤ Check pockets for raw seam edges.

✤ Check the point at which belt loops attach to the waistband. In ultra-high-end trousers, this will be hemmed clean. In lesser-quality trousers, a bit of rough edge may appear. In no-quality trousers, this spot will be frays galore.

PANTS

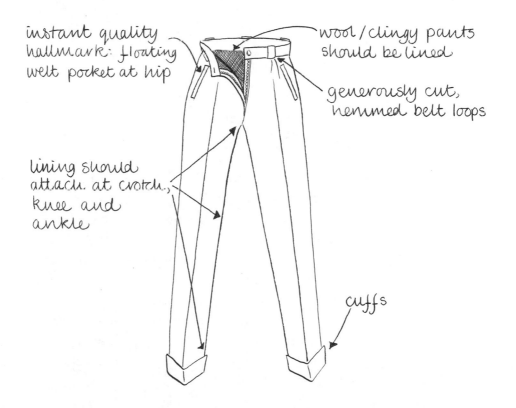

instant quality hallmark: floating welt pocket at hip

wool/clingy pants should be lined

generously cut, hemmed belt loops

lining should attach at crotch, knee and ankle

cuffs

- ❖ Belt loops should be generous—in cheaper trousers, they tend to be skimpy.
- ❖ If waistband is elasticized, gathers should be uniform.
- ❖ The edges of the fly's zipper tape should be concealed behind the lining.
- ❖ Check around any rivets for signs of rust.
- ❖ Any big tag on rear waistband of jeans should be real leather, not plastic or cardboard.
- ❖ Extra-plush corduroy is unusual and generally a sign of good quality.
- ❖ Corduroy shouldn't show signs of wear at seat or knees.
- ❖ Leggings should have spandex content to prevent bagging.

Instant quality hallmark: Floating slashed pockets at the hip (see page 77).

> *When a man says he likes*
> *a woman in a skirt, I tell him to try one.*
> —Katharine Hepburn

Jacket
- ❖ The key quality hallmarks of sports, activewear, and casual jackets are even stitching, a distinctive silhouette, contemporary fabric, and effective hardware.
- ❖ Look carefully at the color of white activewear jackets. Sometimes these have been treated with special brighteners that can be stripped out by improper dry cleaning, leaving the color dingy.
- ❖ The more tailored the jacket, the more important the inner structure (interlinings, padding), since these help the piece conform to the body.
- ❖ With tailored jackets, the meeting point of the sleeve and shoulder should be as sleek as the lines of a Porsche, with no bumps, ridges, or wavering seams. Generally speaking, the closer set-in sleeves hang to the body, the better the construction. Watch out especially for the outline of shoulderpads—you shouldn't be able to see them from the exterior. A hollow or dimple under the end of the shoulder is especially bad.

JACKET

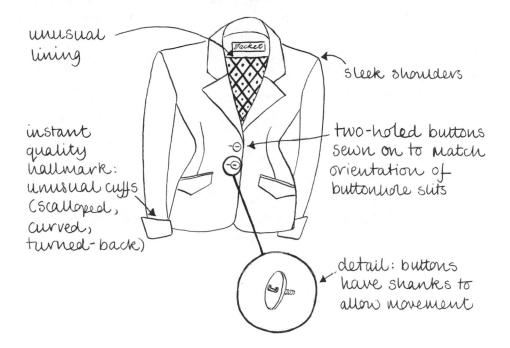

unusual lining

sleek shoulders

instant quality hallmark: unusual cuffs (scalloped, curved, turned-back)

two-holed buttons sewn on to match orientation of buttonhole slits

Jacket

detail: buttons have shanks to allow movement

- Some couturiers (notably Yves Saint Laurent and John Galliano) like to build padding into sleeve caps (the point at which the sleeve meets the shoulder), so that they are slightly peaked. Work of this kind should show no dimples or breaks.
- The attachment points of epaulets and other doodads should be hemmed clean.
- An eye-catching tweed (multitextured, possibly incorporating unexpected materials) points to a standout garment.
- In exquisitely well-made jackets, two-holed buttons will be sewn on to match the orientation of the buttonhole slits (vertical or horizontal).
- In superior tailored jackets, buttons will be attached to fabric with twisted shanks of thread, allowing some play of movement.

- The lining of the finest jackets may be quilted (stitched down in a square or diamond pattern, often seen in Chanel).
- Look for a pleat down the center of the back panel of the lining. In very well made tailored jackets, darts are oftentimes placed to either side of midline.
- In finer tailored jackets, the collar may be hand-sewn onto the jacket body.
- A felt lining underneath a collar is a tailoring detail that indicates ambitiousness on the part of the manufacturer. It must be invisible when the collar is in normal position, and any visible stitching should be attractively done.
- The interlinings should be neither visible (ripples) nor audible (crackles) when you handle the fabric.
- Lapels should have enough substance so they don't fold or droop. In the best jackets, they are constructed to gently roll toward the chest.
- Collars in a contrasting fabric (such as velvet) are costlier to incorporate, and so are a good tip-off to a better-made piece.
- Real suede or leather patches at the collar or elbows are another excellent quality indicator (beware, though, such pieces can be the devil to clean).

  Instant quality hallmark: Unusual cuffs (for example, scalloped, curved, or turned-back).

Sweater
- The component pieces of "fully fashioned" sweaters are preshaped on the knitting machine to conform to the finished outlines of the garment (rather than being "cut and sewn" after knitting is completed). With fully fashioned sweaters, inconspicuous ribbing appears wherever the width of the sweater changes, for example at the shoulder seams. Such sweaters tend to be more tailored and have less bulky seams than cut-and-sewn.
- With wool and cashmere, the finer the knit, the more refined the quality. Sometimes, though, a bulkier, toasty Shetland may be the better buy, depending on wardrobe needs.

SWEATER

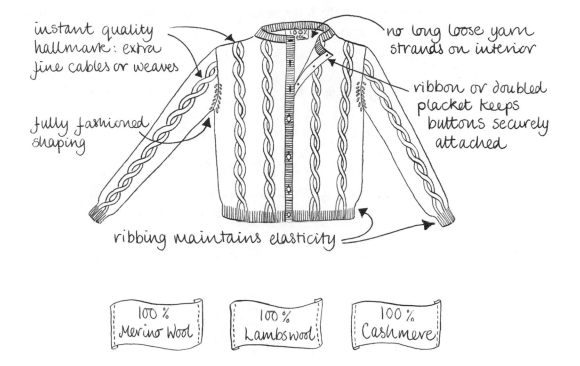

instant quality hallmark: extra fine cables or weaves

no long loose yarn strands on interior

ribbon or doubled placket keeps buttons securely attached

fully fashioned shaping

ribbing maintains elasticity

100% Merino Wool

100% Lambswool

100% Cashmere

- ❖ Cotton knit sweaters tend to look like hell once they've been through the dryer. Check such garments carefully for signs of fading.
- ❖ Check the inside of highly colorful sweaters for long stretches of floating yarn. In a well-finished sweater, these will be anchored (technically speaking, "stranded" or "woven") after every five loops or so. This is to prevent the strands from snagging.
- ❖ Intricately patterned ribs, cables, and stitches are part of the knitter's art, and should be sought out.
- ❖ A true "fisherman's knit" cable allows a careful pinky finger underneath a braid that appears to be attached flat to the garment.
- ❖ Make sure the top edge of a turtleneck isn't rippling.

- ❖ Buttons and buttonholes on better cardigans will have reinforcement in the form of a fabric or ribbon placket to prevent sagging.
- ❖ Yarn used to overlock the seams of sweaters is ideally the same as that used to knit the garment. Otherwise, it should be as close a match as possible.

Instant quality hallmark: Extra-fine cables or weave.

Coat
- ❖ Coats should be cut generously enough to allow for your bulkiest outfit underneath.
- ❖ Linings should also be generous. Look out for signs of wear around underarms (though linings can be replaced fairly easily).
- ❖ Extreme softness in a wool coat indicates the presence of cashmere.

COAT

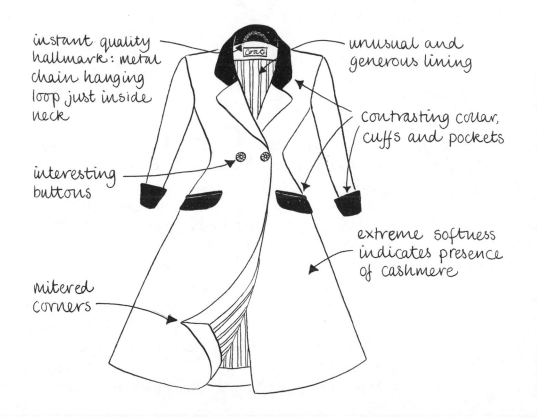

instant quality hallmark: metal chain hanging loop just inside neck

unusual and generous lining

contrasting collar, cuffs and pockets

interesting buttons

extreme softness indicates presence of cashmere

mitered corners

- Capes are so rare in the States that those you see will tend to be of fine quality. Consider them for between-season wear.
- A detachable wool lining in raincoats is a sign of good quality.
- On casual coats, look for heavy-duty hardware.
- Many lesser-quality trenchcoats have cheaply made and attached epaulets, patch pockets, foldover lapels, etc. Check the attachment points and seams very carefully to distinguish the great from the pretenders.
- With suede and leather, the stiffer it is (check especially around the collar), the dirtier—or poorer the quality.
- Due to fur's fall in popularity, it now abounds at resale and thrift stores. Especially with older furs, be on the alert for gaping seams, moth-eaten patches, stiffness in the pelts, and general lack of gloss. Unless you enjoy terrorizing small children, don't buy furs with heads and paws still attached.
- Look for a heavy fabric loop inside the coat collar for hanging. But try not to hang a fine coat with this attachment; use a hanger whenever possible.

Instant quality hallmark: Metal chain hanging loop just inside neck.

> *The trick of wearing mink is to look as though*
> *you are wearing a cloth coat.*
> *The trick of wearing a cloth coat*
> *is to look as though you are wearing mink.*
> —Pierre Balmain, couturier, 1955

Chapter Six

✧

Tag, You're It

*H*ere comes a curve ball: after all the earlier advice to ignore the names on labels, this chapter covers nothing but. Now that you're able to judge clothes on their own merits, the unvarnished truth can come out. Names do count. Not so much for you and me, but for much of the rest of the world. Many people rely on labels as the *sole* key to value—including some of the people setting prices at resale stores. If you know better than they do where a name really ranks, you have the advantage. It means you can:

✧ target bargains where they exist, and
✧ avoid paying more than you ought to

So knowing your labels can help you shop smarter. But, as the old saying goes, a *little* knowledge is a dangerous thing. You want to know *more than most.* Stuff like:

✧ the differences between upmarket and downmarket diffusion lines
✧ instances when respectable names may produce substandard goods
✧ how to spot counterfeits

WHEN THE NAME DOESN'T RING A BELL

Here's a specific example of how a little knowledge can lead to a big mistake: label-struck shoppers often bypass terrific pieces simply because they don't recognize the name on the tag. Given the thousands upon thousands of brands out there, it's easy to understand the urge to be selective—in fact, it's practically a survival tactic for women pressed for time. But it's also easy to narrow down too far. Some women are so eager to get to the CK, DK, and RL they blow right by Adeline André, one of the newest members of the haute-couture club, or Amanda Wakeley, a designer favored by Princess Diana. If your list of must-haves is *too* short, wonderful buys may be missed.

Rule #5 of Resale: *Never ignore a garment because the label is unfamiliar.*

The reason is twofold. Given the ease of global travel (and the strength of the dollar), foreign treasures often crop up at resale stores. So do fine private-label pieces from far-flung department stores in the U.S. Every day shoppers snub these wonderful buys because they literally don't know what they're missing. Maybe this has even happened to you? After finishing this chapter, that kind of oversight will be history.

WHY WE LOVE LABELS

There are 101 reasons. Here are five:

Status: In remote parts of the world, wearing spots, stripes, and scales is a way to show off one's rank in society. In developed parts of the world we've advanced past that, preferring designer logos instead.

Buying into genius: For some, buying a designer garment is like acquiring a work of art. All the better, since it's hard to get Pablo on markdown.

Fashionability: Buying cool (in the form of a Prada jacket) is a lot easier than being cool.

Lack of shopping time/interest: People with money to burn often buy top-status brands as a way to cut down decision-making. (These people are no fun to shop with.)

Style: Sometimes a designer's vision is perfectly in tune with your own sense of style (this is the best reason of all to love a label).

The Time-honored Tradition of Designer Hype

You often hear that designer mania is a new phenomenon, arising in the 1980s as part of that decade's obsession with wealth and status. In fact, couturiers have been doted on for centuries. Rose Bertin, dressmaker to Queen Marie-Antoinette in the late 1700s, was, as Rachel Kempner puts it in *Costume,* "famous enough in her day to be regarded as something of a minister of fashion." France set the style for European fashion, and Bertin's fame quickly spread. Soon she dressed royalty as far away as Madrid and Saint Petersburg—until history's wheel turned. With the French Revolution, the frivolity of worrying about fashionable necklines became bitterly clear to Bertin's clientele. She managed to escape to London, where she embarked on a writing career, "padding out her considerable profits from scandalous and generally unreliable memoirs of the *ancien regime.*"

A hundred years later, the dressmaker Charles Worth had a similarly starry career, minus the rude interruptions. Prickly as a pincushion, he set a tone that has lasted to the present day. According to Diana de Marly, in *The History of Haute Couture, 1850–1950:*

> So keen was he to raise the study of dress to a new level that he adopted a completely unprecedented attitude towards his customers. A lady did not go to Maison Worth as she would to an ordinary dressmaker and say that she wanted a dress in green silk by Friday. First she made an appointment (for Worth was an extremely busy man), which was most unusual, and when admitted to his presence she would find that her own ideas counted for nothing. Worth would study her, note her colouring, her hair, her jewels, her style and then he would design a gown which he thought suited her. Anyone going to Worth had to submit to his taste, while his overseas customers had to rely on his taste completely, it did not matter if they were the Empress Marie Feodorovna in St Petersburg or Mrs J. Pierpont Morgan in New York, they were sent what Worth judged would suit them best.

Another historian has a sharper opinion of Worth's contribution to design history. Colin McDowell, in *Dressed to Kill,* says:

> High fashion required a dictator who would show how much he scorned his clients for their lack of fashion culture. By treating them abominably and over-charging them disgracefully, Worth ensured the lasting success of the breed he had brought into existence.

THE HAUTE COUTURE

Once upon a time, the activities of Worth and his followers directly concerned only a razor-thin slice of society—women with the money and leisure time to have frocks made to measure in Paris. So it remained until recent decades, when haute couture became of interest to all. Along with the popularization came a blurring of the term's meaning. Now merchandisers happily slap the "haute couture" label onto everything from panty hose to pet collars. Yet it really only means one thing: garments made by hand, over the course of several fittings, by a limited number of design houses in Paris—sold directly to buyers rather than through stores.

The list is strictly controlled by the Paris-based Chambre Syndicale de la Couture et des Createurs de la Mode, which acts like a union for this crème de la crème industry. Up until a few years ago, the membership requirements were very strict. Haute-couture houses were obligated to have a significant presence in Paris, employing a specified number of *mains* or "sewing hands." (This explains why the Milan-based Giorgio Armani and others, while certainly capable, are technically not haute-couture designers.) Moreover, fashion shows had to be presented every season, featuring a set number of garments. But now the rules are loosening, in an effort to bring in fresh talent and interest.

The Chambre is fighting for the life of this old-line industry because, by some counts, there are as few as 70 steady haute-couture customers in the entire world. Though these ladies are the walking, talking version of cash machines, even they cannot keep the business afloat. Haute couture is always a money-losing operation. How could it be otherwise, when ten people are employed to hand-sew itty-bitty real pearls all over a mermaid-inspired dress? Or marvels produced like a jacket with no visible point of entry?

The very thought of such clothing makes all of us giddy, but reality must enter in: *haute-couture pieces rarely make it to resale.* In part because they cost their owners too much simply to toss aside, in part because the couture houses' free alteration service means nobody has to grow out of them, in part because they wear beautifully for decades, and in biggest part because they usually get donated to museums instead. Still, *rarely* isn't the same as *never*. It pays to be on the alert, for you just never know. A Nina Ricci couture jacket recently showed up at my local thrift for $80—a few decimal points west of where it was priced originally. Tragically, it didn't fit.

THE HAUTE-COUTURE LABELS

The following names represent the ultimate in the art of high fashion. Please bear in mind, though, that these designers and those on the pages that follow are not cast in stone. If there's one thing fashion is known for, it's change. The best way to keep abreast of who's who and what's what is to regularly read magazines such as *Vogue* and *W.* One more thing: while *you* surely pronounce the names perfectly, your sister might appreciate the guide...

Adeline André (Ad-uh-LEEN Ahn-DRAY)

Balmain (BALL-meh)

Chanel (Sha-NELL)

Christian Dior (CHRIS-tee-ah Dee-OR)

Christian Lacroix (CHRIS-tee-ah La-CWAH)

Givenchy (GEE-vahn-SHEE)

Hanae Mori (Ha-nay MOR-ee)

Jean-Louis Scherrer (Shawn Loo-EE SHER-ay)

Jean-Paul Gaultier (Shawn Poll GO-tee-ay)

Josephus Thimister (JO-sephus THI-mister)

Lecoanet Hemant (Le-co-ah-nay
   AY-mahn)
Nina Ricci (NEE-nah REE-chee)
Ocimar Versolato (OH-chee-mar
   Ver-so-LAH-toe)
Paco Rabanne (PAH-co Rah-
   BAHN)
Pascal Humbert (PAH-scahl
   OOM-ber)

Per Spook (Per SPOOK)
Rochas (ROW-chah)
Ted Lapidus (Ted LAH-pee-duss)
Thierry Mugler (Tyeh-REE
   MOOG-lay)
Versace (Ver-SAHCH-ay)
Viktor et Rolf (VEEK-tor ay Rolf)
Yves Saint Laurent (EEV Sahn
   Low-RAHN)

THE INTERNATIONAL SET

Besides the one-of-a-kind pieces they make for the wealthiest women in the world, most haute-couture houses also produce ready-to-wear (or prêt-à-porter) lines every season, distributed through boutiques and department stores. The prices of individual garments usually top out in the low thousands, attracting a steady stream of customers and offsetting some of the losses in couture. Which is not to say buyers abound. A limited number of them vie for a limited number of pieces. Exclusivity is a big part of the allure.

At this level of fashion, haute couturiers share the stage with prêt-à-porter designers from the world's other major fashion centers. New York, Milan, London—they, along with Paris, are the major launch pads of the ready-to-wear collections. "Collection" is another fashion term that gets flung all over the place, but in the strict sense it means only one thing: the most deluxe store-destined pieces a big-name designer offers—in other words, the top of the line.

The following elite group of prêt-à-porter designers has achieved such success that they are instantly recognized all over the world. Top consignment-store owners, whether they're in Geneva, London, or Palm Beach, warmly welcome them as names that need no introduction.

Alaïa (Ah-la-EE-a)
Alberta Ferretti (Fer-RETT-ee)
Alexander McQueen

Anna Molinari (Mow-lee-
   NAHR-ee)
Balenciaga (Bah-len-chee-AH-ga)

Bill Blass

Calvin Klein

Cerruti (Chay-ROO-tee)

Chloé (CLO-ay)

Claude Montana (Clawed Mon-
    TAH-nah)

Dolce & Gabbana (DOL-chay ay
    Gah-BAH-nah)

Donna Karan (CARE-an)

Emilio Pucci (Ay-MEE-lee-oh
    POO-chee)

Escada (Es-CAH-dah)

Fendi (FEN-dee)

Geoffrey Beene

Gianfranco Ferré (Gee-ahn-
    FRAHN-co Fer-RAY)

Giorgio Armani (Jor-GEE-oh Ahr-
    MAH-nee)

Gucci (GOO-chee)

Guy Laroche (Key La-ROASH)

Helmut Lang (HELL-moot Lahng)

Hermès (Air-MEZZ)

Hervé Léger (Air-VAY LEH-jay)

Isaac Mizrahi (Mizz-RAH-hee)

Issey Miyake (EE-say MEE-yah-
    kay)

Jil Sander (Jill SAHN-dare)

Karl Lagerfeld (LAH-ger-feld)

Kenzo (KEHN-zo)

Krizia (KREE-zia)

Loewe (LOW-vay)

Louis Féraud (Loo-EE FAY-row)

Louis Vuitton (Loo-EE VUEE-
    tow)

MaxMara (Mahx MAH-ra)

Michael Kors

Missoni (Mee-SO-nee)

Mondi (Mown-dee)

Moschino (Mos-KEE-no)

Oscar de la Renta (de lah
    RENT-a)

Prada (PRAH-dah)

Ralph Lauren (LAW-ren, not
    Law-REN)

Rifat Ozbek (REE-faht OZ-beck)

Romeo Gigli (Ro-MAY-o
    GEE-lee)

Salvatore Ferragamo (Sal-vah-
    TOE-ray Fair-reh-GAHM-o)

Sonia Rykiel (REE-kay-ell)

Tocca (TOE-cah)

Trussardi (True-SAHR-dee)

Ungaro (Un-GAHR-oh)

Valentino (Vah-len-TEEN-o)

THE ALL-AMERICANS

If any of your favorites were missing from the list above, it may be
because the following higher-end American ready-to-wear labels,
while loved far and wide across the United States, don't carry the
same buzz at an international level. Not that they are in any way
inferior, just not as hugely popular abroad. Yet.

Adrienne Vittadini (Vee-tah-DEE-nee)

Anna Sui (SUE-ee)

Antonio Fusco (FOO-sko)

Badgley Mischka (Badge-lee MISH-kah)

Bob Mackie

Carolina Herrera (Hey-rah-rah)

Daryl K

Diane Von Furstenburg

Fabrice (Fa-BREECE)

Halston Signature

Joan & David

Joan Vass

John Bartlett

Lily Pulitzer

Marc Eisen

Marc Jacobs

Mary McFadden

Nicole Miller

Norma Kamali (Kah-MAH-lee)

Patrick Robinson

Rebecca Moses

Richard Tyler

Scaasi (SCAH-see)

Todd Oldham

Tommy Hilfiger

Tse (Tsay)

Vera Wang

Vivienne Tam

Zang Toi (TOE-ee)

Zoran

FOREIGN FINDS

On the flip side, many, many top European names aren't distributed widely in the States, so they don't have instant name recognition. The clothes still make their way into resale stores thanks to shopping vacationers, selective adoption by talent-hungry retailers like Bergdorf Goodman in New York, and other means. To give you an idea of their niche in the fashion world, most of the pieces sell between $200 and $1000 at retail—in other words, on the pricey side. Please note that while the list isn't comprehensive (there are simply too many designers to include one and all) these are among the best-loved in their own countries.

United Kingdom

Antonio Berardi (Bay-RAHR-dee)

Aquascutum (Aqua-SCOOT-um)

Bella Freud (Froyd)

Ben de Lisi (duh LEE-see)

Burberry

Clements Ribiero (Ri-bee-AY-ro)

Daks

Edina Ronay

English Eccentrics

Ghost

Hussein Chalayan (HOO-sane CHAL-ah-yahn)
Jaeger (Yay-grr)
Jasper Conran
Jean Muir
John Rocha (RO-sha)
Joseph
Julien MacDonald
Katherine Hamnett
Harrods
Harvey Nichols Collection
Liberty
Linea (Li-NAY-ah)

Margaret Howell
Matthew Williamson
Mulberry
Mulligan
N. Peal
Narciso Rodriguez
Nicole Farhi (FAH-ree)
Paul Costelloe
Paul Smith
Pierce Fionda
Tomasz Starzewski (Star-zev-ski)
Uniform

France

A.P.C. (Ah Pay Say)
Agnès B. (Ahn-yes BAY)
Atsuro Tayama (AHT-soo-ro Tah-YAH-ma)
Cacharel (CAH-shah-rell)
Chantal Thomass (Shawn-TAHL TOE-mahs)
Daniel Hechter (DAH-nee-ell ECK-tay)
Diapositiv (DEE-a-poe-sa-TEEV)
Dorothée Bis (Do-ro-tay BEE)
Emmanuelle Khanh (AY-mahn-u-ell KAHN)
Equipment
Et Vous (Ay Voo)
Galeries Lafayette (GAH-la-ree Lahf-eye-ETT)
Gerard Darel (JAY-rar Dah-RELL)
Georges Rech (Raysh)

Ines de la Fressange (EE-ness duh lah Fray-SAHN-juh)
Irene van Ryb (EE-ren van REEB)
Jacques Fath (Jock Fahth)
Les Copains (Lay Co-PEH)
Lolita Lempicka (Lo-LEE-ta LEM-pee-kah)
Lucien Pellat-Finet (LOO-see-ahn PAY-lah FEE-nay)
Martine Sitbon (SEET-bow)
Plein Sud (Plan SUE)
Popi Moreni (Poe-pee Mow-RAY-nee)
Regina Rubens (Ray-GEE-nah ROO-bens)
Rodier (ROH-dee-ay)
Teenflo
Tehen (TAY-hen)
Vertigo (Ver-TEE-go)

Germany	Basler (Bahz-lair)	Olsen
	Bogner (BOWG-nair)	Rena Lange
	Fink	Searle
	Joseph Janard	KS/Steilmann (Style-mahn)
	Joop!	Strenesse
	Lancaster	Yarell
	Marc Cain	

Italy	Basile (Bah-SEEL)	Loro Piano (Lo-ro Pee-AH-no)
	Byblos (BEE-blows)	Malo (MAH-lo)
	Enrico Coveri (Co-VER-ee)	Mila Schön (MEE-lah SHINE)
	Etro (AY-tro)	Nino Cerruti (Chay-ROO-tee)
	Fendi (FEN-dee)	Simonetta (SEE-mo-NAY-tah)
	Genny (Jen-ee)	Trussardi (True-SAHR-dee)
	Laura Biagiotti (BEE-ah-gee-OH-tee)	

Spain	Adolfo Dominguez (Do-MING-ez)	Roberto Verinno (Ver-EE-no)
	Antonio Alverado (Al-ver-AH-doh)	Sybilla (SEE-bee-lah)
	Marguerita Nuez (NOO-ez)	Vittorio & Luchino (Vee-TOH-ree-oh ay Loo-KEY-no)
	Nacho Ruiz (ROO-eez)	

Belgium	Anne Demeulemeester (Duh-MULE-uh-MEES-ter)	Veronique Branquinho (VAY-ron-eek Brahn-KEE-no)
	Dries van Noten (DREES van NOH-ten)	

Canada	Alfred Sung	John Fluevog (FLOO-vogue)
	Angi Venni	Lida Baday
	Dénommé Vincent (Duh-NUM-may Van-sahn)	Marilyn Brooks
	Dominic Bellissimo	Marisa Minicucci
	Il n'ya que Deux (Eel nee-AH cuh duh)	Nina Mdiviani (Muh-DEE-vee-ahn-nee)
		Robin Kay

Vivian Shyu (Shee-you)

Jean-Claude Poitras (Sean-clawed PWAH-trah)

Marie Saint-Pierre (Ma-REE San Pyair)

Merulla (Meh-ROO-la)

Michel Desjardins (MEE-shell DAY-jar-deh)

Muse

Parachute

Vénéré (VAY-nay-ray)

PRIVATE LABELS ON PARADE

Sometimes, tags go unrecognized at resale because they adorn "private label" (own-brand) merchandise from unfamiliar department stores, possibly based in other regions of the country. With some higher-end lines, the store's own name also features on the label. Other times, the origin may be mysterious, as is the case with the Charter Club brand sold by Macy's, Lazarus, and other stores in the Federated Merchandising Group.

Private-label clothing once had a downmarket reputation, considered second best to the big-name designers. But times are changing. Today, a private label may be overseen by a star name such as Louis Dell'Olio, who produces Dei Tre for Nieman Marcus. Or the store might hire its own in-house creative talent, putting together a team to rival those of outside organizations. According to *Women's Wear Daily,* "at Henri Bendel [a top-drawer department store in NYC], a whopping 50% of merchandise is private label, designed by a staff recruited from the likes of Donna Karan, Cerruti, Gucci and Ralph Lauren." Moreover, these clothes are often made in the same factories as designer pieces. Barney's Collection leather goods, for example, are put together by the same hands that assemble for Prada and Gucci.

Whether the source is an ultra-exclusive department store or a mass-marketer like Kmart (producing Jaclyn Smith), it pays to know private labels, especially from local retailers. Here are some of the more prominent names:

Barney's New York Collection

Bergdorf Goodman Collection

Charter Club (Federated Stores)

Classique Entier (Nordstrom)

CO-OP (Barney's)

Dei Tre (Neiman Marcus)

INC International Concepts (Federated stores)

Real Clothes Saks Fifth Avenue

Saks Fifth Avenue Collection

The Works Saks Fifth Avenue

Sport, Spa, and Body (all three from Bendel's)

Style & Co. (Federated stores)

> *With private-label buyers scouring the catwalks*
> *and going directly to designers' "secret"*
> *sources for materials, Gucci and Prada*
> *are inspiring what was once mediocre*
> *department store merchandise.*
> —*Vogue,* September 1997

DIFFUSION CONFUSION

The big-name designers are very much aware of the glitter factor surrounding their names. They are also aware that only a small segment of the buying public can afford a $1,500 collection suit. That is why, in the 1980s and 1990s, many designers began to create spinoff lines. The pieces in these secondary lines are made for customers who crave the labels but can't afford the whopper price tags on high-end prêt-à-porter. Lower in price, these pieces are also produced in large volumes, in order to reach as many buyers as possible.

The spinoffs are sometimes called "bridge" lines, because their price tags fall between those of the collection pieces and the "better women's wear" that once dominated department stores. We won't call them that, though, because bridge is more accurately used to categorize a slightly different kind of clothing. A better term for the megadesigners' offshoots is "diffusion" lines. The lines come from the same "name" as the collections, but are focused in a different direction, at a different market. They also bear their own distinct brand identity (unlike the between-season "resort" collections, another means by which designers produce less pricey clothes).

✳ Spanning the Gap ✳

True bridge lines consist of the mid-to-upper priced clothing made by such department store fixtures as Ellen Tracy and Jones of New York. Here's how *Women's Wear Daily* describes this layer of the fashion cake:

> Bridge sportswear started out as wear-to-work clothing for the growing female work force, priced above the better market, but well below designer lines.... Soon, though, that woman wanted more than work clothes. And in the last five years, a slew of new companies have launched labels that come in at the bridge price point, but have a distinctly unworkwear look.

Even though many bridge designers hold catwalk shows, they are not considered part of the same fashion galaxy as the big-name designers—probably because bridge lines tend to be cheaper. This shouldn't influence your opinion of the clothing; the quality is often superb. Some of the best-known bridge lines:

Albert Nipon	Gianni
Barry Bricken	Jill Stuart
Cynthia Rowley	Jones of New York
Dana Buchman	Rene Lezard
Eileen Fisher	St. John
Linda Allard/Ellen Tracy	Susan Lazar
Episode	Tahari

Sometimes the relationship between collection and diffusion can be very close. Yves Saint Laurent's Variation line is a good example. According to *Draper's Record,* since its creation Variation has been directly inspired by the couture collection produced two seasons previously, but has been priced about 30 percent lower, thanks to volume buying of fabrics and the use of less costly detail and trims.

The diffusion concept has been a gold mine for most designers. So much so that many have not stopped with one or two offshoots, but are now offering lines three, four, and five price levels removed from the collection pieces. These often have the words "jeans" or "sport" somewhere on the label. Usually targeted to younger customers, the prices are low compared with the other lines produced by the designer (though still more expensive than comparable merchandise from nonglitzy manufacturers). The items are truly mass merchandise, produced in the same megavolume as other national brands.

In general, the lower the price point of a diffusion line, the less direct the designer's participation. Sometimes all they do is OK prototypes worked up by subdesigners in the organization. In other cases, the design and/or manufacture is licensed out to other companies altogether. The name on the label means the glitter factor is still there, but otherwise the goods may be indistinguishable from cheaper ones a few racks away. Buyers either don't know or don't care. They gladly pay a $30 surcharge for a few grains of stardust.

The abundance of diffusion lines means designers' names are omnipresent. The key question is, how to tell collection pieces from those intended to dress junior-high school girls? Here secondhand shoppers face quite a challenge. Say there's a world-famous fashion designer named Nick Mason. He oversees a collection (Nick Mason Couture) and three diffusion lines—in descending order of price and quality of fabric and manufacture: NM Nick Mason, Nick Nick, and Nicky! In department stores, these lines are displayed on different floors, in deliberately segregated "price zones." From location alone, buyers know roughly what Nick Nick and NM will cost. At resale, however, pieces from all four lines are usually on the same rack, and price step-downs may not be there at all. Granted, many consignment-store owners are savvy enough to sort it all out, tagging diffusion merchandise according to its quality level. But others are hoodwinked by the label game. That's why understanding the differences between a collection piece and its diffusion third cousin is a critical aspect of our shopping abilities. To consistently buy at rational prices, you need to rely on your own judgment. There are three ways to avoid overspending:

1. Know your quality.
2. Remember that a collection label *looks* different from one on a diffusion piece. The name also changes: Nick Mason Couture does *not* equal Nick Nick.
3. Become familiar with the relative merits and demerits of diffusion labels. Quite a few are great, offering serious quality at a reasonable price. A few are so bad it's insulting. As quality level often varies from season to season, it would be misleading to rate them here. Talk to store owners and see what they think, and above all, trust your own eyes and hands—now you know how.

Again, lines come and go at a dizzying rate, so the following list will change over time. As of this writing Isaac Mizrahi's collections are sadly defunct. Still, they may have a thriving afterlife in your local consignment or thrift store.

Alberta Ferretti
    Philosophy
Anna Sui
    Sui
Anna Molinari
    Blumarine
Anne Klein
    Anne Klein II
    A Line
Bill Blass
    Blassport
Christian Lacroix
    Bazar de Christian Lacroix
    Lacroix Jeans
Calvin Klein
    CK
    Calvin Klein Jeans

Cerruti Arte
    Cerruti 1881
    Cerruti Club
Dolce & Gabbana
    D&G
    Dolce & Gabbana Jeans
Donna Karan Signature
    Donna Karan New York
    DKNY
    D
    DKNY Jeans
Escada/Margaretha Ley
    Laurèl
    Escada Couture (eveningwear)
    Escada Elements
    Escada Sport
    A Priori 7

Geoffrey Beene
    Beene Bag
    Geoffrey Beene Sport
Georges Rech
    Synonyme
    Unanyme
Gianfranco Ferré
    Ferré Studio 000.1
    Ferré Jeans
Gianni Versace
    Istante
    Versatile (eveningwear)
    Versus
    Versace.intensive
    Versace Jeans Couture
    Versace Jeans
Giorgio Armani
    Giorgio Armani Borgonuovo 21
    Le Collezione
    Mani
    Emporio Armani
    Armani A/X
    Armani Jeans
Helmut Lang
    Helmut Lang Jeans
Jean-Paul Gaultier
    Junior Gaultier
    Gaultier Jeans
Jones New York
    Jones New York Country
    Jones New York Sport
Isaac Mizrahi
    Is**c

Karl Lagerfeld
    KL
Kenzo
    Kenzo Jeans
Krizia
    Krizia per Te
Liz Claiborne Collection
    Lizwear
    Liz & Co.
    Lizsport
    Elisabeth (large-size)
    Emma James
    Villager Signature
Louis Féraud
    Louis Féraud Contraire
MaxMara
    MaxMara Basic
    MM by MaxMara
    Weekend by MaxMara
    Marella
    Marella Sport
    Pennyblack
    Piano Forte by MaxMara
    Marina Rinaldi (large-size)
    Sportmax
    I Blues
    Prisma
Missoni
    Missoni Sport
Moschino
    Moschino Cheap and Chic
Oscar de la Renta
    Oscar

Prada
    Miu Miu
    Granello
    Prada Sport
Ralph Lauren Collection
    Polo Sport by Ralph
        Lauren
    RL
    Ralph by Ralph Lauren
    Polo Jeans
    Lauren
Rifat Ozbek
    Future Ozbek
Sonia Rykiel
    Sonia Rykiel Inscription
Tommy Hilfiger
    Tommy Girl

Ungaro
    Emanuel Ungaro U Collection
    Emanuel Ungaro Parallele
    Emanuel
    Emanuel/Emanuel Ungaro
    Liberté
Valentino
    Miss V
    Valentino Studio
    Oliver
Vivienne Westwood Gold Label
    Vivienne Westwood Red Label
    Anglomania
Yves Saint Laurent
    Rive Gauche
    YSL Variation
    Yves Saint Laurent Encore

THE INSIDE SCOOP ON OUTLET STORES

According to *Outlet Shopping Magazine,* manufacturer's outlets (sometimes called factory outlets) make up the fastest-growing segment of America's retail industry. The first such store in the U.S. was opened in 1936 by Anderson-Little, the men's clothing manufacturer, but it wasn't until the 1980s that complexes housing many different designers and retailers began mushrooming all over the country.

Clothing manufacturers like Gant, Ralph Lauren, and others quickly embraced the outlet concept, for two reasons. First, the stores offer the chance to sell previous-season merchandise, irregulars, and overruns (pieces that retailers didn't buy) that otherwise would have been written off or perhaps shipped to off-price merchandisers like Marshalls and T.J. Maxx. More importantly, outlet malls allow manufacturers to sell goods directly, without having to go through a retailing middleman. So successful were the early outlet pioneers that retailers themselves soon got into the act. This is why you now see Saks Fifth Avenue and Barney's stores alongside Geoffrey Beene Sport.

Sometimes great deals can be found in outletland, but the buyer should always proceed with caution. Suzy Gershman, author of the excellent *Born to Shop* series, notes: "very often, the same—or newer—merchandise is available at your local mall or department store for the outlet price. Or better." What's more, in August 1997, ABC News ran an investigative piece on the shopping villages (a transcript is available on http://archive.abcnews.com/onair/PTL/html_files/transcripts/pt10806.dhtml). Some garments, an expert noted, appeared to be of lower quality than one would expect given the exclusive brand name on the tag. Good luck getting an outlet store to confirm it, but the question must be asked: is substandard merchandise being channeled through outlets, playing on the customers' notion that they are getting real bargains? The deals we think we're getting may not be such a big deal after all.

Why does any of this matter to resale shoppers? Because merchandise sold at outlet stores finds its way into consignment and thrift stores. If it's a beautiful piece, no big deal. But if it's an item deliberately made to sell on the cheap, that is a problem for us all. *Labels may promise more than the garment delivers.* Know your quality, know your quality, know your quality.

COUNTERFEITS!

Once spotting quality has become second nature, you may find yourself laughing out loud at a preposterously bad garment bearing a solid-gold label. Easy-to-manufacture pieces like T-shirts, jeans, and polo shirts are the usual suspects. In Istanbul, there are literally acres worth of outdoor markets selling nothing but knockoffs. Of course, counterfeit gear isn't restricted to Turkey; it's found on sidewalks all over the globe. Folding tables and bogus goods go together like detectives' desks and donuts. What's funny is, for many browsers, the whiff of illegality is part of the allure. They touchingly believe the stuff is real, and authentically stolen. Wake up, guys. It's *never* real.

And contrary to widely held belief, counterfeiting is not a victimless crime. By at least one account, the nuts who blew up the World Trade Center years back helped fund their project by selling counterfeit T-shirts (probably saying I ♥ New York).

Impromptu sidewalk sales aren't the only places counterfeits turn up. Your own thrift store may be selling them, legitimately. In 1996, the U.S. Customs Service pronounced that seized Guess?, Nike, Caravacci, and other counterfeit items were to be donated to local charities, with the permission of the trademark holders. If you got a great deal on Levi's in Arizona that year, you might want to take a closer look at your merchandise.

So how best to defend yourself against the scourge of counterfeits? The label itself is often the giveaway—fake labels are frequently printed rather than woven (remember, printed labels are cheaper to produce). Anyone who believes that Chanel, with its meticulous quality standards, would make a T-shirt with a printed label...well, some people are easily fooled. Labels also point to bogus clothing by their absence—especially the tags indicating country of origin, composition, and care instructions. If you don't see them (or their remains if they've been cut out), red alert—by law they must be included in every item sold through normal retail channels.

Besides counterfeiters, our other nemesis is consigners up to no good. The owner of a glitzy resale store in my city tells a wonderful story about a regular (and *extremely* wealthy) consigner who had too much spare time and not many scruples. In she came to sell a jacket she swore was Chanel. Sure enough, the label confirmed it, and so did the beautiful buttons. Yet our owner remained unimpressed.

"Mrs. So-and-so," he says. "This is not a Chanel jacket."

"Are you insane?" she retorts. "Of course it is. Look at the label, look at the buttons."

"Madame, with all due respect, this is not Chanel."

"How can you possibly be so sure?"

"The lining. You forgot to replace it. As far as I know, Chanel has never used one with 'Jaeger' woven in all over."

Whoops. One more reason to give linings a good look.

If you come across a clear counterfeit while shopping, should you say something to the store owner or manager? It's actually a tough call. If you're a regular customer, then do so, gently (nobody likes a know-it-all). But if you don't know her, you may actually get an argument, because you're basically saying her merchandise (and judgment) is worthless. Here it's often better to consider the piece a learning tool and move on—it's sure to make a less savvy shopper a very happy woman.

PART 2

Finding the Pieces That Work Best for You

Chapter Seven

◆

Getting Great Fit

She looked like she had been poured into her clothes and had forgotten to say 'when.'

—P. G. Wodehouse

Finding great clothes at resale isn't enough. The real goal is finding great clothes that fit beautifully. Bodies being what they are, this is the ultimate test, and, despite all good intentions, it's one that we routinely cheat. Why? Because going home without a purchase, especially after shopping for hours, feels terrible. We'll do anything to avoid it to the extent of summoning up an accomplice, a little demon on our shoulder, who whispers all the wrong answers in our ear:

You: What do you think?
Little demon: Are you nuts? It's Dolce & Gabbana! Buy that pencil skirt before somebody else grabs it!
You (straining to fasten the zipper): I don't know…my backside could use some erasing.
Little demon: The perfect excuse to lose those ten pounds!

But our little accomplice only hangs out for so long. The instant money passes the register, he vanishes. What takes his place? The slow, sickly realization that once again, we've failed the fit test—and are stuck with another barely-passing piece.

✳ Combating the Little Demon ✳

You've been shopping for a few hours and can feel that mania building, a "buy, buy, buy" fever marked by obsessive trawling through racks and agonized stretches in front of a mirror, visions of carrot sticks dancing in your head. Take a deep breath. Truly great clothes are a slam dunk—they shouldn't cause this kind of angst. Soothe the need to score by putting the item back and heading for the jewelry or scarf section. Blow a couple of bucks on a trinket you can really use. This will shut the demon up, and will make you much happier in the long run. Another tactic: put the piece on hold and leave the store altogether. Plan to return in an hour or two, with a cool head. The bother of going back acts like a brisk slap to the subconscious, bringing rationality to the fore. If the item is a must-have, you'll come back; if not, the trouble will hardly seem worth it.

WITH LIBERTY AND SO-SO FIT FOR ALL

If you've ever compromised where fit is concerned, at least you've got plenty of company. Despite the availability of countless makes and styles, despite the media barrage of high-fashion images, lousy fit is widespread. We've largely lost a skill that was second nature back when we all sewed our own clothes—the ability to assess how fabric sits on the body. The proof can be seen on the street, in the corridors at work, at the popcorn stand at the multiplex: women with carefully styled hair, manicures, and makeup, undercutting their looks with poor fit.

Although it's a common problem, it's not *as* common in certain other countries. If you've read other books on personal style, you'll know this is the point where French and Italian women are trotted out in reproach to American dress sense. Writers don't do this just to sound sophisticated. In the big cities of Europe, women *do* seem to know things we don't. Not because they're smarter, not because they're richer, but because they're raised with different notions about how to shop, and more important, how to buy. For them, getting great fit is as important as getting a great deal. Having spent two years in Paris in awe of the native talent, I offer these firsthand observations:

Over there, stylishness doesn't mean having a huge wardrobe. There's more on this in the next chapter, but it boils down to *looking great* every day instead of *looking different* every day—and being much choosier about fit.

They don't try on clothes during lunch. In France, lunch hour is for lunch, or for sitting in the park tanning your legs. Before heading back to the office, the girls may indulge in a quick cruise through a boutique, but only to get a notion of what's there. Real shopping is done on the weekends, and the pursuit is savored rather than rushed.

They shop to educate themselves as much as to buy. In a clothing store, a French woman and a sales assistant will stand in front of a mirror for a good half-hour, debating the rise of the hemline, pinching at excess fabric, molding a potential purchase to the figure. The conversation is open and frank, and matters of a quarter-inch are debated with great gusto. Then what happens? As often as not, the customer walks out of the store, *without buying the outfit.* But it's not like she left empty-handed. Now she's even more knowledgeable than she was before about the shapes and colors that suit her. Maybe she'll return in a few days and buy it after all. Or maybe she'll head out to the Réciproque resale store in the 16th arrondissement and apply that knowledge to her purse's benefit.

They understand the difference between tight and tailored. Tight is sleazy. Tailored is flattering. And once you've decided to try tailored yourself, anything less precise (baggy tops, poorly set shoulders, skirts that slide around the body) feels flat-out sloppy.

They emphasize the good, and disguise the bad. In the fashion capital of the world, women don't give a damn about fashionable hemlines. Their skirts always hit the spot that best showcases their legs. And if their legs aren't so hot, they draw the eye up to more attractive parts, seeing no reason to let one mediocre feature cloud the illusion of perfection.

They look at their bodies realistically. The same kind of cool logic that gave the world the philosophical principle "I think therefore I am" gives French women the ability to say "I think I am too broad in the hips to wear shorts; therefore I am going to wear a skirt instead."

HOW TO GET GREAT FIT

Even those of us without a drop of Gallic blood can learn to achieve fit à la française. It comes down to applying the same cool rationality. Instead of the usual haphazard approach (which takes forever and still offers no guarantees), connoisseurs manage both the process and the outcome by breaking it into five distinct steps:

The first is knowing how current body measurements translate into garment size. (Approximately—even experts can't agree on what constitutes a perfect 10, 4, or 18).

The next step takes place in-store, when gathering an armful of contenders. This is where pitfalls abound. Resale is notorious for missing size tags, jumbled racks, drastic alterations, and odds 'n ends donated by the sideshow the last time the circus hit town. Instead of wasting time putting it all on, connoisseurs use a special eyeballing technique, described below, that helps eliminate no-gos.

Then comes the acid test—the try-on. We connoisseurs do this more carefully than ordinary shoppers, assessing not only the contours we see in the mirror (which can deceive) but specific drape and "feel" cues as well—a logical and holistic approach that is nearly foolproof.

Finding perfect fit right off the hanger is a rarity. This is where the next step comes in—getting clothes professionally altered. This is something every woman *should* do routinely, but many cannot be bothered. If you're in the latter category, you need to be extra choosy at the try-on stage, because there'll be no second chances later on. If, however, you're willing to sacrifice a bit of time and extra cash to get your clothes just right, your wardrobe can be unbeatable.

Finally, there will be times when nothing fits right. On these occasions, the best thing to do is find some inexpensive but fun trinket to reward your hard work—and congratulate yourself for shunning second-best.

> *Trifles make perfection, but perfection is no trifle.*
> —Italian proverb

WHAT'S YOUR SIZE?

Who really knows? We're all haunted by the Ghost of Sizes Past, numbers that were accurate years ago, before childbirth, weight fluctuations, a new exercise regime. The human figure changes, for better and for worse, over time. This is why it's so important to get updated numbers every year. If your weight yo-yos, you might want to take measurements more often. Having an accurate idea of your place on the size chart speeds the process of trying clothes on, and also prevents the ego blows that follow on outdated assumptions.

Honing in on your current size means tracking down a tape-measure. (A chorus of groans lifts from the crowd.) Women hate tape measures for excellent reasons: memories of hot-faced sessions in the training-bra department, Scarlet O'Hara and her 17-inch waist, the vital statistics of brain-dead centerfolds. If it helps, remember that they're only numbers, and nobody needs to know them but you.

Here's where to take measurements in inches (find your notebook; you'll want to jot the numbers down):

Bust: Measure around the fullest part and across back; try to keep the tape as even as possible.

Waist: Hold tape measure comfortably—not tight—at the bend of the waist, not necessarily the belly button. If you're not sure where the bend is, take a quick side dip to find the crease.

Hips: Measure around the fullest part—often closer to the upper thighs.

Inseam: A final important measurement to take. Knowing this figure will help you quickly grab jeans and other casual pants that are sized by inseam and waist inches. The easiest way to do it is to pull out a pair of casual pants that you know hit your ankles just right. Measure from the ankle hem up to the center of the crotch.

	Extra small	Small		Medium		Large		Extra large	
Size	4	6	8	10	12	14	16	18	20
Bust (inches)	34	35	36	37	38.5	40	41.5	43.5	45.5
Waist (inches)	25	26	27	28	29.5	31	32.5	34.5	36.5
Hips (inches)	36	37	38	39	40.5	42	43.5	45.5	47

Now compare your measurements to the chart. Circle the size or sizes that best conform to your figure. Don't be surprised if you're not a uniform 8 or 10 or 16 or whatever—most of us are something on the top and something else on the bottom.

Now that you know your approximate size or sizes, make a note of them in your resale notebook, along with the date, and get ready to learn why you don't have to take them too seriously.

Size Matters, But Only Sort Of

Unlike other units of measurement, like the gallon or the meter, garment sizes have no agreed-upon standard. Why? They're based on national averages that change over time, due to a number of factors. Nutrition is a big one, but, perhaps surprisingly, so is posture, which has had its own modes just as clothes have, and has varied widely throughout the decades. Just ask a vintage aficionado, who sees all these ins and outs as garments transform through the century.

Distance has as much of an effect on garments as time does. From country to country, sizes said to be "equivalent" to ours ain't necessarily so. In theory, French size 40 pants should fit a size 12 bottom, but, because French hips tend to be narrower, their trousers often run small on our figures. Likewise, a British size 12 is allegedly our size 8, but because British women are often fuller-figured on top, American women may find themselves swimming in their clothes. (You'll find an international size chart on page 303.)

To make it more complicated, clothing manufacturers size (or, to use the technical term, "grade") their lines according to widely different formulas. It's often said that top designer clothing is cut more generously than middle-range merchandise, but it's not something you can count on. In any case, there's another rumor afoot that *all* manufacturers are cutting clothes bigger these days, so we can drop a size without any effort. Finally, fit fluctuations may enter in because manufacturers normally allow up to a half-inch leeway between otherwise identical pieces (sewing machine operators can only be so accurate).

All this explains why your size is, at best, a theory rather than a fact. Every garment has to prove itself to meet that theory: you can't take anything for granted. Even brands or designers that once fit like a glove can suddenly go sloppy as an old mitten, for any number of reasons. That's why Rule #6 of Resale is so important:

> **Rule #6 of Resale:** *Always consider clothes one size above and one size below your "true" one. Given the wide variations possible in cut, the off-size is liable to fit perfectly.*

THE ROUGH CUT

So it makes sense to grab a range of sizes to try on. But what if a piece *looks* like a great candidate, but...

❖ the size is snipped out
❖ it's a vintage or foreign item labeled in an unfamiliar way
❖ the size tag and the piece seem mismatched?

Do you have to go through the hassle of pulling the darn thing on, knowing full well it may not fit? Not if you *know how clothes your size hang atop, rather than on, your body.* This is a technique you can apply right in the aisle, one that can save a lot of dillydallying. You probably do it to a degree already. It is, quite simply, the whole-body version of measuring a sleeve against your arm or checking the length of pants down your leg. Note, though, that the information it yields is rough at best, is most reliable with straightforwardly cut, nonstretchy pieces, and counts on your weight holding fairly steady.

To get the gist of the technique, your own garments are once again the best teachers. These should include a blouse (with ordinary rather than dropped shoulder seams), pants, skirt, and dress jacket—all of them nonstretch and a great fit. Once you have them out, and are dressed in a fairly figure-skimming outfit (a leotard works great), stand before a full-length mirror. Item by item, you're going to discover exactly where the sample garments hit your figure. Don't be put off by the wordiness of the instructions below—the draping itself is actually quite simple.

Blouse

We'll start off with a size-check that's familiar. Place the left armhole seam directly over the crease of your left armpit (if you're left-handed, reverse the sides). Letting the sleeve fall naturally down your straightened left arm, notice where the cuff hits the wrist. This point is the *target zone* for future blouses. If a cuff or hem falls much farther up, the candidate is probably too small. Any farther down, and it's probably too big.

Now make sure all the buttons are done up. Holding the blouse taut by the two armhole seams, lay it across the shoulders as though you had it on. See how these seams fall directly atop your armpit creases—these two points are your target zones for shoulder seams on future blouses. If a candidate blouse is too small through the shoulders, the seams will land closer to your neck. On blouses that are too large through the shoulders, the seams will edge down your arms.

Now tuck the collar snugly under your chin. Drape the blouse naturally down your torso and regrasp it by the side seams about an inch below each armpit, so that the fabric rests perfectly smooth across your bust. Your fingertips are now positioned somewhere on your upper ribs—the give-or-take target zones for bustline size. If a blouse's side seams bring your fingertips much closer to your breasts, it's probably too small. If your fingers start heading around your back, the blouse is liable to be too big.

Skirts

Close all buttons and zips. Hold the skirt taut at its waistband, one hand on either side seam, so the skirt hangs flat and is facing front. Drape it from your waist, as though to check length, but instead note where your thumbs hit your middle. These spots are the target zones for future skirts. If, with a rough-cut skirt, your thumbs range closer to your belly button, it may be too small. If your thumbs hit farther back, the skirt may be too big.

Pants

Do the same with the waistband for pants (note that hiphuggers and other low-slung pants will have different target zones than waist-high trousers). Now note where the crotch seam falls relative to your own body (try-on pieces whose crotch falls much higher or lower are going to be very uncomfortable to wear). Finally, to find your target zones for length, hold the waistband at proper height and let the leg fall naturally to the ankle. Remember the spot where the hem lands.

Jackets

Button your best-fitting jacket and drape it against your torso. The position of the armhole seams will give you a rough indication of where these should fall on future jackets.

Again, this technique is approximate—a garment put together by a clever designer might break all the rules but still look and feel great. But if a straightforward piece flunks a couple of these tests, rest assured that it wasn't meant to be.

WHO SAYS THE MIRROR NEVER LIES?

The next stage in the fit process is the try-on, the point at which many of us stumble. And no wonder. Most of us depend on the outlines bounced back by the mirror as the sole evidence of what works and what doesn't. On the face of it, this makes perfect sense. The problem is, when our eyes and mind get together in front of a looking glass, all kinds of mischief can happen. Since the late 1960s, there have been a number of scientific studies analyzing female self-perception in the mirror. The studies routinely show that in Western cultures, we see ourselves as being fatter than we actually are. (While men, rather hilariously, perceive themselves as being more hunky.) At its worst, this cognitive warp can fuel anorexia, but to a less dramatic degree, it distorts our notion of what fits. Due to the misperception of imaginary flaws, some of us may buy garments that are too baggy.

This isn't the only illusion fostered by mirrors. Another one arises when we rely on a single mirror instead of a three-way glass to assess fit. No matter how wide it is, a single mirror lends a two-dimensional, paper-doll effect to the figure. We compensate, of course, by taking a quick turn to profile—posture-perfect, tummy yanked tight. *Very* realistic. Meanwhile, our backsides remain as obscure as the dark side of the moon. Is it necessary to spell out the consequences? In contrast, a good three-way mirror portrays us in the round, as the world sees us. If your favorite consignment store doesn't have one, gently suggest it to the owner. If your favorite thrift is doing well to have a mirror at all, always bring a small pocket mirror to check your back view.

Our Crease to Bear   As we've just seen, the outlines of a garment in a mirror aren't 100 percent reliable. So what's the alternative? Something we're expert in already—spotting wrinkles. Not the kind on the skin. Not the kind due to poor ironing. I'm talking about *tension wrinkles,* the ones that result from bad fit. In catalogues, magazines, and *Fashion Emergency,* these creases don't exist, but in the real world they're everywhere you look: across the back, under the armpits, over the thighs, around the crotch. Tension wrinkles inevitably point to *too little fabric being strained across body parts,* or *too much fabric sagging between body parts.* Unlike the abstract concept of "good fit," they are very easy to spot. Whenever you see one, treat it like a symptom—it's telling you where something's wrong. The fine art of decoding tension wrinkles is explained in Putting It All Together below.

Not for Your Eyes Only   Besides wrinkle cues, there's one other backup for mirror evidence, and it doesn't require a looking glass at all. When a garment hangs impeccably, it *feels* great, like a second skin. There's that "ahhh" factor that clicks the minute it's on. While our eyes can deceive us, our nerve endings never lie. If you can nail down these sensations so that you recognize them time and again, you'll eventually be able to rely on them routinely. That's why it makes sense to systematically use "feel" cues as well as visual and wrinkle cues in the quest for getting great fit.

PUTTING IT ALL TOGETHER

Here's how the techniques come together: the visual and feel cues plus the wrinkle decoder. Using the three systematically in the fitting room should give you a very accurate idea of when you've got a winner.

Blouses   *Proper fit—visual cues*
- Long sleeves hit the wrist bones
- Shoulder seams hang vertically from the notch where arm bone joins shoulder, or, in case of a drop-seamed shoulder, no more than inch or two down the arm
- Front button placket lies flat (no gaping whatsoever)
- Collar rests flat against back of neck
- Darts do not pucker
- Any bustline darts end at most prominent part of the breasts
- Fabric lies smooth across bust and lower torso
- If blouse is to be worn as a tunic, fabric drapes freely over backside and hips

Proper fit—feel clues

❖ You can stretch your arms comfortably overhead and out to the side. When you put them back down, blouse sits properly in place.

❖ Any shoulder pads should rest snugly, not sliding forward, back, or down arms

❖ Top button can be done up without strain (even if you don't ordinarily button this high)

❖ Blouse does not balloon over waistband (meaning you can't grab a handful of fabric)

❖ Tails can be securely tucked in

Wrinkle decoder

❖ Taut horizontal wrinkles in back from shoulder to shoulder = garment is too small across shoulders

  ❖ Taut wrinkles radiating around breast darts *or* taut wrinkles radiating around underarm = too small across bust

  ❖ Taut horizontal wrinkles across back = too small in back

  ❖ Taut wrinkles circling sleeve = too tight in sleeve

  ❖ Taut wrinkles running down sleeve = too tight at shoulder

  ❖ Taut horizontal wrinkles around waist = too tight at waist

  ❖ Slack vertical wrinkles down arms = too big across shoulders

  ❖ Slack vertical wrinkles down chest = too big across bust

  ❖ Slack vertical wrinkles down back = too big in back

blouse too small
across bust

Skirts   *Proper fit—visual cues*

❖ Fabric drops straight down from the most prominent part of backside, rather than cupping the underside of the buttocks

❖ Side seams hang straight

❖ Hem hangs to same length in the front and back

❖ Any pleats lie flat and are straight up and down

❖ Pockets do not gape

❖ Fabric does not mold over stomach, but falls straight down from waistband (don't forget natural two to three pound weight change over course of month)

skirt too small across stomach and hips

Proper fit—feel cues

✧ You can slide skirt on without wiggling
✧ Waistband fits just tight enough to allow two fingers to slip in.
✧ You can sit without stress or strain
✧ You can sit and cross your legs without yanking
✧ Skirt does not circumnavigate waistline while walking
✧ Skirt allows you to take normal strides

Wrinkle decoder

✧ Taut horizontal wrinkles across stomach = too tight across stomach
✧ Taut horizontal wrinkles across hips and thighs = too tight across hips and thighs
✧ Taut horizontal wrinkles across backside = too tight across backside
✧ Excess fabric "ears" appearing at side seams below waistband = too big through hips
✧ Slack wrinkles from waistband = too big at waist
✧ Slack herringbone (v-shaped) wrinkles down backside = too big across backside

skirt too tight across thighs

Pants/shorts

Proper fit—visual cues

✧ Fabric falls straight down backside rather than clinging to lower buttocks
✧ Pleats lie flat and are straight up and down
✧ Pockets don't gape open
✧ Fly doesn't strain open
✧ Standard trouser hems skim front of shoes, and fall about halfway to heel in back
✧ Curve of your stomach isn't obvious from side view (exhale!)

Proper fit—feel cues

✧ Trousers slip on easily over thighs
✧ You can button without inhaling
✧ Waistband fits just tight enough to let two fingers in

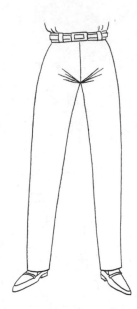

pants too tight in crotch

- Seat isn't baggy (you can't grab handful of fabric)
- Seat isn't painted on (you can pinch an inch or so of fabric)
- Crotch rides comfortably when walking
- You can sit without stress or strain

Wrinkle decoder
- Taut horizontal wrinkles at waist and hips = too small at waist and hips
- Taut horizontal wrinkles at hips and thighs = too small at hips and thighs
- Taut horizontal wrinkles across bottom = too small across bottom
- Taut "smile" wrinkles running up from crotch to hips = too tight in crotch
- Taut wrinkles circling calf = too tight here
- Slack diagonal or vertical wrinkles running from waistband = too loose in waist or hips
- Slack "frown" wrinkles from crotch to thighs = too loose in crotch
- Slack herringbone wrinkle on backside = too loose across backside

pants too loose on backside

Jackets   *Proper fit—visual cues*
- Sleeves extend to wrist bone
- Armhole seam sits vertically rather than slanting toward body or arm
- Shoulder pads are invisible, not hanging clifflike over top of arm or puckering
- All buttons close without gaping or strain
- Fabric lies smooth against back
- Collar lies flat against neck

❖ Fabric falls gracefully over torso and waist
❖ Back vents lie flat rather than gaping open

Proper fit—feel cues
❖ When you shimmy shoulders, you can't feel shoulder pads
❖ You can move arms easily to the front and sideways
❖ Your arm bends freely at elbow
❖ You can bend at waist with buttons buttoned

Wrinkle decoder
❖ Taut horizontal wrinkles from shoulder to shoulder = too small across shoulders
❖ Taut wrinkles radiating around breast darts *or* taut wrinkles radiating around underarm = too small across bust
❖ Taut horizontal wrinkles across back = too small in back
❖ Taut wrinkles circling sleeve = too tight in sleeve
❖ Taut wrinkles down arm = too tight across shoulder
❖ Taut horizontal wrinkles around waist = too tight at waist
❖ Slack vertical wrinkles down arms = too big across shoulders
❖ Slack vertical wrinkles down chest = too big across chest
❖ Slack vertical wrinkles down back = too big in back

jacket too large across chest

Dresses   *Proper fit—visual cues*
❖ If it's button-front, the placket does not gape
❖ Neckline does not strain or gape
❖ Shoulders are in proportion with rest of fit, shoulder pads fit snugly and are invisible
❖ Fabric does not mold to backside
❖ Back drapes smoothly
❖ If a belt is called for, it can be worn without sloppy-looking gathers above and below

Proper fit—feel cues

- ❖ Dress is easy to get into and out of
- ❖ All buttons can be closed without strain or gaping
- ❖ Waist sits properly, at your natural bend rather than too high or too low (do a side bend if not sure where this is)
- ❖ Arms have full freedom of movement

Wrinkle decoder

- ❖ Taut horizontal wrinkles from shoulder to shoulder = too small across shoulders
- ❖ Taut wrinkles radiating around breast darts *or* taut wrinkles radiating around underarm = too small across bust
- ❖ Taut horizontal wrinkles across back = too small in back
- ❖ Taut wrinkles circling sleeve = too tight in sleeve
- ❖ Taut wrinkles down arm = too tight across shoulder
- ❖ Taut horizontal wrinkles around waist = too tight at waist
- ❖ Taut horizontal wrinkles at hips or thighs = too small at hips or thighs
- ❖ Slack vertical wrinkles from shoulder seam, down arms = too big across shoulders
- ❖ Slack vertical wrinkles down chest = too big across bustline
- ❖ Slack vertical wrinkles down back = too big in back

Tops   *Proper fit—visual cues*

- ❖ T-shirts are neither too tight nor too baggy
- ❖ Fabric falls smoothly at waist, rather than binding tight
- ❖ Enough ease at bustline to prevent "monobosom" look
- ❖ Bra straps do not reveal themselves at neck opening
- ❖ With sleeveless tops, you can lift arm without revealing bra
- ❖ Long sleeves end at wristbone

Proper fit—feel cues

- ❖ Top is easy to pull on
- ❖ Shoulder seam falls at notch between arm bone and shoulder
- ❖ Armholes do not bind

- Tail generous enough to tuck in
- Turtleneck doesn't strangulate
- Bodysuits have plenty of give at the crotch

Wrinkle decoder
- Taut horizontal wrinkles from shoulder to shoulder = too small across shoulders
- Taut wrinkles radiating around breasts *or* taut wrinkles radiating around underarm = too small across bust
- Taut horizontal wrinkles across back = too small in back
- Taut wrinkles circling sleeve = too tight in sleeve
- Taut horizontal wrinkles around waist = too tight at waist
- Taut horizontal wrinkles at hips or thighs = too small at hips or thighs
- Slack vertical wrinkles down front or back = too large

ALTERATIONS

Have you ever noticed how the clothes worn by store mannequins are often pinned snug down the back? Think about it. If a *dress dummy* needs help looking good, we poor mortals have really got problems. But we do have an ally in our quest for perfection, and that is a great alterations person. Call this person a seamstress, a tailor, a dressmaker, or what have you, she (or he) is one of the resale shopper's best friends. This kind of pro can often quickly dispatch small flaws that show up in the fit tests. These problems include:

- jackets or dresses fitting slightly too big over the back, bust, waist, and hips
- sleeves (especially jackets) that are too long
- hemlines that are too long
- waistbands that are too loose
- backsides that are too loose

Bear in mind, though, that massive downsizing rarely works. Seams can be taken in here and there, but the proportions of a complete overhaul will never look perfect—you're better off leaving the piece on the rack.

Enlarging ("taking out") a slightly tight or too-short garment is another alterations option, but success hinges on having adequate spare fabric at the seam in question (usually more than one inch). Specific possibilities include:

- easing snug shoulders or back
- lengthening sleeves that are too short
- lengthening hemlines that are too short
- enlarging waistbands that are too tight
- gaining ease in backsides that are too tight

Here again (here especially), alterations can only be taken so far. If you are considering an undersized garment with the notion of having it taken out, take a hard look at the amount of material at the seams, and consider getting a second opinion from the store manager. Beware, too, that letting down hems may leave a *line of demarcation*. To tell, flatten the material to both sides of the hemline to see if the line is lighter than the surrounding fabric. If so, it may be diminished by dabbing with vinegar or even with fabric dye, but you may be better off holding out for a less demanding piece.

What's the best way to find a great alterations person? First, seek the advice of friends and relatives. In so doing, avoid the temptation to go with somebody's Aunt Bebe and her Ronco Sewmagic. You need a professional, someone who not only knows her basques from her bobbins, but can advise you on fit and drape. Your favorite consignment store is another good source of information. Local boutique and department stores usually have seamstresses on call, but this entails buying at retail to make the connection. Many dry-cleaning operations have a sewer at the shop, but proceed with caution—likewise with people found through the Yellow Pages or the Internet. Try all of them out with simple jobs first. You don't want to leave prom gown or mother-of-the-bride overhauls to an untested stranger.

While alterations are a splendid thing, they require time and effort. Getting the clothes to the pro and paying the charge is, for many, a psychological hurdle. If you're buying clothes on the basis of getting them fixed, be *sure* that you'll jump it, otherwise the piece will sit unworn in a corner, making you feel guilty. If you're the kind of person who can't be bothered with one more chore, be sure your fit is great without extra help.

SPECIAL FIGURE ISSUES

Women who are unusually short, unusually heavy, or pregnant are faced with particular challenges when it comes to getting flattering fit. If you're a member of one of the first two categories, a relationship with an alterations pro is particularly beneficial. Pregnant women need to do something rather different—envision their figure not as it is, but as it will be, allowing for flexibility yet maintaining style as the baby grows. All of these topics have been covered at length in style guides purpose-written for these issues—some good ones are mentioned in the bibliography. A bookstore, a resource like Amazon.com, or your local library are other excellent sources of information. Specialist magazines such as *Mode* may also prove helpful. In the meantime, here are some points that apply specifically to these shopping challenges at resale.

The Larger Figure Getting great fit has long been difficult for big women at resale, if only because the choice has been so limited. But better days are dawning, for two reasons. Mainstream manufacturers have finally woken up to the spending power and style desires of plus-sized women, and are now producing a solid range of fashionable clothing. There's always a time lag between retail innovations and the resale echo, so the consignment and thrift situation may need a while longer to improve dramatically. But it will.

The second impulse behind improved shopping for larger women is the rise of specialty resale stores. One example is Monica Francisco's Not a Small World in Walnut Creek, California. "The challenges of plus-size shoppers," she says, "are getting better thanks to stores like mine that cater only to them.... Now a woman can come to my shop and be delighted that there are clothes in it that are too big for her!" Scour the Yellow Pages for such specialty shops and, if you have access, investigate the Internet (see also page 257).

Another fine approach is beating the bushes locally. Consignment-store owners are an invaluable resource for you. Call, or better yet, visit the stores in your area and investigate the kinds of garments they're getting. Be sure to inform the manager that you'll be a good customer for quality merchandise if the size is right, and leave her with your name, number, and size details. This alone may spur her to find consignors who meet your criteria—creative matchmaking is what the business is all about. Thrift stores won't be nearly as responsive, of course, but it still may be worthwhile to investigate whether your locals get donations of larger-sized clothing.

The Shorter Figure   Here again, secondhand stores tend to magnify the poor selection of styles available in the larger retail world. But don't despair. Many of the same strategies used by larger women can work for you, especially calling around and finding out what the consignment stores in your area are stocking. Again, your interest alone may encourage a savvy store owner to seek out more petite consignments.

You should also take heart in the fact that you have it all over your bigger sisters when it comes to shopping vintage, especially if you're fond of the gorgeous delicacies of decades long past. Where today's average-sized women would split the seams, you can slip into an Edwardian lace blouse, a flapper gown, or amazing tapestry slippers with ease. Take advantage of the styles that the rest of us can't get into.

The Pregnant Figure   Congratulations. No, for the other reason: thrift stores were made for your expanding waistline. Where else will you find drawstring pants, blousey tops, extra-large leggings, and other fabulous gear for a mere fraction of the prices at those wretched maternity shops?

Granted, specialized maternity clothes are the best way to go when it comes to business suits, bathing suits, and panty hose, but

❋ A Note on the Future of Fit ❋

At the time of writing, a small revolution is brewing in how clothing is made for the mass market. Increasingly, manufacturers are looking to computer-aided design (CAD) as a way to custom-make clothes for a buyer's individual measurements, rather than producing "average" sizes for the widest possible customer base. Levi's has pioneered the concept with its tailor-made jeans; other makers are sure to follow over the course of the next decade.

An interesting question is how this will affect secondhand clothing. In the future, it may be more difficult for us to find items that fit, since merchandise will increasingly be cut for specific figures. Then again, maybe not. Custom-fit merchandise will cost more than traditional clothing, so the trend may not take over entirely. According to a recent article in the *New York Times*, American buyers are notoriously price sensitive and may forsake better fit if it means saving a few pennies.

While it's impossible to predict the future, CAD breakthroughs seem destined to provide a new round of challenges to the dedicated resale shopper. If nothing else, they're one more reason to get back on close terms with your tape measure.

for everything else, resale rules. Elasticized and otherwise expandable waistlines, and tops with some give at the waist, are what you should hunt down. Empire-waisted or trapeze dresses are also excellent options. In the later stages, *men's* shirts and tops may prove a good choice.

Even maternity fashions may be found at certain specialty resale stores—once again, call around to see what your local purveyors are stocking, and check directories for this kind of specialization.

For Men Only   If you were born a he, you probably know more than most about the challenges of getting great fit with women's clothing. Still, it may be difficult to find shops that cater to your needs. Speaking off the record, a number of store owners mentioned having a male clientele,

but said they risked losing female customers if both were to shop
(and more to the point, use the dressing room) at the same time.
Unfair (and possibly illegal) as it is, the reality of resale is that you
may be turned away during usual business hours. But, if you can convince the owner or manager that you will be a good customer, she
may be willing to open up a bit earlier. Contacts within your own
community will also reveal those places that are open to your custom—good luck, and watch out for that herringbone wrinkle.

Chapter Eight

The Elements of Personal Style

In recent years, movie actresses have again become icons of chic, their images buffed to a degree last seen in the studio era of the 1940s. Since they're actresses, the stylishness seems as natural as breathing, but don't think for a second that they're doing it all on their own. For camera-worthy events, most rely on an image guru, a professional who makes sure unflattering colors, ill-judged cuts, and poor proportions are as bygone as their old waitress aprons and pads. That's the Hollywood way to high style.

So how about the rest of us? If feeding the family takes higher priority than hiring a style consultant, the answer is, once again, self-reliance. Let's be our own gurus. We're two-thirds there as it is. Style begins with good quality and carries through with great fit. The last part of the puzzle hinges on buying clothes that *enhance* the figure, coloring, and personality. This chapter is all about pinning down what kinds of pieces those are.

Is it easy? On one hand, yes. With proper direction and focus, it doesn't take that long to learn what kinds of cuts, colors, and combos look best. Yet the random quality of resale shopping means we must search *that much harder* for pieces that fill the slots. Wonder clothes— the kind that fit and flatter and mesh with the wardrobe—simply don't surface every day. In fact, world-class style is hard enough to achieve when money and other resources are limitless. Women attempting to do it at resale have to be ruthless—able to say no to inappropriate pieces (no matter how cute), willing to work through acres of also-rans, and patient enough to try again and again, until those few perfect items are found.

Frankly, most of us don't have the single-mindedness it takes to become true fashion icons. But if you desire to ratchet up your style quotient to even the slightest degree, read on. The style savvy you gain will go a long way to making *your* dress sense the envy of others—especially women who are buying at full price.

THE ONE TRUE FIGURE TYPE: IRREGULAR

Nobody thinks their body is perfect, even Hollywood stars and supermodels (*especially* Hollywood stars and supermodels). Rather than dwelling on the cruelty of fate, which will only make you feel (and look) worse, give fate a hip check and take control. Start taking steps to *manage* the pluses and minuses of your figure. Not necessarily with diet, nor even with exercise, but *with the garments you choose to adorn your body.* The concept has a special term in French, of course. It's called *mettre en valeur,* which roughly translates into "putting your best forward" via clothes.

Few traditions have as long and distinguished a history as *mettre en valeur* (especially where kings and queens were concerned, as you'll see over the next few pages). Not too long ago, this same kind of advice resurfaced in a number of books about dressing to enhance body type. (Which, depending on the author, could be as straightforward as "pear-shaped" or as mind-bending as "curvy triangular.") Here's how the books work: once the reader determines the body type that most closely matches her own, she turns to the many do's and don'ts (for example, don't go strapless if you have a triangular, or broad-shouldered, slim-hipped silhouette). The attraction of the books lies in their easy-to-grasp formula. Yet along with their strengths come some pitfalls:

They never seem to admit that certain styles work for many different figures. To see this in action, look at professional men. They also come in all shapes and sizes, and all look pretty darn good wearing a classically cut suit as long as it fits well and is made with a fine material. By the same token, when a woman's suit is beautifully proportioned, of lovely fabric, and fits, odds are it will flatter many different figures.

The advice in the books can be limiting. "Don't go strapless if you have a triangular silhouette." That's sensible if you're a stocky 5'3", but what if you're built like Elle MacPherson?

Sometimes they reinforce outdated values. All the books treat big bottoms like they're a curse. Granted, in the workplace it's better to show off your accounting skills, but many find an ample bottom, tastefully clothed, far more attractive than, say, a swanlike neck. Off-hours, there's no reason to camouflage *any* part you're proud of.

Body type is fluid. Women gain and lose weight with perverse regularity. Exercise can make the scrawniest shoulder a thing of beauty. Child-bearing does all kinds of colorful things to the figure. Aging shortens the appearance of the torso (by encouraging breasts downward) and lengthens and flattens the backside. A formula that was letter-perfect a couple of years ago could be a disaster today. Buying a garment because it fits the former you won't do the current version any favors.

Style books try to fit an entire produce section into apple, pear, and banana-shaped holes. Take, for example, the classic pear. According to the formulas, this woman has narrowish shoulders, an "average" bustline, and biggish hips. But this doesn't account for the basic pear's countless variations. Some bustlines will be larger, some smaller, some waists narrower, some thighs shorter. While the guidelines may be accurate in a general way, they will never surpass what you determine on your own, with the aid of an unflinching eye and a good three-way mirror.

Which is where the next section comes in. It's a contemporary version of old-fashioned *mettre en valeur.* Rather than head-to-toe formulas for a limited number of body types, these are guidelines on how to downplay specific flaws, found on all kinds of figures. Once they're under the rug, you're free to emphasize what's best, be it slim ankles, a beautiful throat, or womanly curves.

If you're unsure of your pluses and minuses, have a heart-to-heart with a good girlfriend, the person who alters your clothes, or your favorite resale professional. Resist the notion of asking your sister—she may be annoyingly eager to dwell on the flaws. Once you're armed with an accurate sense of the raw material, consult the guidelines below, remembering that they are guidelines only, not firm "do's" or "don'ts." Let your own eyes make the final call. Also remember that at the quality level we're shooting for, designers routinely pull off miracles of cut and drape. A style that ordinarily makes you look like a brick house could turn out mighty mighty on your figure. Happy surprises are one of the ongoing thrills of our kind of shopping.

✳ Looking the Part ✳

A king was supposed to look and act his part. If nature did not endow him with a regal appearance, he felt that he had to make up for this deficiency by dressing for the part he was supposed to play. Any physical defect would detract from an imposing appearance and court dressmakers vied with each other in devising clever means of covering nature's deficiencies...

—Mary Ellen Roach & Joan Bubolz Eicher,
Dress, Adornment and the Social Order

THOSE VERY SPECIAL PARTS OF YOU

Feet Unless you get regular pedicures, don't expect your poor feet to knock 'em dead in slinky sandals. Untended, most women's feet look like hell. A more discreet, covered-up look will be much sexier.

Long feet

Consider: A low-cut vamp (the part of the shoe that covers the top of the foot) and a slight-to-moderate heel. Matching hose color to shoes will help disguise foot length.

Beware of: Spectator-style shoes and any footwear that is lighter than flesh (or hose) color.

Broad feet/bunions

Consider: Styles that emphasize the length of foot rather than the width (in other words, the main decorative elements of the shoe should run *down* the foot rather than *across* it). Matching hose and shoes will also minimize width.

Beware of: Straps that cross the instep, and shoes that are too tight across the instep. Wearing shoes too snug will *not* disguise a wide foot (ugly bulges will appear in the leather) and may cause long-term damage.

✳ Another French Trick ✳

Parisian ladies are unanimous on the subject: panty hose and stockings should match shoe color, rather than the skirt or dress above. The reason? In that city of leg-worshippers, any visual technique that elongates the limbs is adopted *tout de suite*. Shoe/hose matching does just that, by creating an unbroken line from the toe to hem.

Legs, General   Short legs

Consider: Elongating legs with monochrome shoes/hose/skirt or pant combos, and slight-to-moderate heels. Slingback shoes, a low vamp, and a pointed rather than rounded toe will also elongate the leg. If your legs are shapely, consider shorter skirts.

Beware of: Adding width around the legs (with wide-legged pants, full skirts). Some experts discourage pants with cuffs.

✳ Hemlines ✳

Most women buy skirts and let them hang where they may. Convenient, yes, but it passes up one of the simplest style improvements there is. Stylish women make hem length a personal trademark, revealing the legs to their best advantage.

To find your best drop zone, talk to your alterations person or enlist a buddy with a good eye and steady hand with straight pins. The goal is to have the hem hit a particularly attractive point of your leg. For 95 percent of us, it's where the limb curves inward: either a few inches above or below the knee, or below the widest part of the calf. For the sake of wardrobe flexibility, you may want to pick two target spots—one for long and one for shorter skirts. Some more hemline tips:

✿ Once past the age of fifteen, the knee develops all kinds of knobs, fat pads, and dimples that give it character but take it out of the running for the most attractive part of the leg. For this reason, skirts shouldn't ever fall right above or directly across the knees—it's the visual equivalent of an underline. Ditto for the broadest part of the calf.

✿ If you've always had great legs and like to wear your skirts short, take a reality check every year or so—the backs of the thighs have a way of developing unattractive landmarks that can go undetected for years.

✿ Uneven hemlines are a particular problem with vintage dresses and skirts from the 1930s and 1940s. A good alterations person should be able to straighten them out.

✿ Before buying any dress or skirt, be sure there's enough hem available to lengthen it to your desired level, and make sure that there won't be a line of demarcation (see page 140).

✿ Don't forget that shorts can also be hemmed, and should be if they're dressy.

Lower Leg   Chunky ankles

Consider: A low heel will be more flattering than flats. Matching hose to shoe color will create a longer line. A low vamp will draw the eye down from the ankle.

Beware of: T-straps, mules, clogs, ankle boots, or any other shoes that lure the eye up toward the ankle rather than down toward the toe. Ankle bracelets are not a stylish choice.

Thick calves

Consider: Streamlining legs by matching hose to shoes; slightly sheer hose will be more flattering than opaque.

Beware of: Very high heels and/or poorly balanced shoes (which cause calf muscles to bunch), flats, kneesocks, knee-high boots, tight and/or light leggings, and light or patterned hose.

Skinny calves

Consider: Textured and/or dark hose.

Beware of: Very high heels will emphasize lean calves; lower heels may be more flattering.

Upper Leg   Heavy thighs

Consider: Hemlines that fall below the knee. When wearing leggings or form-fitting trousers, pair them with a tunic or jacket that skims over thighs. Longer skirts with a slit to the knee are another stylish option.

Beware of: Any horizontal lines that fall over and therefore emphasize this area—either in a garment's pattern or from its own hemline.

Cellulite/varicose veins

Consider: If you favor short skirts, be sure hose has enough color and support to smooth any irregularities.

Beware of: Light-colored and/or skimpy stretch garments, which may mold to and emphasize bumps and ridges.

Hips/Bottom   Wide hips and an ample bottom are feminine traits celebrated throughout civilization. But if nature was in a *very* generous mood, these tips
can help.

Broad hips

Consider: Tops and tunics with fabric that floats or drapes prettily
over the hips. Choose garments with strong vertical lines or pattern.
Long jackets and vests will draw attention upward, as will light or
brightly colored tops. Trapeze dresses and A-line skirts (wider at the
bottom than at the top) can work well. Pleated pants are usually
more flattering than flat-front styles. If your waist is slender, draw the
eye up with a beautiful belt. Emphasize neckline with scarves/jew-
elry. Consider small shoulder pads to balance proportions.

Beware of: Tops (including sweaters and jackets) that end on the
roomiest part of the hips. Also, if your backside isn't toned, avoid
stretchy or flimsy fabric that clings to this area.

Jutting hipbones

Consider: Pleats and side pockets can minimize the prominence.

Beware of: Hiphuggers, flat-front, or side-zipper pants, and tight
skirts.

No hips

Consider: Hiphuggers, flat-front, and side-zipper pants, as well as
any pants or skirts with gathers below the waistband. Pleated all-
around skirts and kilts will also look good.

Beware of: Straight skirts that cling.

Big bottom

Consider: As with broad hips, above. Also, be sure underwear fits
well to avoid framelike panty lines.

Beware of: Bold patterns.

Flat bottom

Consider: Skirts and pants gathered all around the waist can add fullness. Patterned pants and skirts are another good option.

Beware of: Drawing belt too tight—this will place unattractive puckers above bottom.

✳ Looking the Part, Continued ✳

…Shoes with long points came into favor during the reign of William Rufus because one of his court favorites, Count Fulk of Anjou, had feet misshapen with bunions which he was very anxious to cover up. The king was so pleased with this novel method of concealment that he eagerly accepted the style and a fashion was thus established which lasted for nearly three centuries…

Dress, Adornment and the Social Order

Waistline   Do the terms "short-waisted" and "long-waisted" confuse you? If so, join the club. If only fashion writers would say what they mean—"short-midriffed" and "long-midriffed"—they'd spare us all a lot of confusion. What's being measured here is the stretch of torso between the bottom of the breasts and the natural waistline (where the body bends). If you can fit a handspan or more there, you're long-midriffed (-waisted). If you can't, you're short-midriffed (-waisted). We all go in one direction or another—at least until older age sets in, when, due to the descent of the breasts, everyone tends to get shorter here.

Short midriff

Consider: Tops and buttoned jackets that skim over waistline and end near the hips are preferable to garments that are tucked into or end at the waist. Draw attention upward with scarves and jewelry.

Beware of: Thick belts, unusually high waistbands, and strong color differences between top and waistband.

Long midriff

Consider: If waist is slender, cropped tops, bustiers, chunky belts, and high waistbands can be worn to flattering effect.

Beware of: Hip-hugger and drop-waisted styles, which may look unbalanced.

Pot belly

Consider: A top made of more fluid, draping fabric will be more flattering than one of clingy material. Choose a waistband with gentle gathers. Empire (high)-waisted styles and trapeze tops are also excellent for this common figure problem.

Beware of: Styles where belts ride on the most prominent part of the stomach. Also avoid light-colored, stretch tops worn over stretchy skirt or pants—this only emphasizes curvature.

Bustline

As with big bottoms, most style books urge you to "normalize" very small or very large breasts. The truth is, either can be extraordinarily attractive if they are clothed with good taste and flair (i.e., small-breasted women can wear beautifully cut halters or bustiers for evening, large-breasted women can play up décolletage.) During the day, the right bra will do wonders to counter any visual imbalance. Otherwise:

Large breasts

Consider: Double-breasted jackets and v-necks, which will lay angles over the curves, minimizing them. Vests have the same effect.

Beware of: Piped pockets or decorative buttons on breasts. Clinging sweaters. Busy or very light fabric may draw eye to breasts.

Small breasts

Consider: Pockets and other trimming details on bust lend visual impact. Vests are often very flatter-

---

⁂ Looking the Part, Continued ⁂

…Long skirts were brought into favor because the daughters of Louis XI of France had misshapen legs and feet. Charles VII adopted long coats to cover ill-shaped legs, and Louis XIII, who was prematurely bald, used a peruke [wig] made in imitation of long curls. Hoop skirts were said to have originated with Madame de Montespan to conceal defects produced as a result of an accident…

Dress, Adornment and Social Order

---

ing. Attractive jewelry at base of neck will draw eye upward. Well-draped scarves are another option.

Beware of: Bulky shoulder pads that emphasize curves on shoulder to detriment of those below.

Shoulders Broad shoulders

Consider: Halters, v-necks, and scoop necks, which all draw eye toward the neck.

Beware of: Shoulder pads, as well as any detailing along shoulder that draws eye to this area. Very thin straps or no straps may be problematic, depending on your figure and the garment's other characteristics.

Narrow shoulders

Consider: Small shoulder pads will help balance your lines, as will boat (wide-cut) necklines.

Beware of: Drop-shoulder styles, and v- and scoop necklines. Be particularly wary of long pendant necklaces that echo slope of the shoulders.

Neck Overly long neck

Consider: Standup or other high collars, scarves, and jewelry at base of neck, dangly earrings.

Beware of: Collarless jackets or tops, scarves or necklaces that hang very low.

✳ **Looking the Part, Continued** ✳

…Queen Elizabeth, in spite of the homely appearance which historians accord her, was exceedingly vain and ordered the court dressmakers to produce fashions which would cover up her defects and make the most of the good features she possessed. One of her naturally good features was her small waist and in order to enhance it she used a corset to constrict the flesh to thirteen inches. Cloth proved to be too weak, so whalebone was used to reinforce it. The high neck ruff which is so characteristic of that period, was adopted by the Queen to cover up a long, thin and unshapely neck.

Dress, Adornment and the Social Order

Overly short neck

Consider: V-neck or scoop-neck openings, long necklaces, collarless styles.

Beware of: High or standup collars, choker necklaces.

Double chin/weak chin

Consider: High (but not tight) turtlenecks, collars. V-necks and v-forming necklaces also can be flattering. Scarves draped around neck can be lovely.

Beware of: Round-neck styles, high neck styles that squash skin under chin.

WHAT'S YOUR COLOR?

Color analysis burst onto the scene in 1973 with the Color Me Beautiful and rival programs. Whether based on "seasons," warm/cool theory, or another principle, these systems exploit the fact that everyone has good and bad colors, based on a given hue's interaction with hair, eye, and skin color.

If you're unsure about your best colors, professional assessment can be helpful—as long as you find a pro who knows what she's doing. Like hair stylists, color analysts have varying degrees of talent. It's always best to go with a personal recommendation from someone whose color choices are always dead on. A less pricey route is the one to your local library, which will almost certainly have a few color guides to delve into. Easier still is following the guidelines below:

Shortcuts to Your Best Colors

Your skintone is the most reliable clue. Everyone's skin is either warm-toned (with yellow-beige-brown-olive undertones) or cool-toned (with blue-rose-pink-purple undertones). Warm-toned women generally look best in clothes in the yellow-red-brown family; cool-toned women in the blue-green-purple family.

- ❖ In general, if there is a strong contrast between your skin/eye/natural hair color (for example, light eyes/dark hair, or pale skin/dark eyes, hair) you can get away with punchy colors. If, however, your hair/skin/eyes are close to the same intensity, more muted shades will best become you.
- ❖ You are likely to look fabulous wearing any of the colors that are visible in your eye's pupil (check under natural light).
- ❖ Believe it or not, some experts hold that the colors of your inner membranes (inner cheek, for example) are also flattering—why not give it a try and see?
- ❖ Ask your hair stylist or colorist what *they* think would suit you.
- ❖ Go through old pictures and pull the ones where you look dynamite. Was it the color you were wearing?
- ❖ Pick a stylish celebrity with coloring similar to yours and watch her choices like a hawk (believe me, she's getting expensive advice on the subject).
- ❖ If your coloring is typical of your ethnic forebears and you're feeling ambitious, hunt down some sources illustrating typical dress in that country (picture books, travel magazines, travel guides), and note the kinds of colors people tend to wear there.

Knowing your best colors doesn't mean basing your *whole* closet on these hues. For one thing, it's hard enough to amass decent basics in black and white, much less in pine green or plum. For another, your two or three ideal colors might not mesh well with each other. A smarter strategy is to base your wardrobe on flattering neutral tones instead, reserving your best colors as *highlights or accents* (in the form of face-framing scarves, tops, and necklaces). This strategy also counters the frustration of color limitations at resale. While you'll rarely find a lemon-yellow cardigan that is beautifully made and fits just right, a gray version is a decent possibility. Pair this with a lemon scarf or T-shirt, and you've achieved the good looks without all the hassle.

The user-friendly nature of neutrals is old news for fashion readers—every style guide worth reading advises assembling a wardrobe in this way. The reason is obvious: it vastly simplifies both shopping and getting dressed. When everything you own goes with everything else, your wardrobe stops being item-based and becomes outfit-based, a real blessing when the alarm goes off at 6:30 A.M.

Despite their soft-spoken nature, neutrals aren't boring—there's an entire hushed rainbow to choose from. If your accent colors lean toward bright jewel tones, you might consider black, white, taupe, dark gray, or navy as your base neutral. If you are flattered by more muted shades, black, cream, beige, or light gray might be better options. Pick one or two neutrals and stick with them, at least from season to season. Life is so much simpler, and good style so much easier, when color matching stops being a big issue.

> *It's beige! My color!*
> —Fashion designer Elsie de Wolfe,
> upon first sight of the Acropolis

More Colorful Tips   They say we can distinguish 10,000 different colors. Keep this in mind when trying to team separates, especially those made of like fabrics. Even if a skirt and jacket appear to be a close color match in the dressing room, their differences will be obvious in sunlight, and you'll look clueless rather than chic. It's actually better to pair decidedly different textures or colors—say, a black chunky-knit cardigan with smoothly woven wool pants, or a cream jacket with beige trousers.

- The best tailoring in the world is worthless if the color makes you look ill. Buy such an item only if you will religiously wear a scarf or other intermediary piece to offset its effect.
- Bright solid colors (say magenta and yellow) can work wonderfully together, but it takes an especially sharp eye to pull them off. For inspiration, check out the picture books on the great couturiers.
- Two different colors in one outfit often benefit from the addition of a patterned scarf or jewelry that picks up the tones of both. The accessory acts as a "peacemaker," harmonizing the contrasting aspects.
- Heightened makeup will let you go brighter than usual—but beware the fine line between heightened and clownish.
- If you're considering a garment with a multicolored pattern, hang it up against a neutral background and look at it from ten paces away—the resulting color meld might not be ideal for your complexion.
- Every so often, try on a shade you usually skip. Coloring changes slightly over time, and you may be very surprised by the outcome.
- Always check colors in natural daylight. Ask to bring a piece near a window or even outside to consider the hue (this will also highlight any stains).

PROPORTION

Designers spend ages working out proportion when creating a suit or dress: widening a lapel here, downsizing a button there, trying to get it all balanced. Architects do the same thing when they draw a building, as do graphic artists when they develop a new logo. Good design makes it to the catwalks, into *Architectural Digest,* onto a can of cola. Bad design, most of the time, ends up in the wastebasket.

Unless it's homegrown: the kind that crops up when amateurs like you and me try to assemble outfits out of separate garment pieces. Unlike designers, we do not have a highly educated understanding of what lines and shapes work best together. As a result, it's rare to see a casual outfit that clicks brilliantly in all of its parts. Need it be said that the resale mode doesn't help matters any. Our separates are *really* separate, sometimes even decades apart.

Still, it's possible to create lovely proportions with a hodgepodge of pieces. The trick lies in knowing something about the innate rules of visual harmony. Without doubt, the most important is the "golden section." Why is this one so special? Because its principles are practically hardwired into our brains. For example, when people are presented with a rectangle and asked to divide it into two parts, they hardly ever cut it in half, nor do they cut it into one very big piece and one very small. Instead, the dividing line falls somewhere at a point in between.

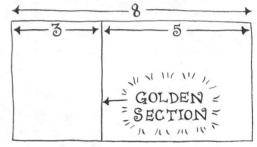

This intermediate point is *so* attractive to *so* many people that it was mathematically fixed thousands of years ago by philosophers in ancient Greece. They determined that if the rectangle is 8 units in height or length, the dividing line will fall about 3 units along, leaving a second segment of 5 units. In honor of its popularity, they called the 3:5:8 ratio the golden ratio, and the division it describes the golden section.

The ratio was first put into formal design practice in the Greeks' temple to Athena, the Parthenon. Its appeal hasn't diminished with

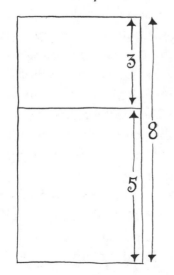

time—we continue to see it all over the place. On cereal boxes, for example, and paperback books, where the lettering typically falls about a third of the way down. It's not just visual designers who love the golden section—scholars have discovered that creative minds as diverse as the Roman poet Virgil and the Hungarian composer Béla Bartok used it subconsciously when setting up the structure of their masterworks. Nature, too, inclines toward the golden section, causing trees to branch and rocks to fracture in patterns conforming to the principle.

This is the long way of saying that there's something about the golden section that's innately pleasing to the eye. It makes sense to apply its principles when putting together an outfit of separates. In simple terms, *the pieces making up the whole should be just different enough in length and volume to create an eye-pleasing balance together*. To clarify this, take a look at what happens when the golden section is ignored. Remember those infamous "dress for success" suits of the 1970s? Even back then they looked dowdy. Why? A boxy, hip-length jacket paired with an A-line, knee-length skirt results in components of near-equal (4:4) visual weight. Zzzzzzzzzz. Compare that to the sharper, unequal-yet-harmonious combos we see today and you start to understand what good proportion is all about. Here are some more examples:

✤ The eye appreciates harmonious differences in volume as well as in length. In general, roomy (and especially A-line) tops look better with slimmer pants and skirts, while baggy or flowing bottoms tend to click better with close-to-the-body or belted tops.

✤ Likewise, separates don't look stylish when there's *too great* a difference between the component parts. The problem is best summed up in two words: Ally McBeal. Never mind the professional shortcomings of her teeny skirts. The real issue, the one that really bugs us on a subconscious level, is the fact that they're proportionally out of whack with the jackets. The same problem occurs when a few inches worth of dress or skirt peeps out below a long winter coat. It just looks ungainly, period.

- ✤ The same kind of imbalance is often seen with lapels—when a too-skinny blouse lapel or collar is placed over a broad-lapeled jacket, the effect on the eye is uncomfortable. Here it would be better to tuck the blouse all the way under.
- ✤ Earlier in this century, the French architect Le Corbusier discovered that the human body is split according to the golden section, with the head to the navel equaling 3 units, and the navel to the foot equaling 5. Therefore, any outfit that splits your body neatly at the waist (top and pants, top and monochrome skirt/hose/shoe combo) is likely to fall into pleasing proportion.
- ✤ Ideally, the 3:5 relationship should echo throughout the outfit— with breast pockets proportionately smaller than those at the hips.
- ✤ Moreover, breast pockets appear slightly more refined if they sit about one-third of the way from the shoulders to waist rather than exactly halfway.
- ✤ The 3:5 proportion also works upside down (think about traditional Asian garb). In Western wear this translates into tunics over slim pants or skirts.
- ✤ The great designers consciously play death-defying balancing acts with the 3:5:8 and less-perfect ratios—it's wisest to leave this sort of thing to the professionals.
- ✤ Accessories fall prey to proportional problems too. If you're wearing a wide belt over a blouse, be sure there's enough fabric showing below the belt to balance its visual weight.
- ✤ Colors and contrast also play a role in proportions. White and bright colors have more visual weight, a heavier punch, than black and muted colors. This is why long stretches of light-toned leg revealed by a short skirt can look girlishly overexposed, while when dark-toned, the same legs look chic. It's also why a priest's white collar/black robe looks sharper than an oversize white sweater with a black turtleneck underneath.
- ✤ Shoes also play a role in the proportion equation. Generally speaking, the more delicate the fabric above, the more slender the heel, while heavier fabrics are better balanced by a chunkier heel.
- ✤ While designers paired Winter '98 long skirts with a nearly flat

heel, most of us are better off with a slightly higher heel if a skirt or dress falls to the calf or lower.

❖ When knee-high boots are worn with a shorter skirt, the slice of visible leg catches the eye and disrupts proportions. Unless that slice is *fabulous,* it's best to tone hose color in with the boots.

❖ Familiarity plays a *major* role in the acceptability of certain proportions. What may look bizarre at the beginning of a season can look perfectly normal come final markdown. Beware of trendy proportions at resale, however—by the time they hit consignment and thrift stores, these one-season wonders can look hopelessly out of date.

Proportion is complex, even for professionals, but it does come more naturally with experience. If you'd like to build your sense of it, scour fashion magazines and catalogues to see how the experts put lines and shapes together. Try to be aware of proportions in your everyday world. And if you have a friend in a visually creative field like design or flower arranging or the fine arts, talk to her about how she does what she does—the added insight may be invaluable.

GET UP ON THE SCALE

There's one final visual element to bear in mind when putting looks together in a stylish way: the scale, or size, of the patterns and textures you favor. Some women (usually big of stature or personality) look great in loud patterns and gutsy textures—it suits their approach to the world. Other women (usually smaller in size and persona) feel more at home in more discreet patterns and surface qualities. Give scale some thought, if you haven't already, and decide what kind of volume level you prefer. Your personal style will be sleeker and more refined if you don't send out scrambled scale messages.

Of course, a number of you mix scale and other style elements up on purpose, going for a *totally* different look every day. This is particularly true of vintage clothes lovers, who tend to have a heightened, more costume-y approach to getting dressed ("if it's Tuesday, I must be Mata Hari; if it's Thursday, Buffalo Girl"). All in all, this is a good thing—you bring zest and imagination to what is essentially a dull clothing world. You, however, will be bored rigid by the upcoming section, about crafting a cohesive look. This part of the chapter is addressed to women who, due to time limitations, professional constraints, or personal taste, take a more conservative approach to getting dressed—yet yearn for a touch of your memorability.

IT'S SO YOUR STYLE

If you're idling somewhere in wardrobe limbo, getting to stylish can be a long haul. And all resale shoppers face the same roadblock. There are so many pieces to be had (*especially* if we compromise on fit and quality), the natural impulse is to buy buy buy, simply because it's so much fun fun fun. Which quickly leads to wardrobe overload—a collection of clothing that is "eclectic" to put it kindly, and "one big mishmash," to put it not.

Does this sound familiar? Depressingly familiar? If you've had enough and are ready to make a break from sartorially schizophrenic to stylish, you'll need to get your head around an entirely new shopping

---

✳ **Sample Mishmash Wardrobe** ✳

Two oxford cloth shirts ✿ leather bustier ✿ Thierry Mugler megashoulder jacket ✿ grampa tee ✿ Mexican wedding skirt ✿ shetland sweater ✿ Gap skinny cardigan ✿ shawl-collar silk blouse ✿ boy-scout shirt ✿ fringed suede pants ✿ hiphuggers ✿ wool culottes ✿ white pantsuit ✿ four pairs of khakis ✿ satin baseball jacket...

approach. Instead of random buying, make a sincere effort to build your wardrobe around two or three distinct looks. Initially, this may sound like a drag, especially if you're into sport shopping (bagging trophies just because they're new and different). But in the long run, you'll wonder why you ever did it any other way. In addition to revved-up personal style, a unified wardrobe brings these benefits:

- ✧ It means less decision-making early in the morning.
- ✧ It's easier to look wonderful every day.
- ✧ The money you save can be better spent on yoga classes or in some other personally enhancing way.
- ✧ You can focus on buying the best, instead of scattering pennies on the mediocre.
- ✧ You can wear the stuff again and again for years (try that with a sequined jumpsuit).

Finding Your Best Look... The designer Betsey Johnson and the late fashion editor Diana Vreeland exemplify polar opposites of personal style. On the minimal end was Vreeland, who, despite having the fashion world at her fingertips as an editor at *Vogue* and *Bazaar,* was said to limit her daytime wardrobe to black cashmere turtlenecks, gray wool trousers, and special handmade shoes replicated over and over again by Manolo Blahnik. Now, myth was as powerful as reality in this fashion doyenne's life, and the severity of her garb may be an exaggeration. But the basic point is clear—Vreeland knew her look, and wasn't going to follow the whims of fashion just because her magazines said so.

At the other pole is Betsey Johnson who, in a recent magazine article, is said to own 300 pairs of shoes, and claims to buy six of everything, "wearing neon orange Mongolian sheepskin, and embroidered peasant coats, over her own tight, stretchy dresses." Her style, she says, is "spontaneous and uncontrived. But I do try hard to make my uncoordinated look work." While at first this may seem a classic case of mishmash, it's not really. There's probably not a single conservative piece in that closet, making her look rambling, but unified.

In their own ways, both women are icons, sharing two characteristics that define their wardrobes (and those of every woman who achieves great personal style):

Consistency: Even if Vreeland woke up one morning and felt like throwing on a lime-green halter top, she knew better. Part of her image rested in the iron control of her look. If she compromised that, her very identity as a style maven would begin to chip away. Likewise, Johnson wouldn't be caught dead in a boring old suit, because this would dilute her own message as an avant-garde, free-spirited designer. Which relates to:

Style as an expression of one's innermost soul: We've all seen ladies whose individuality is hidden under a swarm of designer logos. True style doesn't work when it's simply put on. It has to spring from within. If your spirit feels most at home in delicate lace, you will never be (or look) totally comfortable in corporate armor until you mold it into your own image (perhaps with frilly camisoles underneath, or an array of beautifully detailed lace pocket squares). In a world that revolves around designer whims, true style comes from charting your own course.

> *Know, first, who you are: and then adorn yourself accordingly.*
> —Epictetus, *Discourses,* 2nd century

Nailing Down Style

It's not necessary to go to Vreeland's or Johnson's extremes in charting a course to personal style. But they do point the way toward the destination. If your style focus is murky, grab a pencil, find yourself 15 minutes or so of quiet time, and give some serious thought to the following questions.

If, like Vreeland, you restricted yourself to *single outfits* that you religiously wore for:

1. work
2. casual time (one outfit for summer and one for winter)
3. going out

...what would those four different uniforms consist of? The answers could be garments you already own or an imagined ideal. Don't skip ahead yet—think hard and write your selections down.

Switching gears now—if, like Johnson, you could fill your closet with clothes that tell the world who you are, what would the message be? Drapily romantic? Sleek 'n chic? Retro? If you get stuck on this one, it may help to mentally page through some well-known brand images (such as J. Crew preppy, Laura Ashley feminine, Thierry Mugler hard-edged, etc.), or to borrow the look of a friend or admired public figure. Again, break the answers down into: (1) workwear; (2) casualwear, summer and winter; (3) going out.

Now, somewhere in between the two sets of answers rests your prototype personal style. The first answer—your preferred uniform—describes the *kinds of pieces* you like (or would like) to wear. The second answer—your preferred theme—pins down the *mood* you want to go for.

Now join the two elements together. To help, here's a few hypothetical profiles:

Workwear: Minimalist pantsuit with T-shirt, reminiscent of Jil Sander
Casualwear: Thick knit sweater and cords, reminiscent of the Lands' End catalogue
Going out: Slinky cocktail dress, reminiscent of your sister, New Year's Eve '97

Or maybe you're more this kind of girl:

Workwear: Pastel double-breasted suit and pearls, reminiscent of Princess Di
Casualwear: Pencil skirt and minimalist top, reminiscent of Cameron Diaz
Going out: Little black dress, reminiscent of Audrey Hepburn

Or this one:

Workwear: Coordinated knits with gold buttons, reminiscent of St. John
Casualwear: Fleece and wickable nylon, reminiscent of Patagonia
  catalogue
Going out: All-out velvet, reminiscent of Oscar de la Renta

Get the picture? Once you do, you will have *style templates* to build wardrobes around. The next step is to acquire one or two ensembles that match your templates exactly, and then, when considering additional pieces, buy only if they act *in support of,* rather than *in conflict with,* these central outfits. In this way you'll develop a theme and variations— an efficient, streamlined, yet highly wearable selection of clothes.

How much you develop each of the three subwardrobes depends on how much time you devote to each area of life. Those with stay-at-home responsibilities will weight casual clothes differently than those who are working in an all-encompassing sales job; just as those who entertain a great deal in the evening will have different needs from those who go fancy just a few times a year.

Shopping takes on a whole new aspect once you have some style templates to stick to. Now, instead of randomly buying whatever seems to work, you're *collecting* within a fairly tight framework, as a connoisseur does. You may find it very helpful to keep a running list, either written down or in your head, of any major gaps within your categories. Having three or four pieces on an ongoing *needs roster* (khaki skirt, dressy evening jacket, black cotton cardigan, red turtle-neck) will not only make your buying style more efficient, it will also help you resist the devilish temptation of nonessentials.

It will take a fair amount of shopping time to build your wardrobe up to the kind of consistency that marks personal style. In the meantime, here are a few shortcuts to reinforce it.

Classics
You've surely heard it before, but the reminder never hurts—you can't go wrong investing in pieces of irreproachable classic style. The

truly stylish, truly beautiful pieces will cost a small fortune (even secondhand), but will pay you back by wearing well for years:

* Monochrome, clean-lined pantsuit in impeccable lightweight wool
* Handstitched slip-on shoes
* Midheel pumps in alligator or calfskin
* Little black dress (again, as simple as possible, but in deluxe fabric)
* White button-down blouse, in Egyptian cotton
* Wool dress trousers for winter
* Linen-blend trousers for summer
* Perfect white T-shirt
* Dark wool skirt, neither too short nor too long
* Cashmere sweater in appropriate neutral color
* Beautifully made trenchcoat
* Great handbag
* Small collection of top-rate scarves

Trademarks

These are the unique markers, the points of interest, that women adapt to distinguish themselves from the herd. Prime examples include the hats worn by the late congresswoman Bella Abzug. Or designer Carolina Herrera's polka dots, a motif that appears regularly in her designs and also adorns her namesake perfume. A fashion trademark is not only fun to devise and collect, it also piques the inner life of those around you (what kind of pin will she have on *today?*).

Fashion Blackout

Less a style than a way of life, wearing black makes for easy matching, automatic street cred, and implied creative depths. It has the disadvantage of being dull and unflattering (fixable, though, with wisely chosen accessories). While many women wear black to get away with cheap fabric and make, don't follow their lead—when fabric and make are all you've got, you've really got to go for the best possible.

Era-specific

If you're a vintage fan, you can automatically set personal style by dressing only in pieces originating from a certain period. While the approach itself is minimalist, the resulting look is dramatically memorable.

Designer-specific

One final way to hook into style is to borrow it altogether, limiting your selection to a single designer. This is an extremely demanding option for resale shoppers—most of us don't have the time to hunt down every last Lauren (or god forbid, Junya Watanabe) within a hundred-mile radius. But if you're in an urban center that is replete with the look you love, or if your favorite consignment store happens to have a consignor who shares your size and taste, then you may get lucky.

✳ A Last Few Words on Style ✳

Only God helps the badly dressed.

—Anonymous 19th-century Spanish quotation

The expression a woman wears on her face is more important than the clothes on her back.

—Dale Carnegie

So who's right? You won't catch me taking sides; they both make a good point. The question of how much importance to attach to personal style is one that has flummoxed serious women throughout history. How you resolve it is your business. Do try to remember that valid choices lie to either side of the divide. Stylishness is neither foolish vanity nor the mark of a real woman—it's simply one way (of many) to express yourself.

Chapter Nine

◆

Flaws:
The Not-So-Bad, the Bad,
and the Very, Very Ugly

Once you've discovered a promising item—one that looks great, fits, and meshes with the rest of your wardrobe—take a deep breath and get as far from the register as possible. The time to find any flaws is now, before you get past the point of the no-returns policy.

Given the worldliness of resale garments, they're subject to a wide range of flaws. Some are so easily fixed they are easy to forgive (the not-so-bad). Others require some more spending and/or effort, possibly overwhelming any bargain factor (the bad). Still others are beyond hope (the very, very ugly), and are grounds for instant rejection.

We all have our own standards. You, your sister, and I will have different tolerance levels for different kinds of problems. At one extreme are perfectionists, who only buy pieces that are or look brand new. More easygoing souls accept minor booboos like missing buttons, knowing that quick work with a needle and thread will turn another woman's reject into a treasure. And then there are the buccaneers who don't mind challenges like grit and grime, and are willing to attack with detergent and muscle power to return garments to their former glory.

Due to our varying standards, you may have some quibbles with the following categorizations. That's fine—healthy dissension is why resale flourishes at the highest and the lowest ends. What's really important is being dead sure of the kinds of flaws *you yourself* will tolerate, so you don't make a purchase you'll later regret. Given the strict no-return policies at most stores, there are very, very few second chances. Being a connoisseur means knowing exactly what you're getting yourself into.

Rule #7 of Resale: *Never buy an item before spot-, hole-, and wear-checking every last inch.*

THE NOT-SO-BAD

This type of flaw may spook retail shoppers, but by and large it leaves us serene. The problem is either so minor it can be fixed at home, or it can be dispatched inexpensively by a professional sewer. By the way, it's a good idea to ask your alterations person for a price list of routine alterations such as letting down hems, zipper repair, relining, and other chores you wouldn't do yourself. This way, you can accurately calculate the true end cost of a garment that needs a little attention before it blooms into full glory.

Wrinkles
As we saw in the last chapter, tension wrinkles indicate how a garment sits on the body. The other type of wrinkles—the plain old unpressed kind—may interfere with the all-important fit check, but otherwise are no big deal.

Unpressed garments rarely show up in good consignment stores, whose policies mandate dry cleaning. If you do find a crinkly piece, ask the owner—diplomatically—if the item was indeed cleaned prior to consignment (if not, you may be able to bargain on price). Next, see if a steamer can be brought out to get the article hanging straight and true.

If you find a wrinkled garment in a thrift or a vintage store, bear in mind that it may have been that way since the Eisenhower administration. Don't rush to buy until you've made sure that the crevasses are free of discoloration or fading.

If you've gotta have it: Once you get home, carefully determine the type of fabric and its ironability. If it can be pressed and there are no visible stains, give it a shot, being sure to use the correct iron temperature (see Chapter 12). If the item is silk or wool, a hot steam in the bathroom may be a better alternative. If neither approach gives great results, take the piece to a dry cleaner for professional pressing.

Missing Buttons

While buttons gone AWOL add a couple of dollars to the cost of the item and require some of your free time, they are a minor fault, provided you know how to attach them yourself (a skill every die-hard secondhander should master).

If you've gotta have it: Take the garment to your local button counter (found in sewing stores and the notions departments of good department stores). See if you can match the missing link. Can't do it perfectly? Then find replacements for *all* the buttons (look for real beauties), and sew them on while watching TV. It's important to do this chore as soon as possible—otherwise the garment will languish in the to-do pile and you'll feel like a lazy so-and-so every time you look at it. TV time is perfect for minor repair work, because two mindless activities somehow add up to a highly productive evening at home.

> *I have always sewn on my own buttons...*
> *I am forever changing the buttons on my clothes,*
> *usually for the same reason that I correct a drawing*
> *or shift colors around in my paintings:*
> *it sharpens the total effect and creates harmony.*
> —Jim Dine

Offline Hemlines

The pants fit perfectly, except for the length, which harks back to the advanced-placement math class come a high rain. Most trouser hemlines are easy to shorten when too long and, *sometimes,* can be lengthened if too short. Ill-fitting sleeves are a more serious problem. But, for a price, a good tailor may be able to work wonders.

If you've gotta have it:

Raising hems on pants: As long as the pants are of a sturdy material, you can do this yourself, following the instructions in a good home-sewing book (helpful for a connoisseur to have handy). Basically it involves measuring carefully, pinning the fabric in place, and making sure the stitches catch only a few threads at a go.

Lowering hems on pants: Before purchase, turn the hem inside out to see if there's enough extra fabric to drop to the right length. Allow for at least a half-inch to be hemmed back up inside afterwards. Also, take a good look at the current crease line. Cotton, velvet, and suede tend to get lines of demarcation that can be tough to eliminate once the repair work is done (see also page 140).

Adjusting hems on skirts: Unless you're a practiced sewer, leave this to a professional, because uneven work can result in an unattractive boxy-looking hemline. Bear in mind that a slit on the back or side will become a weird little flap if the fabric is taken up too high. If a skirt has pleats, a tulip-style front opening, or another kind of curving hemline, don't get your hopes up for successful alteration—hemming these can be a nightmare, even for a professional.

Adjusting sleeves: For professionals only. Shortening is fairly straight-forward. Lengthening is probably possible if it's only a matter of a half-inch or so, but note that the expense may hardly be worth it.

Broken Zippers

> *Is there anything more deadly*
> *than a zip that turns nasty on you?*
> —Agatha Christie,
> *Come, Tell Me How You Live*

She was exaggerating—a bad zipper is annoying but hardly lethal. A good home-sewing book will offer instructions on how to replace a worn or broken zipper, but most of us are more comfortable leaving this to a professional.

If you've gotta have it: As long as the construction of the garment is straightforward and you're willing to pay for the repair, go ahead and buy. After consulting the alterations person, you may wish to purchase the zipper yourself to ensure the best color match and quality.

Hair
While it's a big yuck for most of us, hair—human or animal—is harmless, unless you are prone to allergies. If you find one of Cousin It's castaways at a consignment store, alert the owner—dry-cleaned garments shouldn't carry any hair. (Though it could have come off a previous customer.)

If you've gotta have it: If the garment is otherwise perfect, wash or dry-clean it and don't give the hair a second thought.

Torn Linings
Winter coats, in particular, are subject to torn or frayed linings—the fabric is fairly vulnerable to snags, and the underarm areas undergo a lot of wear and tear.

If you've gotta have it: Put the item on hold. Your alterations person can tell you the approximate cost of replacing the lining, as long as she knows the size and style of the garment. If you decide to go ahead and it's in keeping with your personality, pick out a replacement fabric with real dash.

> *There was a young belle of old Natchez*
> *Whose garments were always in patchez*
> *When comment arose*
> *On the state of her clothes*
> *She drawled "When ah itchez, ah scratchez."*
> —Ogden Nash, 1902–1971

THE BAD

Stains

In consignment stores, where dry cleaning is usually mandatory, any visible stains are likely to be so long entrenched you can count on living with them forever. Paradoxically, stains on clothing from thrift stores may come out more easily, simply because nobody's ever given it a real go (not true of old underarm stains, which are not only gross but incredibly stubborn; see page 182).

If you see a stain yet still love the garment, take a harder look. Do you see any evidence of a cleaning attempt (in other words, is the mark shadowy and grayish rather than crisp)? If the stain looks like it's already been in the wash, your chances of eliminating it are poor. Many stains set forever once they have been laundered at high heat. If, on the other hand, the stain has some color and texture, for example makeup on a collar, it may be fresh enough to offer hopes of removal. One way to test is to carry a travel-size bar of white soap in your purse. If you see a stain, moisten a corner of the soap and rub it lightly against the fabric (ask permission first, or you might be accused of putting the mark there in the first place). If the color lifts or fades, odds are good that the stain will come out.

> *Out, damned spot; out I say.*
> —Shakespeare, *Macbeth*

If you've gotta have it: The best (if priciest) option for removing stains is the dry cleaner. With at-home attempts, the appropriate product can work wonders on fresher stains (see Chapter 12). But be warned—none of these options is guaranteed.

Odors

One of the worst old clichés about resale clothing is that it smells. On the rare occasions when it's true, this can be a very, very ugly. All the same, it's not a reason to reject clothing outright, for some odors are fairly easily eliminated. It all comes down to the source. Old perfume usually responds well to dry cleaning. Embedded perspiration usually does not. Mustiness due to storage in less-than-ideal conditions often goes away after a good airing. If the odor lurks in the lining of a coat or jacket, replacing the lining may do the trick.

Sometimes, too, clothing smells because of its nature. The "waxed" waterproof country coats so popular in England do a terrific job of keeping out the rain, but are quite smelly due to the natural oils impregnating the fabric. Heavy woolen fisherman's sweaters, when wet, develop much the same kind of aroma, due to the activation of the lanolin coating the hairs. There's no good way to get rid of the smell of such pieces, and you really wouldn't want to, for this would render them ineffective against rain. Some stuff is just meant to be worn outdoors. Besides, with a couple of shot grouse in the back pocket or a cod or two hanging from your neck, the smell of the outerwear isn't nearly as noticeable.

If you've gotta have it: Again, a good relationship with your dry cleaner will pay off. Put the garment on hold, and give him or her a call. Describe the fabric, its age, the location of the odor and try to describe it. Is it musty, like old newspapers? Pungent like skunk? Faintly sweet, like L'Air du Temps? If you give your cleaner regular business, you should get the straight dope on getting the smell out.

As a perfume doth remain
In the folds where it hath lain
So the thought of you, remaining
Deeply folded in my brain,
Will not leave me: all things leave me
You remain.
—Arthur Symons, "Memory"

Pilling

Knitted wools and fuzzy synthetics have the unpleasant habit of pilling when they're rubbed the wrong way. Opinion varies over whether pilling relates to the quality of the piece—all I know is, every cashmere sweater I've ever owned eventually developed a few bobbles. Constant abrasion lifts the fibers up, they become entangled, and then, under the continued force of abrasion, roll into little balls that cling tight to the surface of the knit. While not repulsive, they do indicate age and wear.

If you've gotta have it: Pills can be removed successfully. Not by pulling them off—that's the worst thing to do, because it draws out more fibers, leaving them vulnerable to further pilling. Instead, stretch the sweater flat over a pillow and carefully clip pills off with nail scissors, or buy one of those pill shavers from a gadget store or catalogue. By trimming the bobbles, you can dramatically freshen the look of a sweater, but remember, they always come back.

Moth Holes

Moth holes are devilish—they often go unnoticed until you've gotten the item home and are trying it on again, then...$%^&!!! This is why, before you purchase anything made of wool, you need to go over it meticulously. Especially a sweater that otherwise looks pristine—the very reason it's at resale could be because a chompy moth got there first. The most effective way to inspect is with a miniflash-light in a dark corner, running the light up the insides of the sleeves and legs. If you see pinholes of light, gotcha.

Actually, it's not the moths themselves that do the damage but their offspring, caterpillars, especially those of the breed *Tineola bissel-liella.* The little buggers thrive on the protein keratin, found in wool fibers (they also require generous side orders of food stains and per-spiration, one more argument for keeping and storing clothes in a meticulously clean state). About four generations can breed in one year, wreaking untold havoc in your closet.

If you've gotta have it: If you find a motheaten garment in a consign-ment store, alert the owner and remind her where it was hanging. Any live animals could seriously eat into her profits. For your part, if you can live with the holes, the first thing to do, before letting that piece anywhere near your own precious clothes, is get it to the dry cleaners to remove any lingering eggs or (yes) larvae. A somewhat less reliable but much cheaper wipeout technique is to hang the gar-ment in bright sunlight for an entire day (the dark-loving larvae liter-ally die away in the rays). Be sure to open out any pockets, unfold any creases, and turn the garment inside out at least once, then brush vigorously. Once the item is all clear, take an extra-fine needle and wool thread in an identical match, and loop the hole closed. In some cities there are even professionals (called "reweavers") that will do this for you, but the price is likely to be high.

Mothballs are not completely effective unless the storage space is airtight. Cedar chips are more ecologically friendly but less effective still. The chips or blocks should be sanded once a year to ensure enough oils are on the surface to drive the moths away. Strong-smelling herbs such as bay leaves, hung in bunches, also help repel moths.

. . . AND THE VERY, VERY UGLY

Here are the flaws that should make you drop the garment and move smartly along—possibly right out of the store. Nobody needs this kind of aggravation, even if the piece started out as a couture wonder. Go ahead, be a snob, these clothes deserve it.

Critters

While moth holes rest on the border zone of acceptability, other kinds of bug infestation, meaning the small, gray, pinhead-sized egg casings that house lice—or worse, the animals themselves—are repulsively different. Please note that clothing carrying body lice is unlikely to *ever* make it past a store's sorting and tagging operations, because typically it was worn day in and out for weeks without being washed. In the rare instances where the staffers zoned out, you certainly won't. Immediately alert the store owner or manager if you find an infestation, and strongly consider alerting your local health department.

He can see a louse as far away as China but is
unconscious of an elephant on his nose.
—Malay proverb

Buckled Seams

On a less drastic, but still reject-worthy note, puckering along seam lines happens for a variety of reasons. Every now and again, designers deliberately work it in (for example, in cargo pants, or certain makes of preppy-slovenly oxford-cloth shirts). Nine times out of ten, though, it's the unhappy result of ill-chosen materials or shoddy assembly. Who needs more wrinkles?

Washed-out Knits

Cotton knit sweaters are lovely to have in the wardrobe, especially come cool summer evenings. Unfortunately, one accidental spin in a hot dryer and their good looks can simply fade away. Racks and racks of washed-out sweaters can be found in every thrift store in the country. They're not worth good money—newer, brighter versions are also plentiful and will look good much longer if given proper care.

Boiled Wool

Like faded cotton knits, this flaw indicates that the previous owner had little clue about how to care for her clothes. Amateur boiled wool (as opposed to Austrian loden coats, which are purpose-boiled by experts) has a hard, tight feel that is extremely unpleasant. It's said that these pieces can be brought back to life with a second round in the washer, but perfect reincarnation is not guaranteed. This is another case where passing is the smartest shopping decision you can make.

Overstretched Knits

Like their boiled and washed-out cousins, knits that droop at the neck, cuffs, and waistband do your appearance no favors. There's absolutely no reason to purchase an underachiever like this when there are so many beauties awaiting discovery. Put a clamp on your wallet and wait for the best.

"Shattered" Fabric

According to vintage expert Donna Barr of Victorian Elegance, "shattering" describes the breakdown of fibers in a very old fabric, especially silk. The telltale signs are slight tears that run with the grain. Pulling at the fabric even slightly will cause it to rip, meaning it is practically useless as a wearable item. As beautiful as it may be, give it a pass, unless you want the item for display purposes only.

Bad Alterations

There are a lot of well-meaning but completely incompetent people wielding a needle out there. Unfortunately, once misstitching is done, little can repair the damage. Signs of bad alterations include: sloppy, oversize, or irregular stitching at the seams; jagged hemlines; uneven pants or sleeve lengths; odd bunching at the waistline. It's particularly important to check inner seams—you can see the mischief before you try on the garment.

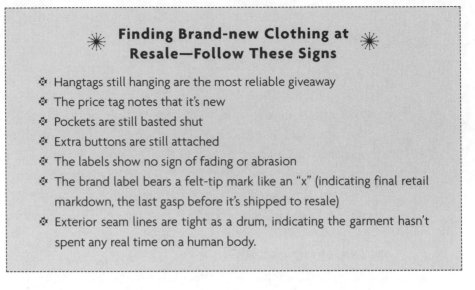

Fraying

While a frayed lining can be replaced, a frayed cuff or collar is another story. Even the slightest hint of fringe means the piece is on its way to the rag bin.

Yellowing

Sometimes yellowing occurs after a garment has done many tours of duty in the washer dry, or after only one mistaken go-round with colored items. Other times the fault lies not with the consumer but with the dry cleaner. If instructions are not carefully followed, a white item can yellow in the dry-cleaning process. Careful bleaching may restore sparkle to off-tinged items, but it can also result in graying, which is just as bad. Always examine clothing in natural sunlight, where any off-tint will be evident.

Sweat and Blood

Old bodily stains are not only gross, they're the devil to get out—the proteins lock into cloth at high wash temperatures. Certain clothes-care advice books recommend removal by dabbing with vinegar or even a solution of crushed aspirins, but is this the kind of project you really need? Think hard. If not, give this stuff a pass and a good rid-dance.

Shininess

Certain tightly woven fabrics, particularly those that contain syn-thetic materials, develop a sheen when they've been pressed at too-high heats or rubbed constantly over the course of long wear. Seats, elbows, and lapels are the usual locales. A shiny suit is a suit that's past its wear-by date. If there's one in your wardrobe, you may be able to temporarily restore it by gently stroking the spots with fine sandpaper or dabbing them with a vinegar solution, but this won't fool anyone for too long. Don't buy anything this worn—it's not worth the money.

Chapter Ten

Glorious Accessories

Looking good gets you appreciated. *Not looking beautiful.* Looking put-together, well-groomed, what the French call soignée. Doors open, you get attention instead of attitude, you're treated like a somebody because you *look* like a somebody, a woman who takes pride in her appearance. If this reaction doesn't normally come your way, you're probably wondering what kind of tiresome prep work it takes. Actually, it couldn't be simpler. Put on nice accessories. As often as you can, not just on dates and job interviews. Jewelry, scarves, a great pair of shoes, the finishing touches to a fine outfit. As advice goes, this may sound straight out of the Stepford Wife manual, but honestly, it works. Accessories have this weird power. The reasons are mysterious, but maybe it's because once upon a time, charms and amulets were worn to guard against evil and to signal status in society. The doodads we hang on our bodies, even today, may arouse an atavistic, in-the-bones form of respect. Or perhaps accessories' attraction lies in their attractiveness, plain and simple. Back in the days when women dressed up for a trip to the corner store, the little extras were standard issue: earrings; matching shoes, gloves, and bag; a cunning hat. But as the decades passed, the codes of personal appearance began to give way. The gloves came off, and looks that were once hidden behind closed doors, like ripped jeans, became fashion statements. These days, the old codes of public appearance are gone altogether. Mature people of both sexes routinely dress like toddlers—on airplanes, in nice restaurants, on the streets of the most sophisticated cities of the world. Needless to say, accessories (apart from fanny packs and marshmallow "athletic" shoes) are widely missing in action.

Given the forces of casual at work, eye-catching refinements carry great force. Wearing lovely accessories is a form of public beautification, like a clean-swept sidewalk. Fellow citizens take it as an unspoken compliment, and old-fashioned courtesy is their way of saying thanks in return.

LOOKING GOOD = FEELING GOOD

Let's not kid ourselves—wearing heels instead of flip-flops does mean a tradeoff in comfort. But it doesn't mean buying into the old saying that "women have to suffer for good looks." Leave that to the supermodels, who get paid for it. Any discomfort *you* feel dressing well should be low to nonexistent, as long as you:

* acquire pieces that fit, made with great fabrics
* wear quality shoes that cushion your feet instead of cheap ones that set your dogs barking
* think about your posture so that slouching doesn't artificially tighten clothes' grip
* adjust jewelry so that it hugs rather than pinches

Accessories shouldn't cause much financial pain either, because secondhand offers such reasonable prices. Sure, a Hermès scarf will set you back $100, but a lovely no-name copycat may be tagged at $3. Earrings routinely turn up for less than $5. Astonishing belts are there for the grabbing because other shoppers don't recognize their allure. Build a great accessories collection and you effectively double your wardrobe. And with prices like these, it only makes sense to go for the best.

KEEP IT CLEAN

As with all matters of style, there's a fine line between looking done and looking overdone. Accessories are like the flicks of a brush an artist uses to bring interest and depth to a portrait. If they go on too thick, in glaring colors or in poorly judged combinations, the sitter is overshadowed by the special effects. Keep this in mind if you choose to wear a standout accessory, such as a beautifully bold necklace. It should be the star of a relatively simple outfit, with other pieces playing a supporting role.

It's all too easy to over- or underdo it with accessories, because none of us was born knowing how. If you'd like inspiration on how to put subtle looks together, the *Chic Simple* books by Kim Johnson Gross and Jeff Stone are a wonderful reference guide. Their ensembles tone colors, textures, and shapes into harmonious wholes. The overall image is decidedly classic—perfect for more conservative situations and environments.

If you hunger for more dramatic assemblages of jewelry, hats, and shoes, have a good browse through the glossy retrospective books on Yves Saint Laurent, Christian Lacroix, or John Galliano (on the Fashion/Design shelves in good bookstores). Especially at the haute-couture level, these designers go all out to dazzle the eye. You will find countless images to set your imagination racing—looks that may be directly applicable for party situations, and, with careful editing, for daytime wear as well.

One more general tip on accessories: color-matching your bag, belt, and shoes sometimes works wonderfully and other times doesn't at all, depending on the colors and textures. If they're all the same low-key shade (black, brown, gray, cream), a two- or three-way match usually looks great, especially if the textures are different. But, if the color is offbeat, like lavender, yellow, or even white, a perfectly matched shoe, belt, and bag combo risks looking too prissy and "done."

THE LAST WORD ON SHOES

Top saleswomen in pricey boutiques always knows what's afoot. They see shoes as an index of buying power, and before you can say Prada kitten heel, Spring '99, they've got the customer pegged. Sure it's superficial, but it also makes sense. The well-shod shopper is clearly willing to spend top-to-toe on her appearance. She's not going to settle for second best. That describes you as well, right? The difference is, instead of putting thousands into footwear, you'll invest cunning, good taste, and patience.

New, well-made shoes regularly turn up at consignment stores, especially in the bigger cities. They're usually some other woman's mistake, so when you find them, proceed with caution. Be sure they're there because they didn't fit their former owner. A more dia-bolical problem, like a rough inner seam or an unusually narrow arch, is going to haunt you as well.

New shoes are easy to detect because their soles are as smooth as a baby's bottom. With *slightly broken-in footwear,* you'll see moderate abrasion of the soles and heel and some erasure of the print on the insole. No matter how easygoing you are about mileage, you don't want to buy *goners* (shredded toe, cratered insole, leather as wrinkled as a Shar-pei puppy). Why?

* they're not going to look better once on
* they've absorbed more perspiration than you care to know
* they're probably at the tail end of a style cycle, and nothing looks more over than out-of-date shoes

As bad as worn-out shoes are, ill-fitting ones are worse still. When it comes to buying shoes, lots of women temporarily go dead from the ankle down (and the neck up). Let's stop the madness right now.

Rule #8 of Resale: *Never buy shoes that rub the wrong way. By the time the blisters heal, the season will be half over anyway.*

Quality Considerations

- ✤ The very best dress shoes are made entirely of leather, right down to the heels. They are so designated on the sole with a hide-shaped insignia bearing the words "vero cuoio" (Italian for real leather), "cuir" (French for the same thing), or an English variation of "all leather."
- ✤ Shoes of the next-best quality rank consist of leather uppers (the part above the sole) with a synthetic sole and heel. Here again, the content is stamped on the sole of the shoe, usually as "all-leather uppers."
- ✤ Synthetic uppers run a poor third. While they're fine as foul-weather shoes, they make feet smell even on the driest days.
- ✤ Fabulous shoe leather feels plump and yielding when pinched, like a ripe cherry. Cheap shoe leather feels thin and stiff like cardboard.
- ✤ The finest pumps have no seam at the instep.
- ✤ The leather in fabulous shoes is stitched together (Hermès, Ferragamo, and Dooney & Bourke still do this). Further down the quality scale, the leather is glued. Stapling is grounds for instant dismissal.
- ✤ The shoe should flex back and forth easily at the point at which the big toe would flex away from the foot.
- ✤ The interior of a fine shoe is perfectly smooth—no ridges, bumps, or bulges. All visible seams should turn inward.
- ✤ Patent leather holds its own against rainy weather but it can dry out easily. It requires regular care with patent-cleaning polish (though in a pinch, a good rubdown with some petroleum jelly will bring back its luster).
- ✤ If heels, outer soles, or inner soles are worn down, they can be replaced, but be sure to factor this work into the total cost of the shoes. Also, be sure that there's enough life left in the upper to make the time and investment worth it.

✧ Boots with exposed zippers may snag hose or the linings of your clothing. A narrow flap covering the zip is a sign of superior quality.

To kiss, pretty Saki, thy shoes' pretty tips,
is better than kissing another girl's lips.
—Omar Khayyam

Fit Considerations

✧ Shoes should allow a half-inch between the big toe and end of shoe. You should be able to flex your toes.

✧ Your heel should be gently cupped. If it's shifting, buy an insert.

✧ Boots should fit snugly at the ankle.

✧ Walk around the entire store a few times before buying a pair of shoes. If the shoes feel tight, for heaven's sake, throw them back.

✧ Remember that feet swell toward the end of the day, and this is when try-ons are most accurate.

✧ The smaller the area on which you stand (in other words, the tinier the shoe's footprint), the more unstable you'll feel. Skinny sandal straps only add to the precariousness. Unless you're a practiced wearer, or you won't need to walk more than twenty feet, go for wider heels and platform soles.

According to Temple University's School of Podiatric Medicine,
women today "experience four times the number of
foot problems as men due to high heels, poorly fitting footwear,
or other abuses in the name of fashion."

Some of the most exclusive names in women's shoes, usually sold in boutiques or deluxe department stores, are:

Bottega Veneta

Céline

Chanel

Charles Jourdan

Christian Louboutin (note lipstick-red soles)

Gucci

Hermès

Jimmy Choo

Manolo Blahnik

Maud Frizon

Prada

Robert Clergerie   Stephane Kelian
Roger Vivier (vintage)   Susan Bennis/Warren Edwards
Salvatore Ferragamo

More top-ranked names, usually found in the designer shoe department of better department stores:

Amalfi   Gina
Anne Klein   Giorgio Armani
Bally   Isaac Mizrahi
Botticelli   Patrick Cox
Bruno Magli   Richard Tyler
Casadei   Sigerson Morrison
Cole Haan   Sonia Rykiel
Diego Dolcini   St. John
Donna Karan   Vanessa Noel
Ernesto Esposito   Vera Wang
Fendi   Walter Steiger
Fortuna Valentino

Coming in at a slightly lower price point are the designer's diffusion shoe lines, as well as traditional midpriced favorites:

Adrienne Vittadini   Enzo Angiolini
Armando Pollini design   Gofreddo Fantini
Bally   Hush Puppies
Bandolino   Isaac
BCBG   Kenneth Cole
Caressa   Marc Jacobs Look
Cheap and Chic   Nickels
CK   Nine West
Cynthia Rowley   Paloma
D&G   Paul Green
DKNY   Sacha
Donald Pliner   Sergio Rossi

Stuart Weitzman   Via Spiga
Unisa   Who's
Van Eli

Shoe-care Tips

- ✦ Try to find shoe trees at a thrift store near you. These help restore and preserve the shape of shoes after a hard day's wear. Rolled-up socks are a second-best substitute. Rolled up newspaper will help prevent knee-high boots from sagging.
- ✦ It's worth investing in a good shoe-shining kit (with appropriate brushes and polishing cloths) to help keep footwear in top form. The kit will last a lifetime—and your shoes will last longer too.
- ✦ Shoes should be polished with cream or wax shoe polish on a regular basis. This not only helps them look great but protects against splashes and grime.
- ✦ Restore the luster of patent leather by rubbing it with a dab of petroleum jelly. Be sure it is thoroughly wiped clean before wear.
- ✦ Marks on suede can usually be lifted with a clean white pencil eraser. If that doesn't work, try gentle rubbing with a bit of fine sandpaper.
- ✦ Try not to wear shoes for two days in a row. The feet sweat a great deal, no matter what the time of year, and shoes require adequate time to air out.
- ✦ Be stringent about maintenance. Have your shoe repairer attach heel and toe taps as soon after purchase as possible—taps cost less than replacing an entire heel later on. Also, try to buy shoes just large enough to accommodate a cushiony insole. This will protect the interior against wear, keep shoes smelling fresh, and improve your chances of reselling the shoes later on.

BELT IT OUT

A great belt, properly cared for, is one of the most enduring pieces in a woman's wardrobe, easily lasting for a decade or longer. Since belts hang around for so many years, it only makes sense to buy the absolute best, even if it means spending more than you're used to (beware, though, of belts bearing designer names or logos in gold—these tend to look cheap no matter how much they cost). In consignment stores, the finer belts are usually showcased under glass. In thrift stores, they're found on a rack at the back of the store, sportily mixed in with the vinyl.

Quality Considerations

- ❖ The maker's name, and occasionally the type of leather, are printed or stamped on the inner side. Names to watch for are the same as for fine bags and shoes.
- ❖ The inner side is a key checkpoint of an excellent belt. Leather belts should be lined with leather whose quality and attractiveness matches that used on the outside (it may be a different color). If the interior is raw suede or vinyl, the belt is of inferior quality.
- ❖ The best belts have a buckle and fittings made of solid metal (these feel more substantial than the cheaper hollow or metal-plated versions). If you detect a silver buckle with tiny hallmarks stamped onto its surface, congratulations, the metal in question is sterling.
- ❖ Great belts are sewn together (with tiny, tight stitches). Cheap belts are glued.
- ❖ Alligator, crocodile, and snakeskin belts are actually more durable than those made of calfskin (the finest belt leather).
- ❖ In the best belts, the holes are punched clean as a whistle.
- ❖ There should be no cracks running from the holes on the inner side—this means the belt is on its way out.
- ❖ Studded belts fly in and out of fashion. Don't spend a lot of money on one.
- ❖ If you find a gorgeous buckle on a worn-out belt, it's possible to replace the strap—a good shoe repairer should be able to do the job. Unfortunately, the work will probably cost more than the belt itself.
- ❖ Don't forget to check the men's and boys' areas of resale stores, which often hold wonderful well-made belts.

❖ Never buy a belt without trying it on. It may be too *long,* which is as bad a problem as too short.

❖ If the belt only buckles on the very last hole, remember that weight gain or bulky tops may make it a useless dustcatcher.

❖ New holes can be punched by a shoemaker, but be sure the extra measure of strap will go through your beltloops and/or won't droop.

❖ Be sure that the belt's width works with the loops you currently own—even the greatest belt doesn't deserve its own wardrobe.

❖ To keep your belt gleaming, supple, and crack-free, treat it every so often with a good leather cream.

HEY, BAG SPENDER

Call it a pocketbook (in medieval England, a small, book-shaped holdall carried in the pocket), purse (from the ancient Greek *byrsa,* "to hide"), or handbag (in Victorian England, a largish piece of travel luggage, like an old-fashioned doctor's bag), this wardrobe element speaks volumes about personal style. Some women go for a full-blast effect with a Chanel gilt 'n quilt, Louis Vuitton LV-fest, or Prada black nylon. Others prefer the more discreet (but no less expensive) offerings of Trussardi, Gold Pfeil, or Tanner Krolle. Still others like the classic image of Coach, or the extravaganza of styles possible with vintage. No matter what *your* leanings, you can't go wrong carrying a beautifully made bag that complements your overall look.

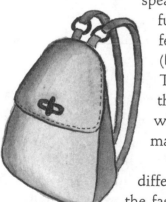

While it's admirable to have a wardrobe of bags to match different outfits, changing them daily is beyond the budget and the fashion discipline of most of us. That's why it makes sense to spend heavily on a few really great bags that match the main neutrals in the wardrobe. Bag switches are made easier, by the way, by regularly clearing out debris and keeping makeup in its own holder.

Formal evening events are the one occasion where a bag switch is mandatory. A day bag, no matter how nice, will undercut your gala

look. Even if you don't go formal very often, it's worth investing in a
simple satin or velvet number that will carry you through such events
for decades.

Quality Considerations

- Top-quality leather bags have several layers of padding and support in between the interior and exterior, giving the leather a plush, cushy feel (see the description of Leiber bags, page 195).
- As with a great suit, the interior of a top-of-the-line bag is as beautiful as the exterior. The best examples are lined in fine suede or silk. Lesser bags are lined in nylon. At the lowest end, they're unlined.
- The surest giveaway of an inferior bag is cheap hardware. Make sure all buckles, clasps, zips, and bolts are solid metal rather than cheap molded or plastic substitutes, *especially* on hot-name nylon bags, which are easy to counterfeit.
- Finer bags often have magnets helping clasps grip.
- The clasps on great bags usually "thunk" together in a heavy, satisfying way, while on cheaper bags the attachment is flimsy.
- The finest framed bags (those designed to keep their shape no matter what) often have four rounded metal "rests" on the underside.
- Real leather takes a tiny scratch (do this discreetly on a hidden part) and smells like leather. Vinyl resists scratching and smells like nothing.
- Straps should be stitched together rather than glued.
- All stitching (unless decorative) should be tiny and regular.
- If you opt for a straw bag, select one with a distinctive pattern and tight weave, with all raw edges carefully bound.
- Beaded and sequined bags are so common at vintage it makes sense to hold out for perfection. Metallic mesh is a sturdier alternative.
- Fabric bags should show the same kind of seaming and overall workmanship seen in fine clothing.

Style Considerations

- How will you wear the bag? Over the chest, bandolier style? Over the shoulder, clutched in hand, slung over a wrist? Will you be happy carrying the bag all day, or do you prefer your hands free? These questions should be carefully considered *before* purchase.

✳ **The Making of a Judith Leiber Handbag** ✳

…the first operation consist of cutting a paper pattern and then cutting every part of the bag, completely by hand, in whatever material is being used. After that, the skins or fabric are gathered, folded, shirred, quilted, or trapunto puffed before marriage to their interlinings and later attachment to their frames. Whenever a pattern requires bending or stitching, the leather is skived, or thinned, to the necessary degree. If a fabric is used, particularly a tartan, each section is carefully matched.

A latex machine, similar to one utilized in shoe factories, is used only for putting interlinings together. The interlinings are one of the truly hidden secrets of a Leiber bag, with as many as seven in a single design. Among the interlinings used are paper, muslin, flannel, horsehair, foam rubber, canvas, and wadding. All of them go into some bags and at least several go into every bag. The soft bags usually take an extra layer of a stiff material.

Once the interlinings are put together, they are cemented to the outside material by hand and the various parts are sewn together. Many operations—shirring is one—that theoretically could be done by machine, are done by hand so that the leather remains soft. Machine work for such details can work well but the outcome is more chancy, a risk Mrs. Leiber is not prepared to take. If the bag is a soft one, it is piped, turned over, and the lining—silk or leather—is dropped in, not quite literally but almost. Backed by the multi-interlinings, the lining is, to a great degree, what makes the difference between a sleek bag and one without distinctive form.

—Judith Leiber, *The Artful Handbag*

❖ If your wardrobe leans toward crisp lines, go for a geometric bag. If your look is softer, a scrunchier bag is more on target. If you're a vintage queen, you have the widest range of all.

❖ Petite women can get shoulder straps shortened (by a good shoe repair shop) so that the bag hangs at a comfortable spot.

❖ Beware of a bag with flimsy straps. It's easy pickings for a purse snatcher.

- ✧ The quickest way to downgrade the looks of a great bag is to over-stuff it. Bag volume is *always* smaller than it looks.
- ✧ Knapsacks kill the lines of a good suit, but are great on weekends.
- ✧ Nothing undercuts a great look faster than a schlepper totebag, which people *do* notice, even when it's at the end of your arm. If you need to transport bulky papers to and from work or school, get yourself a stylish carryall.
- ✧ New mothers: there's no rule that says you *have* to carry one of those cartoonish diaper/toy/catchall baby bags. A roomy nylon bag in a sleek shape is light and waterproof, and looks ten times smarter.
- ✧ Be aware that designer initials turn off as many people as they impress.

MARV SCARVES

There are almost as many styles of scarf—square, oblong, pocket, shawl, muffler, wrap, bandanna, kerchief—as there are ways to tie them. They're unusual accessories in that the best ones easily make the jump from casual to professional and even to formal wear, which is why you can hardly have too many. It's good to mix them up in terms of fabrics and styles. Silk and cotton are the usual suspects, synthetic metallic are great at night, and there is nothing more luxurious in chilly air than a pashmina cashmere shawl (which sadly costs a fortune, even at resale).

Quality Considerations

- ✧ The best dress scarves are made from ultraheavy silk. Hermès, Ferragamo, Gucci, Tiffany, and Versace are some of the names to watch for.
- ✧ The designs on most silk scarves are screenprinted, which means every single color required a separate procedure to put it there. The more colors in a printed scarf, the more complicated the production, and the higher the intrinsic value. Hermès scarves are among the most colorful, featuring up to 25 different hues.

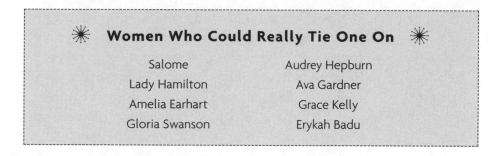

✳ **Women Who Could Really Tie One On** ✳

Salome	Audrey Hepburn
Lady Hamilton	Ava Gardner
Amelia Earhart	Grace Kelly
Gloria Swanson	Erykah Badu

❧ With printed silk scarves, the coloration is usually less intense on the reverse side, but if there's a major difference, be on alert. Silk absorbs color brilliantly, rayon less so—and this may be a sign that the scarf is counterfeit.

❧ The finest silk scarves have hems that are rolled and sewn by hand. Odiana Dauman of Bis Designer Resale in New York points out that Hermès is so proud of the beauty of its hem it is meant to be worn facing outward.

❧ Odiana also notes that a hand-sewn hem should be slightly puffy rather than flat. If it is flat, the scarf has suffered callous pressing. This detracts from its value.

❧ Dry cleaning and pressing kills the luster of silk, which is best washed by hand in a gentle detergent, then steamed wrinkle-free.

❧ Carefully clip the label off a scarf—it's unattractive when left in place. But if the make is excellent, keep the label handy in case you eventually choose to resell.

❧ With wool/cashmere/other animal-fiber scarves, be on the lookout for moth holes.

*A heavy shawl called a manto
was worn on the head and shoulders in
16th-century Spain, as widows and young women
were allowed to show only one eye.*
—Alice Macknell, *Shawls, Stoles and Scarves*

*Style
Considerations*

- ✧ Few women can pull off the Audrey Hepburnesque teeny scarf knotted at the base of the neck. But if you have a graceful neck, go for it.
- ✧ Pick your knots carefully. The *cub-scout neckerchief* works fine with sweaters and tops, but with button-down blouses a high knot can look fussy—a looser, lower knot may be more appealing. The *choker* works with almost every type of open collar, but may look odd with a dress, and isn't right for women with short necks. Avoid knots that turn scarves into droopy *loops*—another turn around the neck usually prevents this, or tethering with a carefully placed pin.
- ✧ If you work in a conservative environment where "statement" jewelry is frowned upon, scarves can be a style lifeline. Wear one just peeping out around the opening of a jacket, or use a pocket square to enliven jacket and blouse.

BATTY FOR HATS

*People still see hats as an old-fashioned accessory.
I disagree. Hats are a form of expression and people love a hat
whether they are a connoisseur of fashion and style or not.*
—Philip Treacy, *Financial Times*

It's hard to put it better than that. In England, women wear hats with mad abandon, but over here we get shy, saving them for church, the beach, and temperatures below freezing. It's a shame, because few items in the wardrobe carry their drama. Whenever you shop resale, don't overlook the hats. Whether they're sporty, demure, or dashing, wearing them provides great pleasure to onlookers, and it's a rare hat that goes unappreciated.

*Quality
Considerations*

- ✧ Felt hats are made from wool, or, in superior-quality toppers, a wool–rabbit fur blend. The latter are much softer and finer-feeling, rather like velvet.

- Great felt hats, like great clothes, are substantially constructed. Cheap versions are flimsy and easily crushable.
- At the top end of the range, straw hats are made with so-called Panama or Manila straw, which is very fine and glossy, or Italian (also called leghorn) straw, which consists of strands braided, then woven, together. At the lowest end, straw hats are made with recycled paper fiber.
- The finer the straw and tighter the weave used in a summer hat, the better the quality. Authentic Panama hats are so well constructed they can be rolled up as tight as a cigar and will instantly pop back into shape.
- The quality of the label used in a hat is an excellent overall indicator.
- Flowers and other doodads can add greatly to the charm of a hat. Examine these extras carefully. Cheap plastic flowers are a minus; unusual feathers add value.
- If you're inclined to wear all-fur hats, be vigilant for cracking and other signs of wear.
- To restore a battered felt hat, hold it over a steaming kettle and brush vigorously. Steaming also lets you change the shape of the crease or brim—be careful not to burn your fingers.
- Be wary of a hat with a fraying ribbon band—it's probably not of high quality.

Fit Considerations

- When considering a hat, keep it on your head for at least five minutes. If it's even slightly small, it will begin to itch or otherwise irritate your forehead.
- For fitting accuracy, it's best if your hair is styled as it would be while wearing the hat for real.
- Don't worry too much about hat sizes, which vary depending on the make and style.
- A slightly large casual hat can be cute. A slightly small one will be a torment.
- If you love a hat but you're worried about cooties, relax—you're more likely to catch them off the back of a movie seat, and you

don't worry about that, do you? (You *do*?) Then buy the darn thing, put it in a plastic bag, stick it in the freezer for a couple of days, defrost, and give it a good brush inside and out.

❖ Never buy a hat without checking it out first in a full-length mirror. Some women can't carry really big ones; others can't carry really small.

❖ To tighten a too-large hat, or to keep an irritating crown away from the forehead, get some adhesive-backed Velcro tape, cut a few inches and stick it on just where your forehead hits, keeping the hook and loop parts of the tape attached together.

> *Hats are the most unnatural of all items of clothing;*
> *they are the least necessary but most powerful.*
> —Colin McDowell,
> *Hats: Status, Style and Glamour*

Style Considerations

❖ A man's hat, especially a fedora or trilby, looks smashing with trenchcoats, and is often of better quality than similar models made for women.

❖ After trying on a hundred hats, you'll know which shapes work best for you. That's why it's always worthwhile to spend a minute or so sampling, even if you're not in hat-buying mode.

❖ Generally speaking, the lines of the hat ought to complement the lines of the outfit. A clean-cut overcoat will look best with a crisp hat, while a curvier jacket can take a scrunchier chapeau.

❖ If you find a hat that is not quite an exact color match for its intended outfit, consider glue-gunning on elements like a new band, flowers, or feathers that *do* match, to better harmonize the whole look. Hat notions can be found in fine sewing stores, craft stores, and even stationery departments (ribbons, bows, etc).

❖ If you're wearing a hat to complement a dress or suit, keep other accessories fairly quiet.

❖ "Hat head" is the one downside of wearing a topper. The best way to minimize it is to style hair smooth and straight back from the forehead.

✿ There are few occasions, apart from funerals, where dark veils can be carried off successfully. But if your destination is a sophisticated club, your outfit is chic, and you have the nerve, why not? Classy men adore a touch of mystery.

Some Great Names in Hats

Stephen Jones	Frederick Fox
Philip Treacy	Patricia Underwood
Borsalino	Tracey Tooker
Philippe Model	Victoria DiNardo
Gabrielle Cadet	Olivier Chanan
Carlos Lewis	Marie Mercié

World-class names in hats do occasionally show up at resale, but you're more likely to come across the work of local hatmakers. Millinery (to use the formal term for the art) is undergoing a renaissance in many cities. Wildly creative and technically impeccable examples pour forth from these artisans, who may only distribute to a few neighborhood boutiques. If you're a hat lover, it's worth getting to know the local all-stars, so you'll recognize the names when they crop up in your favorite stores.

JEWELRY, JEWELRY, JEWELRY

Discovering fine gemstones at resale is a high-risk pursuit, best backed by training in gemology. Gold, silver, and other precious metals are a slightly safer bet, but you still can't be sure of authenticity—even items with all the right stamps could well turn out to be bogus. The point is, don't splash out on jewelry because you're bewitched by the carat count—do so because you're dazzled by the piece. That way you'll never be disappointed.

Au-inspiring Gold works hard for its sparkling reputation. According to Fleming and Honour's *Dictionary of the Decorative Arts,* this most precious of metals is so easy to tool it can be hammered to a mere four-millionths of an inch thick, yet so heat-resistant it won't start to melt until temperatures climb over 1000°C. Gold's miraculous properties, along with its beauty, led the Aztecs—better known for human sacrifice than for poetry—to call it the "excrement of the gods."

Pure gold (otherwise known as *24-carat* gold) is too soft to make durable jewelry, so it is always blended with copper, copper and silver, or platinum. When the blend reaches half gold, half another metal, it is called *12-carat*. The highest-quality pieces are generally *22-* or *18-carat* gold. In some European countries, such as Italy and France, any alloy below eighteen can't be called gold at all.

By law, all gold jewelry must have the content stamped somewhere on the piece. On rings, it's usually inside the band; on necklaces, on the flat oblong loop near the catch. Sometimes, instead of a carat designation, you'll see a numeric symbol:

916 indicates 22-carat
750 indicates 18-carat
585 indicates 14-carat
375 indicates 9-carat.

But again, don't count on any stamp if you see one at resale—to get a 100 percent guarantee, you should limit purchases to reputable jewelry stores.

Hi-ho, Silver!   Like gold, pure silver is too soft to be easily worked and worn—it is usually alloyed with copper for increased strength. The percentage of silver varies depending on the time and place of manufacture. *Sterling,* the best quality, is generally somewhere around 93 percent pure. The number 958 or 925 is occasionally used to designate sterling. There's also another method—hallmarks. These are the tiny stamps silversmiths use to designate a piece's origin. To learn more about a specific hallmark, see if your local library has a guide. One other way to tell silver from lesser metals such as pewter or nickel is the presence of tarnish—a result of a reaction between its molecules and oxygen. But lesser-quality *silverplate* will also tarnish; see below.

Going Platinum

The rarest of precious metals, platinum has been used as a setting for precious stones since the early part of this century. But in recent decades, it has emerged from a supporting role to become a star in its own right. The number 950 or the word *plat* stamped on a light silvery metal indicates that a piece is of platinum, but at the risk of sounding like a broken record, don't bet the farm on its authenticity at resale.

Precious Metal Jacket

Both gold and silver looks can be produced on the cheap by a process known as electroplate. Here, laboratory fiddling enables base metals such as copper or nickel to be coated with a thin layer of gold or silver. With time, the coating wears away, revealing the metal underneath. Before that happens, your skin can be a better bogus detector than your eye. If skin near the piece starts turning green, you've got a case of electroplate-itis. Don't worry, it's harmless, and will go away shortly after the jewelry is removed from the spot.

Costume Party

Where resale jewelry really shines is in the costume department. At thrift stores, extraordinarily fun stuff can be had for pennies, especially ethnic-style beads and those wonderfully fake paste starbursts from the 1950s. A sharp eye can often detect pieces of real value as well, jumbled together with the junk. Vintage stores offer an even more bountiful array of faux baubles, from the marcasite-and-silver combos so popular at the turn of the century to 1970s-era mood rings. The prices at vintage will surpass those at thrift, reflecting the pieces' age (some are true antiques, over 100 years old) and collectability (there is a thriving market for period jewelry of all kinds and quality levels). Consignment stores, for their part, tend to specialize in big-ticket contemporary costume—the stuff usually found under the pricey counter at department stores. If you're shopping for a big night out, this may be exactly the place to find the perfect finishing touches for your outfit.

According to Deanna Farneti Cera's excellent reference *Costume Jewelry,* the rise of costume pieces closely follows the evolution of clothing in the 20th century. She categorizes faux pieces as follows:

Bijoux de couture (couturier's jewelry): At the richest end of the costume scale are the limited-edition pieces commissioned by haute couturiers, meant to be worn with specific outfits from their collections. Coco Chanel was the great pioneer of this kind of adornment, and this house's pieces still carry a lot of cachet. Other classic names in couturier jewelry include Schiaparelli, Balenciaga, and Dior—their early works are among the most coveted. The tradition of couturier jewelry continues today. Sporadically before the 1950s and consistently afterward, such pieces have been "signed" (in fact stamped) with the name of the commissioning couturier.

Costume jewelry for ready-to-wear (also called bridge jewelry): Produced in greater volume than the models above, this group tends to follow fashion rather than set it. Still, the level of craftsmanship is often superb. Certain pathbreakers from the past, such as Miriam Haskell, Fulco di Verdura, and Jean Schlumberger, produced pieces that are as sought-after today as the best of the couturier baubles. Other makers, such as Trifari, Pennino Bros., Napier, Adele Simpson, and Kenneth Jay Lane, are collected at an equally avid rate. Like the couture pieces, ready-to-wear also tends to bear the signatures or marks of its manufacturers.

Inexpensive costume: Also called trinkets, these pieces were and are produced in the hundreds of thousands to be sold inexpensively as lighthearted adornments. Riding the fashion tide, the styles appear in department stores, street fairs, mail-order catalogues, and the like. They disappear just as quickly, washing up sooner or later under the glass cases of vintage and thrift stores. Rarely signed, they are usually not worth much to collectors, but that's not the important thing. If you love something and will put it to good wear—that's what counts.

Countless women accumulate jewelry like magpies, only to hide it away in the jewelry box or closet. One of history's most striking examples is memorialized at the Royal Museum in Edinburgh, Scotland, in the jewelry collection of an ordinary woman of the earlier part of this century. Like a lot of us, she spent most of her lunch hours out shopping, scouring her favorite shops and secondhand stores. She was an avid and meticulous collector, carefully noting the origin and price of every piece. But instead of ever wearing the jewelry, she kept it all squirreled away. Even her closest friends were astonished when, after her death, the hundreds of treasures were revealed. You can't help but think how much brighter her life might have been with some of that razzle-dazzle at her neckline and wrists.

The lesson? Don't wait for special occasions to wear your accessories. When you start dressing as though life were occasion enough, special times will come right along with it.

PART 3

Tender Loving Clothes Care

Chapter Eleven

◈

The Well-Tempered Closet

*A*h, the ambiance of a packed resale store—some of us love it so much we have a home version in our very own closet. But what a disservice this does to beautifully made clothes. To look their best, blouses need elbow room, pants need expanse, garments need the final frontier. In James Wagenvoord and Fiona St. Aubyn's book *ClothesCare,* Elise Gaubert, a real lady's maid, recalls how she "once looked after a woman who had enough closet space to leave six inches between each garment. Nothing was ever crushed…which reduced the need for pressing, ironing, and cleaning." *Six inches.* For most of us, this is about 5⅞ inches beyond our wildest dreams. All the same, when times get tight in the wardrobe, there are steps we can take to make sure clothes hang properly and breathe.

Here's a simple test to tell when your closet has reached maximum capacity. Will a blouse stay hung even if its hanger isn't touching the rail? If so, it's time to clear the decks via a full-scale storage overhaul. Admittedly, this is a chore only Martha Stewart could love (as if *she's* short of hanging space), but the end result is worth the half-day of effort. Why?

❖ You'll be able to dress faster in the morning (in other words, an extra five to ten minutes of sleep)
❖ Your clothing won't need as much maintenance and repair

❖ According to the principles of feng shui, the ancient Chinese art of spatial organization, the less mess in the closet, the clearer and happier the mind.

Done right, an overhaul consists of three parts:

1. Emptying and cleaning the closet and dresser
2. Sorting through the clothes to weed out substandard and little-worn pieces
3. Reorganizing the wardrobe in an orderly and pleasing way

Doing the whole job at one go is the smartest tack, for it gives you an overview that helps you streamline and unify. For the same reason, a systematic approach like the one outlined in the following pages is better than diving in unprepared. Take heart: you've been nosing through your closet so often as part of your quality research you've subconsciously done a lot of the groundwork already.

Before you begin, read this chapter through once to get an idea of the steps involved and what you can do to prepare. If you share your closet with someone else, consider doing the closet cleanup as a team. Finally, check out a household organizing store or its catalogue to learn about storage options and equipment. You may find a gizmo that revolutionizes the way you keep order.

STAGE 1: CLOSET CLEAROUT

To purchase/prepare ahead of time: Household cleansers, cedar blocks/mothballs, fragrant sachets/potpourri, shelf liner.

The plan: First, clear any nonwardrobe items off the flat surfaces in the bedroom—you're going to need all the space you can get. Then throw the closet doors open and start in. Every hanging item should be draped on the bed (it's easier if you keep clothing on the hangers, but beware of snagging neighboring garments). Dressers, bureaus, and any other containers should also be emptied on the bed. Finally, shoes, belts, scarves, etc. should be brought out in plain sight.

After the closet and dresser are entirely empty, they need to be cleaned. Dusted, vacuumed, shelves swiped down, old mothballs, potpourri flakes, and what have you swept up (wear rubber gloves for the mothballs), burned-out lightbulb changed, old love letters read over, etc. If you are hypermotivated and have the space to temporarily stash the clothes elsewhere, you might consider repainting the closet's interior.

Once the closet and drawers are spotless, strew the mothballs or nail up the cedar blocks (both far enough away from clothing so they won't come into contact—the mothballs are toxic, and cedar oils could cause yellowing). Apply fresh contact paper and toss in the lavender, taking pleasure in the thought of all those fresh smells that soon will infuse your clothes.

STAGE 2: SURVIVAL OF THE CHICEST

To purchase/prepare ahead of time: Decent hangers (wood, padded, or well-shaped plastic; avoid wire). The best hangers for skirts have rubber-dipped metal or plastic clips (those with hinged crossbars tend to crease waistbands and are a pain to use). If you have the room to hang pants full-length, hangers with clips are also a good option. If you need to hang pants folded, hangers with a crossbar are your best bet. For dresses, look for hangers with notches for dress loops. If space is very tight, think about buying multitiered hangers for pants, shirts, and skirts. For long-term storage, look for heavy plastic garment bags (not the clear ones used by dry cleaners, which are terrible for your clothes), old suitcases/trunks, etc. If you have delicate vintage pieces, consider purchasing some acid-free boxes. Also get a fresh roll of garbage bags for discards.

The plan: At this point, the pile on your bed would strike fear in the heart of a skilled Sherpa guide. Don't be daunted—you can conquer the mountain all on your own, doing it step by step. Start by separating the items (shoes and accessories included), into four separate piles, according to the following guidelines:

1. Discards

These are the clothes, shoes, and other accessories that you know, in your heart of hearts, have come to the end of their useful life. Typically, they have one or more of the following characteristics:

* The quality now makes you cringe
* The flaws are so bad even a starving moth won't touch it
* Your style has moved on
* The fit leaves more to be desired than George Clooney
* It's been two years since you've worn it

Put the stuff of low desirability (in other words, thrift store-bound) straight into a garbage bag. If you're thinking about consigning the better pieces (and you should be), weigh the cost of dry cleaning against the profit you could realistically earn (see Chapter 16 for more on reselling clothes), then set these clothes aside as well.

> *There comes a time when you have to let your clothes go out*
> *into the world and try to make it on their own.*
> —Bette Midler, *People,* 1981

2. Deep Storage

These are the items that you probably should throw out, but for various reasons, ranging from the fairly rational to the borderline psychotic, don't want to. They include:

* Ethnic garb picked up on vacation that you may need for a costume party someday

- Anything you haven't worn for a full year
- Perfectly good clothes that are one size smaller than the current-model you, if you're taking steps to lose the weight
- Athletic clothes, if you're not
- Old T-shirts reeking of nostalgia or an ex-boyfriend's CK Be
- Heavy sweaters (if you live in, say, Austin or Orlando)
- Ski and any other clothing that requires an air ticket
- Formalwear (if you haven't been to a formal since Barry Manilow sang the slow ones)

Before storing the clothes, take them off the hangers and assess. Do they need to be washed or dry-cleaned? It may seem bothersome, but believe me, when you unearth them in the fullness of time, you'll be glad you did. Once the clothes are ready for deep storage, carefully fold them and place into appropriate holders. These can be suitcases, trunks, heavy-duty garment bags—even cardboard boxes, but remember that the latter contain acids that will eventually have an adverse affect. Be sure to add mothballs or other critter-preventatives such as bay leaves—in bags so they aren't in direct contact with the clothes. Finally, polish and bag to-be-stored shoes (will they really be stylish in another year or so?) and accessories and put them into storage holders as well. Before shoving the whole shebang into the darkest reaches of your living quarters, quickly jot down the contents on a piece of paper and tape it to the outside. This will spare you lots of hassle if that costume party ever comes through.

3. Menders

Meanwhile, back on the bed, this pile contains everything you ought to be wearing but aren't, because the zipper's stuck, the hem's not right, a button's gone, etc. As soon as you can face another round of domestic detail, stock up on supplies at a notions or sewing store and get to work on fixing this stuff, or take it to your alterations person and let her worry about it.

4. Keepers

These are the pieces that make you proud. Carefully rehang them on appropriate hangers, and refold the ones that will go back into the drawers (have a look at the storage tips on pages 216 and 279–80). As you do this, be sure to give the items a quick once-over to be sure they don't require any cleaning or mending themselves.

Now that you're through sorting, what's left to do? Apart from organizing your hanging space, little except dropping a couple bagfuls off at your favorite thrift, consigning a few items, and figuring out what to do with all the leftover wire hangers. In the spirit of recycling, gather them together with a twist-tie and take them to the one place they'll be warmly welcomed: the dry cleaner.

STAGE 3: ORGANIZING AND HOW TO DO IT

Different people have different notions on how to organize a closet. Some believe arranging clothes by color is best. Others insist on hanging ready-made ensembles. Still others recommend grouping clothing by type. How you do it is a matter of taste and needs. If you're uncertain, the following rundown of advantages/disadvantages may help you make up your mind.

Arranging clothes by seasons: A few experts recommend grouping clothes according to the time of year that they're worn. For example, all winter skirts are in one corner, all summer tops in another.
Conclusion: Seasonal segregation seems a lot less apt now than it did a few decades ago. Today, we're a lot more flexible about what colors are right when, and many fabrics span three seasons of wear. Still, if you live in a part of the country with sharply defined weather patterns, and if you have a huge wardrobe and storage capacity (i.e., a walk-in closet), this method can help bring order to your abundance. Just beware of overlooking wardrobe possibilities (such as wearing a T-shirt under winter wool) due to overcategorization.

Organizing clothes by color: Some women like to open their closet and see a rainbow of hues. Yellow pieces moving through to oranges, then to reds and beyond. In this system, the color rules placement, so a skirt might hang alongside a dress or a pair of pants. Besides pure aesthetics, there's a theory at work: when clothes are arranged by color, matching is easier.

Conclusion: While it makes for a pretty closet, the method has its shortcomings. Valuable space is often wasted when short and long items are mingled together (since there is no room for a second hanging bar below). Also, just because clothes are the same approximate hue doesn't mean they will match—style and proportion also count for a great deal. In any case, the best match is often between colors that are at different ends of the spectrum.

Organizing clothes by ready-made outfits: Advocates believe that tops and bottoms that work beautifully as a team should be hung together (with appropriate accessories slung over the same hangers). They say the method makes getting dressed a no-brainer.

Conclusion: This is a great way to guarantee consistent good looks, because the outfits have proven themselves already. And it gives women with very large wardrobes another way to get a grip. Those with a limited number of pieces, however, may feel too tightly locked in. Also, as with the color method above, it may encourage space inefficiency, as pieces of different lengths must be hung next to each other.

Organizing clothes by garment type: Here, skirts are hung with skirts, pants with pants, etc., progressing from one end of the closet to the other. There's a vague "scientific" air to this arrangement, as it is the one promoted by the closet-organizing companies.

Conclusion: Closet companies like organizing by type because it makes maximum use of minimum space. It also allows for high flexibility in putting outfits together, and makes it possible to detect wardrobe gaps. However, with the freedom comes danger—poor matches may occur because it's so easy to throw any two pieces together.

Ultimately, you know best how you want your clothes to hang. Pick one of the systems and try to stick to it—at least until the next closet overhaul (most experts recommend twice a year).

A few last storage tips:
- Knit dresses should be folded just like sweaters
- Pants can be folded or placed on shelf, or hung two to a hanger, facing opposite directions
- Never fold a sweater lengthwise—the crease will take forever to fall out
- Blouses can be hung or folded
- When buying hangers, be sure the hook is big enough to fit your bar
- If you must use wire hangers, wrap elastic bands around ends to prevent garments from sliding
- A fishing tackle box is an excellent jewelry holder
- Wine racks are good for storing shoes
- Or, store shoes in boxes with the ends cut out so you can see what's inside.
- To prevent cracking, belts should be coiled or hung straight, not left in garments

EXPANDING YOUR STORAGE CAPABILITIES

There's never enough room, is there? Even after the closet is organized to the last inch, overflow may still be a problem. What to do? Forget about hanging items from the shower rail. The following fairly instant, not-very-expensive methods are lifesavers. Besides keeping stuff out of sight, they'll even up the style quotient of your living space.

Hatboxes: Whether antique or brand new, these are a marvelous way to add to the room in your room. It doesn't matter if you never wear

hats. You do surely wear pantyhose, T-shirts, leggings, scarves, and gloves—all of which fold flat and are perfect candidates for tucking away. These containers stack up in a corner or on top of a wardrobe and look great, plus are light enough to fling around easily when you're looking for an item one holds. Be sure to line the box with tissue paper before adding clothes. Hatboxes are often found at thrift or vintage stores, flea markets, and, best of all, in relatives' attics.

Rattan trunks: Also lightweight and fairly inexpensive, a rattan trunk can hold a couple of seasons' worth of sweaters within easy reach of the rest of the wardrobe. Or jeans, down coats, or whatever other bulky pieces don't merit a full-time parking space in the closet. Spray-painted a great color or with a pretty throw on top, they're a classy addition to all manner of decor. The best place to find them is at import emporiums and funky, lower-priced furniture stores.

Antique luggage: A bit pricier are the gorgeous leather pieces that huddled in the hold while their owners sipped champagne at the captain's table. Stack these up against some underused wall space and you've not only got instant storage but a touch of Titanic-style class. Pieces with alligator scales or Louis Vuitton's initials are particularly covetable. The less expensive ones are usually pretty banged up but can be redeemed with some tender loving polish and strategic positioning to hide damage. Antique luggage can be found at vintage stores, antique stores (here you'll pay big), relatives' attics, and thrift stores.

Screen/rolling rack: I once lived in a studio apartment that didn't have a single closet. (If it did, the landlord would have called it a one-bedroom.) The solution? A standard garment rolling rack, hidden behind a nice folding screen. *Voila,* instant walk-in closet. Household organizing stores should be able to supply the rolling rack. The screen can be had from import stores, flea markets, or even made with some plywood, hinges, fabric, and a staplegun.

With a little ingenuity and some careful combing of your favorite resale haunts, you'll not only detect fabulous finds, but also fabulous storage aids to hold them. And even though your own lady's maid is out of the question, nobody will know it from looking at you.

Chapter Twelve

❖

Caring for Your Clothes

In the past, people were famously less fussy than we are today when it came to keeping their clothes clean. The same garment would be worn for weeks (if not months), pressing was infrequent, stain removal was haphazard at best. But before rushing to judge, it's only fair to consider the circumstances. If you think a full hamper is one of life's torments, consider the fluff and tumble of laundry years ago.

RUB A DUB DUB

The very first washing apparatus was simplicity itself: a pair of hands or feet, a river, and a nice big flat rock. When clothes were beaten against the hard surface, dirt and oils would loosen and drift down the current. If this original version of stonewashing was tough on clothes, it was even tougher on the washerwomen's limbs. The introduction of tubs and paddles didn't help. According to Una Robertson's *Illustrated History of the Housewife,* women worked "with their coats tucked up . . . and this not only in summer, but in the hardest frosty weather, when their legs and feet are almost literally as red as blood with the cold. . . ."

In many parts of the world, plants (especially those in the *Saponaria* family) helped get clothes clean. When pounded, their stems release a lathery froth, the forerunner of soap. In the 15th century, the first true soaps were fashioned from plant or animal fats blended with ashes and sodium bicarbonate. By the 19th century, soapmaking was a worldwide industry. Even so, it wasn't standard at laundry time, for two reasons. First, in certain countries and eras, soap was highly taxed, making it prohibitively expensive. Second, it only dissolved in hot water, and so wasn't always practical in the days before electricity. This is why washerwomen from ancient Rome on up to 19th-century England turned to another natural product to get clothes clean and bright: stale human urine. Though this may sound like a bad Monty Python routine, it's actually not that farfetched. Urine contains ammonia, one of the best natural cleaning and brightening agents around. Something else in its favor—it was a cleaning supply that never ran low. Many households had troughs set up in the backyard especially for collecting the raw material.

This pungent chapter in laundry history drew to a close when detergent came into common usage at the beginning of our century. Today, lots of us use the words "soap" and "detergent" interchangeably, but they're actually two different things. Soap is, or at least was, made from natural ingredients. Detergent is made from petroleum by-products.

The laundry saga didn't end with the final rinse—pressing was one more reason women dreaded washday. Before the introduction of specialized tools, clothes were literally pulled or trampled flat, or hung on a line to flap straight (and board-stiff) in the breeze. Heavy irons simplified the job, but what with all the heating and reheating, scorched fabric and fingertips were inevitable. In the 18th century, a contraption called a mangle appeared in wealthier households. Clothes were set on rollers underneath a weighted box, which, as it was cranked over them, flattened the items and pressed out most of the water. Since the box could be up to six feet long and was filled with heavy stones, the mangle could hardly be described as a labor-saving device, though it did lighten up in later years.

So the next time your laundry duties start getting you down, cheer yourself up with some snapshots from the past—chilblains, aching back, burnt fingers, and swishing around in what amounted to a full toilet. The contemporary version—sorting, loading, folding, and ironing, all in the space of two hours or so—is, by comparison, low agitation.

NEW IMPROVED FORMULA

In fact, it's so easy to do laundry these days that lots of us slide by with half-measures. You know what I mean: cheating on sorting, flinging stuff into machines without adjusting the controls, leaving minor stains to take care of themselves, blowing off temperature recommendations. While most of today's clothing is tough enough to withstand the occasional shortcut, doing laundry sloppily with any regularity is certain to increase fading, wear, permastains, and the outright ruination of favorite items. Spending an extra five or ten minutes to do it right points to a woman who truly values her clothes, one who knows that a little virtue come laundry time brings more than its own rewards:

* Drying clothes for the recommended time means they need less ironing
* Dealing with stains before they set means saving big bucks at the dry cleaner
* Keeping an eye on laundry temperatures means colors stay punchier
* Doing it all right means your precious investment endures

Rule #9 of Resale: Great clothing only stays that way with careful upkeep.

The next several pages detail how. If this piques your interest about laundry lore, also have a look at *Martha Stewart Living*'s excellent "Clotheskeeping" issue of November '98 (order via 800-999-6518, or try to find it at your local library). The library is also sure to have books on household tips. While they can be corny, they're also strangely addictive once you get into them.

SEPARATED, BUT EQUAL

In the laundry kingdom, there are three broad classes of clothing:

* machine-washable stuff
* hand-washable stuff
* stuff that must go to the dry cleaner

The breakdown depends on the type of fabric involved and its reaction to water, heat, and agitation. To sort out what's what prior to cleaning, it's best to check the garment's care label. Predictably, though, resale clothing throws in a few wrinkles. The care tags are cut out, for example. Or written in Hungarian. Or, due to the clothes' age, nonexistent in the first place. Not to worry. As long as you know what kind of fabric the garment is made of, you can proceed with confidence. Here's a rundown of the typical care requirements:

Acetate: Dry-clean, or machine- or hand-wash at cool temperature. Do not wring when wet or put through spin cycle in washer. Hang or dry flat (do not tumble dry). Iron while damp at cool temperature.

Acrylic: Machine-wash. Hang or dry flat. Iron at cool temperature.

Corduroy: Wash as per material (usually cotton), turning inside out. Tumble dry. Leave inside out for ironing.

Cotton: Separate lights and darks and machine-wash. Whites may be washed very hot, colors warm. Tumble dry, but remove while still a bit damp or wrinkles will set fast. Iron on hot.

Denim: Wash as per cotton, but the first time all alone so that dye does not stain other clothing. Turn inside out to discourage fading.

Leather: Send to specialist dry cleaner. Spray with protective product once back.

Nylon: Wash by hand or machine at cool temperature with like colors. Nylon's natural hue is grayish and it will revert if mislaundered. Special nylon whiteners can be purchased at the supermarket. Iron cool.

Rayon: If washing instructions are missing, dry-clean only.

Spandex content: Wash at cool temperature. Hang or dry flat, or tumble dry at cool temperature. Iron cool.

Silk: Dry-clean or hand-wash in cool water with Woolite or similar gentle product. Do not rub or a chalky bloom may arise due to broken filaments. Hang or dry flat. Take care with spot cleaning, as this may leave rings. Shirts and blouses should be steamed or ironed on cool on reverse side.

Suede: Dry-clean only. Protect with suede-protector spray once back from cleaner.

Wool and cashmere: Dry-clean or hand-wash. Wool may be damaged by traditional soaps and detergents—better to use Woolite or baby shampoo. Put wool through washing machine or tumble dryer only on settings specifically designated for this fiber. If wrinkled, hang dry woolens in steamy bathroom.

If the garment is older or delicate vintage, see the specific care instructions on page 237.

YOUR PARTNER IN GRIME

Sometimes, due to the nature of the fabric or the delicacy of construction, you simply can't do the cleaning yourself. Here are the main reasons to take an item to the dry cleaner:

—You don't know what kind of material it is
—The garment has interfacings and/or linings

—The garment is made up of two or more kinds of fabric
—The garment is beaded
—The garment has metallic thread
—The fabric is otherwise very dressy, like velvet or taffeta
—God only knows what that stain is
—The laundry-care tag tells you to

Whether you dry-clean clothes once a year or twice a week, try to work with the best outfit in town. Yes, it'll be more expensive, but ultimately it's worth it.

In choosing dry-cleaning professionals, remember that those with equipment on the premises come out ahead, for three reasons. First, store personnel are more knowledgeable, since they're the ones doing the job. Second, you can make any complaints directly, without having to go through a middleman. Third, it cuts down on the chances of items being lost (exasperatingly frequent, in my experience). Something else to seek out: specialization in cleaning wedding dresses and formals, for these people will be comfortable with a gamut of fabrics. Finally, check the door or window for association membership stickers. Dry cleaners that belong to professional organizations are serious about their work, and are more likely to reimburse you if something should go wrong.

Dry Cleaning Inside Scoop

❖ Only dry-clean cotton and linen if shrinkage is a real worry— otherwise detergent and water do the best job. Another reason: some believe these fibers retain whiffs of dry-cleaning solution.

❖ If you must dry-clean jeans, be aware that the pressed crease down the front will soon bleach in permanently.

❖ Work with your cleaner. Point out any stains, describe the source if you can, and mention any special dry-cleaning requirements (it *is* their job to check, but the nudge never hurts).

❖ Garments are professionally ironed in one of two ways: entirely with specialist pressing equipment (faster and less expensive) or finished by hand (pricier, better results). The following signs of careless machine-pressing mean the garment should be redone. If you specified hand-pressing, they're signs that you're being ripped off. Get your money back and don't return.

—Lapel squashed flat against the front of a suit jacket (it should gently curve inward instead)
—Pants cuffs pressed so hard they leave an indentation against the side of the ankle
—Cuffs and collars wrinkled or otherwise distorted (French cuffs are frequent victims)
—Cuffs pressed so hard buttons leave an indentation on the fabric below
—Buttons broken, chipped, or pitted from the heat of the iron. By rights these should be replaced by the dry cleaner. If it's a gauntlet button, make sure they use a smaller one than those at the cuffs.

INTO EVERY LIFE, A LITTLE STAIN MUST FALL

We're all only human, and stains are nature's proof. When it happens to you, don't lose your cool. Most stains are history as long as you treat them as quickly as possible. Even if it means excusing yourself from the table during a job interview or date—in any case, you'll look much more together after some quick work in the Ladies' than with marinara all over your blouse. The point is to do as much as you can before laundering, because washing, drying, and ironing, especially at high temperatures, often lock the mark in for good.

Effective stain removal depends on two things: the fabric's care requirements and the cause. *If the garment is dry-clean only,* try to remove as much of the gunk as possible with a white paper towel (being careful not to rub it in), then get it to the cleaner pronto. (Some clothes-care experts recommend tackling the stain yourself with a store-bought dry-cleaning product, but unless you have total confidence in your abilities, it's best to leave it to the experts).

To treat stains on washable clothing, there are three options:

❖ If it's just a spot, attack it directly with a store-bought prewash product, then wash as usual

❖ If it's a bigger, nastier stain (and the item can go into the machine), run it through the prewash cycle, or

❖ Soak the garment in a bucket (but if it's silk and wool, use only cleaners safe for those fabrics and never soak for longer than a few minutes)

If the item is badly or very stubbornly soiled, the soaking and prewash techniques are preferable, because they prevent gunk from getting trapped in the washer and redepositing on the other clothes. If the stain is protein-based, such as blood, egg, or grass, enzyme-presoak cleaners are helpful. Note, though, that they will eat away at animal fibers such as wool and silk.

Before using any stain remover, test it on a hidden area of the garment, blotting after a moment with a white cloth or paper towel to see if the dye lifts. Also be sure to use the appropriate product. All-purpose stain removers like Spray 'n Wash work best on machine-washable fabrics, while solvent-based products like K2r are intended for dry-cleanables. If you can't get your hands on an all-purpose stain remover, baby shampoo, clear dishwashing liquid, or even hand soap will do.

One thing that regularly blots our reputation is food. Such spills usually don't happen where reference books are handy, so it's a good idea to memorize these general treatment rules for washable items.

For nongreasy stains: Rinse in cool water as soon as possible. Apply a prewash product, stain remover, clear dishwashing liquid, or soap (if you're not sure how the fabric will react, test first). Gently press suds through—rubbing may damage fine fabric. Rinse stain under cool tap, or flush detergent through with spray water bottle. If you're out of the house, press dry with paper towels, or, keeping fabric well away from the heat, hold for a few minutes under a bathroom hand-dryer. As soon as possible, wash garment as usual.

For greasy stains: If feasible, use an absorbent such as talcum powder or cornmeal to soak up the stain, let it sit for twenty minutes, then gently brush off. Next apply a stain- or grease-removing product (testing first on unpredictable fabrics). If greasy stains come your way with pathetic regularity, consider carrying pocket-sized stain remover in your purse. Follow manufacturer's instructions (you may need to repeat several times). As soon as possible, wash in the hottest temperature the fabric can stand.

For combination stains (chocolate, dairy products, gravy): Treat as for greasy stains first. If stain persists, treat with all-purpose product. Wash in hottest temperature fabric can stand.

The methods above are good general remedies for emergencies. There's also a roster of at-home techniques to deal with more specific spots and spills. Many have been used for generations, well before the advent of specialized laundry-care products. If you know the source of your stain and are ecologically minded, you may want to try one of these first, as they are a gentle and responsible way to treat your clothes. Then, if they don't work, move on to the stronger stainbusters.

Alcohol: Even if the alcohol was colorless, the stain will turn brown if untreated (if you remember anything at all the morning after, try to remember this). Sponge several times with white vinegar diluted 1:1 with warm water. Wash as usual.

Ballpoint ink: Flush immediately with cold water, then treat the stain with soap (which is more effective on inks than detergent). Rinse and repeat if necessary. Traditional alternative method: soak stain in sour milk. If you can't wait for milk to sour, try spraying with alcohol-heavy hairspray, then rinse with cool water.

Blood: Soak ASAP in cool, heavily salted water, then dab on liquid detergent, rinse. Wash as usual. If stain remains, consider soaking in enzyme pretreatment (check that fabric will not be harmed first).

Candle wax: Put item in plastic bag in freezer for an hour. Peel solid off fabric; lift any remaining stain with solvent-based product. Wash as usual.

Coffee and tea: Rinse in warm water, then wash in warm soapy water. On wools and silks, first apply glycerine (available at a good drug or hardware store), let stand, and rinse with warm water.

Egg: Scrape off any solids with a dull knife or spoon edge. Turn garment inside out and place towel underneath, then sponge cold water on fabric (never use hot, which will set the stain permanently). If stain is stubborn and item is not silk or wool, soaking in enzyme cleaner is the next resort.

Grass: Treat with liquid detergent rubbed into stain, followed by sponging with rubbing alcohol, if the stain is persistent (test alcohol on an inconspicuous area first!). Treat with enzyme product, if necessary, or dry-clean.

Mildew: Leather stored under damp or humid conditions is especially prone to mildew. After testing on an inconspicuous area, apply antiseptic mouthwash on cotton ball, dab gently.

Mud: Let dry completely first. Remove dry mud with brush or cloth. Presoak if fabric allows, then launder.

Pencil: Rub gently with a soft, white eraser.

Perspiration stains: Sponge old stains with 1 tablespoon white vinegar in 1 cup water. Or apply paste of 1 tablespoon cream of tartar, 3 crushed aspirins, and water. Leave on for 20 minutes. Rinse well.

Rust marks: On white cottons and linens only, stretch stained fabric tight over pan of boiling water and sprinkle lemon juice on top. After a minute, rinse well and repeat, if necessary. Or, again with these fabrics only, spread stain with cream of tartar, hold over steaming kettle. Rinse immediately.

Scorch marks: Try rubbing with the edge of a quarter. If this doesn't work, resort to dry cleaner. Note that bad scorches probably won't come out.

Toner: Do not wet. Try vacuuming powder out; otherwise take to dry cleaner.

Water marks: Hold marks over steaming kettle. Remove from steam, dab mark gently with cloth.

A Brief Word on Bleach   Chlorine bleach is a valuable cleaning aid in certain situations—namely with all-white cottons and linens, where it helps lift stubborn stains and boost brightness. But with colored items and other fabrics (silk, wool, rayon, and permanent-press cotton), chlorine bleach could out-and-out ruin your clothes. Always check care labels before using such a product, and be sure bleach is well diluted—2 teaspoons to 2½ gallons of water is recommended. For colored clothing, nonchlorine bleach formulations (like Clorox 2) are a safe alternative.

SYMBOL LOGIC

Doing wash right means having a firm grasp of the lingo. In the old days, this meant knowing your permanent press from your gentle cycle. But today, it's more a matter of telling your ⊔ from your ⊔̲. Increasingly, in the name of simplification, the clothes-care biz is turning to icons in the place of words.

Cleaning clothes without knowing the symbols is like driving in a land with unfamiliar traffic signs. Most of us can manage without a wreck, but it makes better sense to be prepared. All the more so since as of 1999, clothes manufacturers are no longer obligated to provide written instructions along with the icons on care labels. In other words, you could be faced with a bunch of symbols and no other

guidelines whatsoever. That's why it makes sense to check these
symbols as often as you can. Just as with road signs, the more frequently you see them, the more routine they become.

As ever, resale garments add a few extra curves to the symbol-
reading process. If your garment was made before June 1997, any
care symbols present will look slightly different, as they may if
they're of foreign origin. The following table should sort it all out. (If
you're still confused, ask your dry cleaner.) To further add to the
mystery and drama, some older symbols feature color-coding as well.
Basically, a *green* symbol means proceed with confidence using warm
settings, *yellow* means proceed with caution using low or moderate
temperatures, and *red* means don't machine-wash, dry, iron, or
bleach, depending on the icon in question. Currently, all don'ts are
represented by an x through the icon. If you see this, pay attention,
they're not kidding.

Machine wash, normal: set washer to 65–85°F/30°C. (With this
and all wash settings, older and/or foreign garments may show
the recommended Celsius temperature rather than dots.)

Machine wash, normal: set washer to 105°F/40°C.

Machine wash, normal: set washer to 120°F/50°C.

Machine wash, normal: set washer to 140°F/60°C.

Machine wash, normal: set washer to 160°F/70°C.

Machine wash, normal: set washer to 200°F/95°C.

Machine wash, permanent press (any dots indicate same temperatures as those above)

Machine wash, delicate/gentle cycle: any dots indicate same temperatures as those above. In foreign garments, a single broken
underline may be used instead of a double underline.

Hand-wash

Tumble dry

at high temperature

at medium temperature

⊙ at low temperature
▣ Tumble dry, permanent press
▣ Tumble dry, gentle

▥ Drip dry
▢ Hang to dry
⊟ Dry flat
✕ Do not wring

⌂ Iron
⌂ High: set iron to 200°C/390°F
⌂ Medium: set iron to 150°C/300°F
⌂ Low: set iron to 110°C/230°F
⌂ Do not use steam

○ Dry-clean
✕ Do not dry-clean
Ⓐ Dry-clean with any solvent
Ⓟ Dry-clean with any solvent except trichlorethylene
Ⓕ Dry-clean with petroleum solvent only

✕ Do not bleach
⚠ Do not use chlorine bleach
△ Use any bleach when needed

ANOTHER LOAD OFF YOUR MIND

Phew. Now that you're fluent in the care symbols, let's move on to the heavy equipment. As mentioned earlier, there's a right way and a wrong way to feed the washing machine. The wrong way is to throw it all in come what may. Do this and your clothes will soon resemble that thrift-shop *schmatte* you ordinarily reject out of hand. Taking a few more seconds to do it right means gaining months, if not years, of increased wear.

> ✳ **Why Socks Disappear in the Wash** ✳
>
> The late, lamented "Bureau of Missing Socks" Internet site offered some fascinating theories on this phenomenon. Here are the likeliest explanations:
>
> ✧ Socks are actually the larval form of wire coat hangers
> ✧ The spinning dryer opens up a space/time continuum through which the sock is transported to distant galaxies
> ✧ Socks don't actually disappear, they reproduce—but only have one baby at a time
> ✧ Socks in the hamper feel like they're in jail and plan their escape during laundry
> ✧ Elvis has them

Sorting

Once upon a time, I divided clothes up between colored and white (and was proud of being so fastidious). Then I met my beloved, who, as it turned out, broke them down further into greens, grays, permanent press, towels, each bundle getting a separate turn in the wash. Wow, that's particular, I said when we shared our first hamper (but in truth had another word in mind). Now, though, I'm doing it his way, because sorting this specifically does make sense. For one thing, it lowers the risk of color tainting. For another, it maintains the life of certain fabrics, like perma-press, delicates, and synthetics, all of which require cooler temperatures. Likewise, heavy items like towels do best when washed all together, since they shed a lot of lint.

Before putting anything in, run through pockets to remove any coins, paper, or, God forbid, pens. Also snap snaps and do up zips prior to washing, which will prevent snags and damage to other items in the wash.

Loading

Smaller loads are much easier on your garments than gargantuan piles, and will help keep the washer repairman at bay. To judge load size in a top-loading washer, here's a tip from the American Apparel Organization: a blouse should surface a minimum of five times over the course of a minute. If it doesn't, the load is too large. With front-loading machines, fill the drum three-quarters full.

Choosing your settings

Follow instructions on the care labels, or, if these are missing, the general-care advice provided for different fabrics on pages 212–13.

Washing-machine Inside Scoop

- ✧ If you use coin-op machines, you may be reluctant to waste quarters on subsorted loads. Consider doing your wash with a buddy (or, if you're bold as brass, an attractive stranger) if it will help get you into the habit.
- ✧ If you send your laundry out, the clothes will be washed all together unless you do a subsort beforehand. If you buy a couple of different sacks for this purpose, the process will be automatic.
- ✧ To clean detergent buildup from your own machine (a good idea every few months or so), run an empty load, putting a quarter-cup of white vinegar into the detergent compartment.
- ✧ Using more detergent than recommended will not get clothes cleaner. Big suds do not mean a better wash. In fact, any excess detergent remaining in the fabric will actually attract dirt later on. (Cultural note: like different households, different countries show huge variations in per-wash use of detergent. Australians and Asians use the least but wash clothes more frequently, while Germans use the most but tend to do weekly rather than daily loads.)
- ✧ Try to get wet clothes out of the machine as soon as they're done—this will help reduce wrinkling in the dryer.
- ✧ Safety pins or special sock clips can combat vanishing sock syndrome.

HAND-WASHING

Putting hand-washables in a net bag near the hamper keeps them safely away from the rest of the load, and acts as a subtle reminder to do it. I prefer to handwash at night, so I'm not stepping over (on) the drying items.

- When the instructions say use only warm or cool water temperatures, they mean it.
- Make sure detergent has dissolved completely before adding clothing.
- Don't rub at grime, especially if it's on silk. Gently press suds through instead.
- Don't keep stuff soaking forever—try to remove as per time instructions.
- Rinsing hand-wash is easier and faster in the tub than in the sink. Close the drain and fill a few inches with cool water. Immerse garments, swish around well, drain, and repeat. (Adding a tablespoon of white vinegar will help get rid of the soap.)

"Dry flat only" is the method recommended for most wool sweaters. Why? Because machine-drying will shrink them, and hanging will stretch the arms and torso. To flat-dry properly, first roll the garment up in a towel to remove excess moisture. Then lay the sweater flat (ideally on a glass table, but any even, dry surface will do—use a dry towel as a barrier on floors and carpets). Try to position the garment in the same shape as desired when dry. *Martha Stewart's Living* recommends measuring the garment before washing to ensure the proper length when laying out to dry. If you're willing to bother, God bless you.

- If cuffs or ribbing have become stretched, use wool's shrinking properties to your own advantage. Dampen these sections, then blowdry on hot to shrink back to shape.
- If you have minimal floor space and the garment is almost dry, you can get away with hanging if you do it like this: grab an old pair of

pantyhose or tights and feed through the arms of the sweater. Clip the hose ends to a line and hang.

If a garment can be hung, do so outdoors if you can, for nothing beats the smell of line-dried clothes. Also, sunlight is an excellent natural bleaching agent for dingy-looking whites. Remember, though, that it will have the same effect on colored items, so it's best to hang these in the shade. If hanging wet clothes indoors on hangers, don't use uncoated wire or stained wooden ones, for they may leave a residue on clothing.

GOING FOR A SPIN

When it comes to reading dryer settings, a lot of us are functional illiterates. Still, if you've gone to all the trouble to sort clothes for the wash, it only makes sense to keep up the good work on the back end. Remember that synthetics always do better on cool temperatures than warm. Also, if a care tag specifies hang-dry, don't cheat. Putting it in the machine might strip away special finishes, and leave the piece looking miserable.

Dryer Inside Scoop

✤ Give each item a good shake before putting it in. This will prevent wrinkles, and gives you a last chance to rescue nondryable items from the load.

✤ Don't overdry (it's especially easy in laundromat machines). Better to remove garments when they're the tiniest bit damp—the wrinkles won't be as fierce and the clothes will hold together better over the long run.

✤ Machine-drying causes cotton knits to fade and fuzz up much faster than drying naturally. I always try to hang them instead. They may dry a bit stiffer, but the payoff in added wear is worth it.

Graffiti on broken dryer, Princeton University laundry room:
"It toileth not, neither does it spin..."

PRESS FOR SUCCESS

There's a difference between ironing and pressing—with the latter, a cloth is used between the iron and the fabric to reduce the possibility of damage. Actually, it's always a good idea to use a pressing cloth routinely (any clean white pillowcase will do), for it prevents damage to delicate fabrics, keeps the iron from overflattening the garment, and reduces the risk of raising a shine. You can further protect an item by turning it inside out. Most ironing is simplified if the clothes are lightly damp—keep a mister handy for this purpose.

Ironing Inside Scoop

- Start by ironing at coolest setting first (silks) and progress towards warmest (cottons).
- When ironing blouse collars, always move from the tips to the center.
- Don't use the steam setting on silk—if your iron spits, watermarks may result.
- When ironing pleats, bobby pins can help keep them in place. But avoid running the iron over the pins.
- Never put a freshly ironed garment onto a wooden chair—the polish may transfer onto the warm cloth.
- Always empty steam irons after use so that vents stay clear and mildew doesn't develop. Strictly speaking, distilled water should be used for ironing, to prevent the buildup of gunk in the vents. If you like, add a drop of cologne (just *one* drop, and alcohol-based only) to the iron water to add a delightful scent to pressed clothes.
- Never iron across buttons or zippers; iron around them instead.

CARING FOR DELICATE VINTAGE CLOTHING

*Cleaning and washing can set off a chain of reactions
which may accelerate the decay of a piece, or cause
even more problems than the treatment set out to cure.*
—Naomi Tarrant, *Collecting Costume,* 1983

Gentle treatment with a Dustbuster (with the nozzle held well away from the cloth and the garment placed in a fine-meshed nylon net to prevent accidental sucking away of any beadwork or delicate threads) may be the best method of all for very old or very worn garments. White cotton and linen items can be gently hand-washed. Colored items must be tested before washing (blot with a damp white cloth) to ensure that the dyes won't run. To wash, place the garment in a fine nylon net bag, use warm water temperature and an extremely gentle washing agent like Woolite, well diluted. With a small sponge, press gently on the fabric to push through the suds. Rinse with distilled water. The garment should be dried flat and not ironed. With items such as vintage rayon, a good dry cleaner will be able to offer the best advice and care. That classic Hawaiian shirt may shred in the machine!

KEEPING UP APPEARANCES:
GENERAL CLOTHING CARE

- Always hang just-worn items out overnight so that air can circulate, drying residual perspiration.
- Hanging clothes also allows gravity/the residual heat of your body to gently act on wrinkles, pulling them clear.
- Heavier garments, such as wool jackets, trousers, and jeans, should be gone over with a good clothes brush to remove dust after wear. If dust is allowed to settle in the creases, it will literally grind your clothes apart, fiber by fiber.
- Don't leave clothes in a steamy bathroom hamper for weeks on end. Mildew and perspiration will begin to rot them away. If an

eternity passes between your washloads, keep the hamper some-place dry.

⚜ Lint, dust, dandruff, and hairs can be removed with a piece of masking tape wound several times around the hand, or with one of those store-bought dust-removal rollers. If none of these are handy, a damp sponge will work in a pinch.

⚜ If you've never read the back of a detergent box or the manual that came with your washing appliances, consider taking a look. While they won't beat a good thriller, they will take a lot of the mystery out of doing your wash.

PART 4

Getting the Most out of Secondhand Stores

Chapter Thirteen

Assignment: Consignment

$\mathcal{N}$o one knows exactly how many consignment stores are currently open in the U.S., but the number is certainly in the tens of thousands, with more popping up every day. What they all have in common is a business method that dates to the earliest days of trade. The term "consignment" slips easily off our tongues, but what does it actually mean? According to *Webster's Third New International Dictionary,* one meaning of the word "consign" is: send or address to an agent in another place to be cared for or sold.

And this is exactly how it works. People—or, more rarely, retail organizations—wishing to sell unwanted or unsold goods present them to consignment shops, hoping that the store's marketing savvy and reputation in the community will attract a buyer. Rather than purchasing the piece outright, the store acts as a matchmaker, saving sellers the hassle of advertising, display, storage, and dealing with the likes of you and me. As compensation, the store takes a percentage of the sale. What's important to remember about the arrangement is this: the store owner's obligation to her consignors is as strong as that to her customers. Indeed, owners will tell you time and again that consignors are the lifeblood of the business. Once a steady stream of high-quality, desirable merchandise is flowing in, outflow is all but assured.

So this is what consignment stores have in common. Otherwise, they're as individual as can be. At a point when retail stores are looking more and more alike as "chaining" sweeps over the country, consignment stores are one of the last strongholds of cozy, quirky, one-of-a-kind shopping environments. What drives the individuality is the owners. Their vision filters through every aspect of the business, from how the shoes are displayed to the quality of the lighting, to the kinds of hangers on the rails, to the presence of candy near the register. Some stores have a vibe that says "come on in, have a good browse, don't mind the dog"; others are as exquisite as a jewelbox. Discovering and appreciating the differences is one reason consignment shopping is so much fun.

As for the merchandise, that too is as varied as all fashion itself. Certain shops pride themselves in a dizzying diversity of labels and price points, offering something for every customer. Others purposely limit themselves to the crème de la crème names, or specialize in maternity wear, plus sizes, wedding gowns, and more. The nature of the merchandise usually reflects the tastes and fashion needs of the surrounding community. That's why a store in small-town Oregon may do its best business with Liz Claiborne's A-line, while one in New York City's trendy SoHo sells only model-sized garments—practically still warm from shoots and catwalk shows.

WHAT TO EXPECT WHEN SHOPPING IN A CONSIGNMENT STORE

If you don't have much experience in the consignment store environment, think of it like this: it's a lot like visiting a new town. The more you know about it in advance, the more comfortable you'll feel once you get there, and the more you'll profit from its offerings. To give you the lay of consignment land, here are the most important pointers.

Avoiding Clothes Culture Shock   Especially when time is tight and you have strong ideas about the styles and brands you're after, call an unfamiliar store beforehand to make sure you're both on the same track. There's nothing worse than having your heart set on a new cashmere sweater, only to find that the store speaks nothing but acrylic, or having an extremely limited budget and discovering that the price tags are all in the triple figures. Even before calling, certain clues can help you suss the kinds of merchandise on offer. If the store has a display ad in the Yellow Pages, look carefully at what it says and even how it's designed. The words "cheap," "secondhand," and "bargain" predictably point to the budget end, while "exclusive," "couture," and any other words in French indicate pricier or more upwardly mobile stores. ("Rag" is a weird one, used by both the ritziest and most down-market of shops.) If you own any consignment store directories or guides, this is the point to check them, for they generally offer store profiles. (For more on finding stores, see pages 253–55.)

Another indicator of the marketing niche is the location. As mentioned earlier, a store's offerings tend to reflect the community dress code, so if it's located in a modest-income or unpretentious area, the styles, labels, and prices will follow suit. Likewise, shops in glitzy urban and suburban neighborhoods are more likely to feature the flamboyant (and expensive) goods, as well as more international labels. If *you* live in an area where high fashion doesn't play a big part in the dress code, you may find it hard to unearth the kind of quality this book promotes. Don't get frustrated—get going. Take every opportunity to travel to places where high-end clothing is frequently worn, and hit the consignment stores there. When you take vacations, consider building in resale shopping as part of the experience. Finally, get to know the Internet, which could be the key to getting delightful clothing to even the farthest-flung door.

Keeping up
Appearances Consignment stores, unlike thrift stores, are picky about the kinds of clothes they accept. Veronica Lytle, owner of My Secret Consignment Boutique in Orange, CT, gave kind permission to reproduce the printed guidelines she hands to every consignor:

1. Consignment by appointment only
2. Very current items from the last 1–2 years
3. Gently used clothing:
     No stains or rips
     No broken zippers

✳ Specialty Focus: Bridal Resale ✳

At first, most brides-to-be are reluctant to consider a resale wedding gown. But once past the first blush of engagement, when NATO-quality logistics take hold, the benefits become increasingly clear:

1. Little-known, but true: consignment gowns can be as virginal as those at retail salons. Why? Weddings are called off, some women order more than one dress and settle on another at the last minute (!), local retailers go out of business or want to clear unsold stock…

2. Resale gowns are generally about half the price of their retail cousins. This means an additional $300 to $5,000 (and up) to spend on flowers, food, or the third cousins from Topeka.

3. According to Misty of the Lasting Impressions store in Edmonton, Alberta, in Canada, their shop, like most others, carries a far wider range of labels and styles than do retail bridal salons, which generally only feature a limited number of designers.

4. Most bridal consignment shops stock veils, shoes, even mother-of-the-bride outfits and sets of bridesmaid's gowns, allowing for great savings all around.

5. Whereas most bridal stores require months of lead time for ordering and fittings, most consignment stores can have dresses ready within a few weeks.

6. Nobody thinks twice about the groom going out and renting a tux for his wedding day!

If you've decided to shop resale for a gown, resist the temptation to rush. Instead:

❖ Spend as much time as you can beforehand researching retail possibilities at all price points. This will give you quality benchmarks, help familiarize you with the designers, and give you a notion of the kinds of styles that suit you.

❖ Read the bridal magazines. You'll benefit from the exposure to a wide range of styles.

> ✦ To find stores, see pages 253–55. Once you've located a shop, call ahead to learn about their selection, especially if you're an unusual size or have very specific ideas in mind.
> ✦ Any dress you buy will surely need alterations. Make sure you have a seamstress available or that the store can provide the service for you.
> ✦ Apply your quality detection skills. Gorgeous fabric, embroidery, and other lovely details are what set the finest dresses apart.
> ✦ If it suits your personality and style, consider vintage as well—the Edwardians did a great line in white lace, the 1920s in silk chemises, the 1930s in dramatic bias-cut gowns.

4. Seasonal items only
    February–June—Spring and Summer
    August–December—Fall and Winter
5. Eveningwear and Mother-of-the-Bride accepted all year long
6. Items, including sweaters, must be cleaned, pressed, and presented on hangers so we can view them quickly. (Clothing prepared properly sells best!)
7. No mothball smell, smoke odors, or animal hair.
8. Payment to consignor will be 50 percent of the final selling price which will be set by My Secret.

Reading between the lines, we see that My Secret stocks clothing in excellent condition, new or very recent, and appropriate to the time of year. In this, it reflects the majority of consignment stores. Do bear in mind, though, that it's the rare proprietor who won't accept a mint-condition Escada ensemble just because it's over two years old. The bigger the name, the more flexibility there is in terms of age, especially if the piece is a classic. Do we care? Of course not. If the item is beautifully made and enduringly stylish, it will continue to look good for many years.

How Stores Lay Out Store environments range from the sublime to the ridiculous—thankfully the latter are few. In fact, it's rare to come across a truly awful consignment shop. The most frequent flaw is an environment packed so tight it makes pulling pieces a tug-of-war. Generally, though, clothing is displayed in such a way that you don't need to break nails to get to it. Garments are usually subdivided by type. You'll also find a counter for jewelry, a nook for shoes, a display area for belts and bags, and a special section for markdowns. Pay special attention to the goods here. Sometimes they're true rejects, of course, but more often they're out of season, an odd size or color, or simply don't meet local tastes and needs.

In keeping with consignment's upscale niche, most stores have private dressing rooms with good lighting and mirrors. And then there are the special touches that make every shop unique: magazines and photos displaying fashion trends, fresh flowers on the counters, pleasant music from the speakers, energy-enhancing aromatherapy scents wafting out from hidden sources. The ideal store environment is both stimulating and soothing at the same time, leaving you primed to buy, but relaxed enough to do so with a level head.

With a Smile   Consignment stores are one of the few remaining sources of sincere and personalized customer service. If you become a regular customer at a given shop, here's the kind of treatment you can expect:

⋄ Top-quality assistance by sales help that truly knows the merchandise
⋄ Offers of help with sizes and rehanging unwanted items
⋄ An honest opinion about the right styles for your figure
⋄ Extra-mile efforts à la Prada and Gucci boutiques, such as phone calls announcing that your preferred styles and sizes have come in
⋄ A low-key education in the qualities of the best clothing
⋄ The possibility of flexibility on store hours (but only if you're an excellent customer)

While it's usually best to deal with the owner or manager, many shop assistants hope to own their own store someday, and are consequently very sharp indeed. How to tell the aces from the jokers? Gauge their reaction to a try-on that looks terrible. Great salespeople are honest. Poor ones, for some reason, feel they must fib.

✳ **Indicators that a Salesperson** ✳
Isn't Telling the Hard Truth

1. Narrowing of eyes when looking at the outfit
2. Hesitation before comment
3. Taking a step back (in horror!)
4. Tapping on chin with fingers while thinking of what to say
5. Talking to clothes to avoid eye contact
6. Silence, in order to drive you into a commitment
7. Eyes lingering over the item's worst bits
8. Stumbling over words
9. Folding arms

(by Lauren Libbert, reprinted with kind permission
of *Take a Break* magazine)

HOW THE CASH FLOW WORKS

Like all businesses, consignment stores—even those operated by nonprofit charities—revolve around making money. Understanding the hows and whys of the pricing policy will put you ahead when it comes time to buy. Way back in the first chapter, we spoke of the percentages involved in consignment pricing, but it's worth repeating here so that you have a clear idea of how the game is played. Depending on the label, the condition, and the age of the piece, store owners try to price it at anywhere from one-quarter to three-quarters of the original retail cost. This is a finger-in-the-wind kind of thing, because even the most brilliant store owner can't keep a record of the retail price of every garment ever sold. Usually she depends on her rough sense of the market, as well as the word of the consignor (some of whom, it must be said, inflate like blowfish to reap higher profits). This is why you find consignment store prices that seem to be way under, and even way over, that 25 to 75 percent range. Doing your retail homework puts you ahead of the game. If you know the original cost of the kinds of clothes you hope to find, you can avoid getting burned by so-called bargains that ain't, and can seize the day (and the piece) if it works and is way underpriced.

Meanwhile, back at the register, once you've paid up, the store takes 40 to 60 percent of that amount, while the other portion goes to the consignor. If a piece doesn't sell, it will most likely be marked down on a regular basis, with every owner fixing their own policy. As Karen Ryan, owner of the Stock Exchange in Hilton Head, SC, says, "We mark down around the first of every month. If you know the shop and know their policy, you can really make out." Special sales are another common feature at consignment. Many, many stores, such as Myrna Skoller's Designer Resale in New York City, make a point of alerting regular customers by newsletter and mailouts about beginning and end-of-season opportunities. Such mailings are another great advantage of being a regular, for they give you the jump on walk-in customers. (Always ask to be put on the mailing list if you like the place and plan on coming back.)

> *It feels good to wear expensive clothes,*
> *especially when someone else*
> *paid for them the first time around.*
> —Caterine Milinaire and Carol Troy,
> *Cheap Chic,* Crown, 1975

Haggling Do's and Don'ts   This is a delicate area with consignment-store owners, and understandably so. It's not that they want to deny you a good deal. The problem is, most of the time, the sale price or the profit has been fixed with the consignor, leaving no room for flexibility. This is why some owners get testy if you ask for a discount. Others don't seem to mind. Certain experienced resale shoppers suggest always going for a discount, but my advice would be to do so only when:

❖ There's a flaw with the merchandise that may have slipped notice at consignment time.
❖ You're buying an unusually large or unusually expensive selection of clothes. If many of the pieces came from a single consignor

(check the tickets for matching names or numbers), there may be more room for flexibility.

✧ You have nerves of steel and don't mind a frosty reply.

WHAT TO WEAR WHILE SHOPPING

If it's my first time in an upscale store, I try to dress as well as I can. Over the years I've found that good rapport simply clicks faster if I come in looking sharp. Writer Tom Wolfe, in an interview with the *Times* of London, puts it much more elegantly: "I realized early on that clothes are one of the few honest expressions people make about themselves. It's one of the ways people reveal how they think of themselves and how they want to be treated.... People don't like to admit that these attributes reveal character, or that they are doorways into the soul, which I insist that they are."

Still, practicality also enters the picture. It's good common sense to wear slip-on shoes and clothes with few attachments (meaning no bodysuits or multibutton blouses). It's also better to wear hose instead of knee-highs, even underneath pants. First, you'll get a more accurate sense of the proportions of dresses and skirts, and second, you'll have one less thing to dislike in the mirror (for the same reason, I try to remember to wear attractive, well-fitting underwear). When shopping for an evening dress that may involve support garments, either put them on or carry them along, so you can make the most realistic assessment.

HOW TO BECOME A PREFERRED CUSTOMER

Happily, this more mature stage of your relationship with a store moves away from outward appearances. And, contrary to popular belief, it doesn't mean spending huge wads of cash (though this never

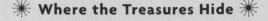

✳ **Where the Treasures Hide** ✳

1. The best merchandise in consignment stores often hangs within eye-sight of the register, sometimes with security devices locking it to the rails. In stores with a good selection of top-ranked merchandise, designers may be sectioned off by name.

2. In the window. Smart store owners put their best stuff on public view to attract passersby. They're also willing to pull items out if there's a chance of making a sale.

3. At extremes of size. If you're an unusual fit, you may benefit where others fail.

4. On mannequins or up on the walls. Why decorate with posters when you've got Isaac Mizrahi instead?

5. In the back room. Oftentimes, premium merchandise is in a holding pattern, awaiting a steam or tag. If you're a good customer on excellent terms with the owner or staff, you can ask if anything wonderful is out back, getting the jump on others.

6. On the formalwear rack. Women, especially society women, turn in formalwear at a much faster rate than other kinds of clothing, so the merchandise here is liable to be in excellent condition.

7. Shoes. Mistakes become painfully evident after only one wearing, so nearly new shoes are a commonplace.

8. On the "hold" rail. If you spy a garment that looks like it might work, ask to try it on, with the understanding that someone else has dibs (some stores may allow this, others may not). If the piece fits, ask the store to call you if the buyer doesn't come through.

hurts). You become a preferred customer by being a clever and considerate shopper, someone who appreciates and returns the store's human touch. In short:

❖ Shop early and shop often. Let the owner get to know you, your tastes, and personality.

- Spare thirty seconds for some friendly chitchat with everyone on deck, no matter how rushed you feel. It will pay off the next time you go in.

- Treat the clothes well. Remember to take your shoes off before stepping into skirts, shorts, and dresses. "My biggest pet peeve," says Phyllis Davis of P.J. London in Los Angeles, CA, "is customers who throw clothes on the floor, in a bundle or ball, after they've tried them on (although I'm sure this takes place in even the finest retail stores)." And, reminds Carol Waldman of Consigning Women in Scottsdale, AZ, "please, please be aware that makeup is most attractive on skin but is most unattractive on clothing!"

- If you must criticize, do it like a diplomat.

- Whenever possible, try to deal directly with the owner or manager. But don't monopolize her if the store is busy.

- Take advantage of the system. Most of the time, the tags hold the names or code numbers of specific consignors. If the same number crops up frequently in your picks, this is your kindred spirit on the other side of the consignment mirror. Tell the owner that you love this person's taste, and ask to be notified the next time she drops items off. This makes the owner a hero twice over.

- If your purchases are sending the owner's kid through Princeton, consider asking for the occasional special (but not outlandish) service. People do like to give favors when they sense it will help bind the relationship for the future.

STORE OWNERS SPEAK OUT

To make the most out of resale shopping, I believe the greatest factor is shopping often. As you probably know, items come in every day. In our store we have gotten next-to-new Dooney & Bourke and Coach purses that a consignor felt were too heavy! . . . This is the only way to shop.
—Monica Francisco, *Not a Small World,* Walnut Creek, CA

If you see something and you like it, buy it!
It's likely not to be there the next time you come in.
—Kevin Raymond, *My Sister's Closet*, Hilton Head, SC

Consignment stores are THE service retail stores of today.
Remember when your Mom or Grandma used to get calls from the
small Main Street dress shop letting them know that an emerald dress just
came in and would be perfect for their retirement party? Well, we do that.
We know our "regulars" and their preferences and their lives enough to know
what they need, why they need it and what would look great on them.
Can you call a major chain department store and tell them you have a
funeral and need a black dress, will they stay late or open just for you?
Hardly. But we'd be glad to. So get to know us so we can get to know you.
—LuAnn Jenkins, Lu's Back Door, Fairport, NY

You can't come in looking for one particular item. I think that's where
people make a lot of mistakes—"Oh, I need a black suit."
Instead, come in every couple weeks and look—not necessarily
to buy every time—that way you won't miss anything.
—Rita Code, Buy Popular Demand, Chicago, IL

Try to count on spending at least an hour in the store.
—Veronica Lytle, My Secret, Orange, CT

My advice to customers is to ask, or at least to converse with the
salespeople. The customers that get the most out of their shopping
experience are those that get personal attention. The item they are
looking for may be separated from the others of the same kind.
Maybe it's in a window, maybe it hasn't been put on the
floor yet, or maybe it's waiting for a quick steam.
—Charlotte's Threads, Woodbury, NJ

Some shops are more expensive for the same item than others—
so be sure to check out three or four shops, at least, when shopping resale.
—Phyllis Davis, P.J. London, Los Angeles

*Normally these stores have someone very good at dressing and
accessorizing for special events. We dress people for the Kentucky Derby,
the Academy Awards, inaugurations—if you ever need special
attention or a head-to-toe look, come right on in.*
—Audrey Patterson, Recycled Rags, Corona del Mar, CA

*Stay aware of retail prices, so you understand
how much of a bargain resale can be.*
—Karen Ryan, The Stock Exchange, Hilton Head, SC

HOW TO FIND CONSIGNMENT STORES

Consignment stores are springing up all over—happily
the directory business is keeping close track. To find
stores in your local area, your best bet is the trusty *Yellow
Pages.* Since different parts of the country list these stores
under different headings, you may have to flip around a bit. Here are
the likeliest classifications:

*Consignment
   Secondhand
      Women's clothing, used
         Clothing, used
            Resale
            Old clothes*

Always call before you visit a store for the first time—if it has
gone out of business or moved, better to find out in the comfort of
your own kitchen.

Another fine resource for dedicated consignment shoppers—and
curious newcomers—is *guidebooks.* One national and quite a few
regional guides have been published in recent years. The national
guidebook is entitled *The Ultimate Consignment & Thrift Store Guide,* by
Carolyn Schneider (Consignment & Thrift Store Publishing, 1997;
www.theclothestree.com/branch/ultimateguide/). The book provides

names, addresses, and merchandise details of a limited number of stores in every state. If you do a lot of interstate travel, this may be a good one for your shelf. The book also features condensed but useful listings of stores in Australia, Canada, England, France, and Ireland.

Then there are the regional guidebooks. Often self-published, often highly opinionated, these have the advantage of broad and deep roundups of resale stores in a given state or part of the country. Resale-loving California leads the pack with the greatest number of books. Typically, regional guides are sold only in local-area stores, but if you know the publishing details, they can be special-ordered at your local bookstore, or purchased directly through an Internet bookseller like Amazon.com (www.Amazon.com). Please note, though, that some of these titles are out of print, making them difficult to obtain through any means.

Never Buy Anything New: A Guide to 400 Secondhand, Thrift, and Consignment Stores in the Bay Area (San Francisco). Charlene Akers, Nate Levine, 1992

Consign Connecticut: A Shopper's Guide to Connecticut's Consignment Stores. Kathleen Bulloch, Heidi Hall, 1996.

Rummaging Through Sonoma County: A Guide to over 275 Thrift Shops, Rummage Sales, Secondhand Stores, Consignment Shops, Flea Markets, Surplus and Salvage in Sonoma County. Holly Harris. PO Box 297, Sonoma, CA 95476. Tel (707) 939-9124, fax (707) 939-9579.

Cheap & Chic Guide to LA's Resale Boutiques. Gloria Lintermans, a Lintermans Publication, 1990.

A Guide to Washington DC's Thrift and Consignment Shops (covering DC, Maryland, and Virginia). William West Hopper. PO Box 42712, Northwest Station, Washington, DC 20015-6112. E-mail: WWHRestoration@Worldnet.att.net

Where to Find Everything for Practically Nothing in Chicagoland: A Bargain Hunter's Guide to Resale & Thrift Shops. Trudy Miller, 1987.

The Sacramento Resale Directory, Sea Miller. P.O. Box 13831, Sacramento, CA 95853-3831. (916) 922-8511.

Another valuable resource exists in the monthly or semiannual *newsletters* specializing in consignment-store shopping. These are frequently published by the same people who put out guidebooks; otherwise they are produced by independent consignment-store fans or the stores themselves. Some examples include:

Secondhand News. Contact Pat Doering at 3120 41st Street, San Diego, CA 92105-4133. E-mail Smiller@AOL.com

Resale Hotline. Contact Jackie Greene, PO Box 314, Garden City, MI 48136-0314. (313) 562-0180.

Rummaging through Northern California. Contact Holly Harris, ed. PO Box 297, Sonoma, CA 95476. Tel (707) 939-9124, fax (707) 939-9579. Includes wonderful articles and tips for consignment, thrift, vintage, rummage queens, and more. See also Harris's Web site, the Internet Resale Directory, details below.

Local organizations like the Consignment Consortium in Washington, DC (c/o Shirley's Consignments, 14834 Build America Drive, Woodbridge, VA 22191; (703) 491-6159) put out pamphlets listing member stores. Have a word with your local store owners to see if any such support organization or literature exists.

Finally, the *Internet* is a gold mine for consignment-store listings. Access Yahoo's Yellow Pages, type in the city you wish to survey, and then search under "consignment," "resale," or "secondhand clothes." Also try typing these same words directly into the various search engines—you find a host of stores that have home pages right on the Web. These days, many are starting to sell over the Internet, with some even scanning in photos of covetable pieces for sale. Quite a few provide return e-mail addresses, so if you have an interest in a particular type of merchandise (Kate Spade bags, extra-wide shoes) you may land a connection in another state (or country!) that is the beginning of a beautiful relationship. Do take sensible precautions, however, before sending money or credit card details to any Internet entity.

✳ **The Way It Ought To Be** ✳

In this passage from *Cupid & Diana,* a delightful novel by Christina Bartolomeo (Scribner, 1998), the author describes the perfect consignment-store owner:

Mary never lied to me about what looked good and what didn't. She never sold a customer an unflattering garment. The clothes in her shop were carefully dry-cleaned, and anything pressed or patchy she put in the circular bin and gave the proceeds to charity. She chain-smoked and dispensed advice, she took in consignments and gossip from her regulars, and when people left, they felt they'd been on a surprisingly pleasant social call.

From Mary I learned the designers who suited me and those who didn't. A "yes" vote to Calvin Klein's clean elegance and flattering necklines; a "no" to Emanuel Ungaro's cheerful prints and whimsical ruffles, adorable as they might be. Like my mother, Mary loved the hidden beauties of good workmanship that are too rare outside designer circles: a hem properly finished with lace basting tape, a lovingly worked buttonhole, a satin lining striped in old gold and rose. Fine craftsmanship brought joy to her heart. When the new genius Richard Tyler came on the scene, she pinned up magazine photos of his line on her bulletin board with the words "This is good tailoring!" inked across the top of the page.

Many a skirt or jacket of mine was sent to the Salvation Army after it failed to pass the test of Mary's searing gaze. Under her tutelage, I spent half of what I used to on my wardrobe, and looked twice as good.

In addition to offering store listings, the Web also hosts an honest-to-gosh consignment community comprising owners, fans, organizations, and more. The following sites are particularly worthwhile:

The Internet Resale Directory: www.secondhand.com
The Clothes Tree Consignment Connection: www.theclothestree.com/
NARTS (The National Association of Resale & Thrift Stores):
   www.narts.org

NARTS deserves special mention as the nonprofit organization dedicated to the education and professional development of the consignment and resale community. In nationwide existence since 1988, it holds regular meetings and seminars for its members. While the membership does not include every store in the country, it's been my experience that shops run by NARTS members take an extremely professional approach to their business. Their logo on a door, window, or business card indicates that the store owner strives toward high professional standards.

Chapter Fourteen

❖

Thrift-o-Rama

*F*or true believers, trolling through thrift stores ("thrifting" for short) is less a shopping experience than a cult activity, complete with its own gurus, Internet specialty pages ("Bad Velvet Paintings"), and more. The thrift-store faithful include a tremendously wide range of shoppers, and their motivations are as eclectic as the merchandise. Most, of course, are there for the rock-bottom bargains. Others thrive in the kitschy ambience emitted by broken Chucky dolls, vinyl pocketbooks, and John Waters lookalikes combing the lingerie aisle. Then there's you and me, drawn because thrifts offer the best quality/price ratios in the known universe. Every resale shopper has heard of a "friend of a friend" who found a Schiaparelli jacket priced in the single digits. Funny, isn't it, how few of these triumphs happen to anyone we actually know. The reason is simple: riches like these are as rare as natural pearls, and finding them is darn hard work. Getting great quality at a thrift store is the sign of an Iron Woman connoisseur. If you've got the stuff, take your marks. But before we ready, set, go . . .

A LITTLE BACKGROUND DETAIL

To make the most out of the thrift experience, it helps to understand the different kinds of stores. Broadly speaking, thrifts come in three categories:

Nonprofit: These include the outlets run by major national charities (Salvation Army, Goodwill, St. Vincent de Paul, Junior League, American Cancer Society, and the like). Also under this heading are one-of-a-kind stores run by local religious groups, charities, or cultural benefactors (like New York City's Out of the Closet, benefiting AIDS-service organizations, or the Disabled American Veterans Thrift Store of Sioux City, SD).

Charity-affiliated for-profit: Relatively new on the thrift-store scene, these include chains such as Thrift Town/NSC and TVI Value Village/Savers stores, which buy clothing from charitable organizations (helping to fund their activities), then sell it for a profit.

For-profit: These include chains such as Buffalo Exchange, which buy/trade goods from individuals and/or wholesalers, and sell at a profit.

What's the difference and why does it matter? To an extent, the store category affects the environment and merchandise—important if you're choosy about the kind of atmosphere you'll shop in, or are pressed for time, or are able to visit just one store on a regular basis. For-profit stores tend to emulate a "normal" (that is, retail-like) shopping environment, with decent fixtures, good-quality lighting, and clear organization of merchandise. Nonprofit stores affiliated with charitable and cultural organizations with a wealthy patronage often attract spectacular donations. The major nonprofit chains have a huge inventory and rapid turnover.

The categories are meaningful in another way as well. All thrifts are worthy in that they keep wearable clothes out of landfills, and afford those with low incomes the chance to purchase at decent prices. But there are some big differences between thrifts as well. When you spend in a for-profit store, your dollars are funding a private entrepreneur. Not that there's anything wrong with that—it's simply a factor worth considering. As for the nonprofits, different charities have markedly different missions. Perhaps you'd prefer your shopping dollars help fight a particular disease? Or fund local programs? Or *not* fund certain politically volatile causes? In the spirit of being an informed shopper *and* citizen, it's good to know where your money is going. To learn more about the activities of charitable organizations, this Internet address can help: Guidestar: The Donor's Guide to Charities and Nonprofits: www.guidestar.org/

Environmental Issues   The thrift-store vibe can be either dire or delightful, depending on who's running the show. Apart from few-and-far-between "boutique" shops (which limit themselves to high-end merchandise), thrifts are typically fluorescent-bright, rolling rail, patchy linoleum kinds of places, infused with that certain *je ne sais quoi* that you stop smelling after a few minutes. The clothing is usually sectioned off by type. Size segregation is rare, and most stores do not bother to indicate the size on the price tag. Even when done, it's likely to be unreliable. In larger stores, the organization of the merchandise tends to disintegrate as the day wears on, thanks to customers' devil-may-care attitude about returning garments to their original spot. Dressing rooms are communal, individual, or nonexistent; most stores have mirrors somewhere on the shop floor. Some places, especially those plagued by shoplifters, have a no-try-on policy, but if you look reasonably normal, you can usually sweet-talk a staffer into allowing you to slip something on over your clothes.

> *Thrift stores, after all, are where fads go to die...*
> —David Futrelle, *Salon,* December 1997

Always in Stock   Like the swallows to Capistrano, certain garments always come home to roost in thrift stores. They are, in no particular order:

Stonewashed jeans
Stonewashed-looking sweaters
Sweatpants with missing drawstrings
Heavy metal concert T-shirts (especially Whitesnake and Motley Crüe)
Shoes looking like they crossed the Sahara and were trampled by camels before being fished from the oasis pool

Then there's the merchandise *we're* after. Treasures like calfskin belts and new Anne Klein trousers, so mysteriously untouched while inferior items fly right out of the store.

Other kinds of garments are location-specific. As with consignment stores, the merchandise in a given thrift tends to reflect the local dress code. This means glittery gowns brighten the rails in the Las Vegas St. Vincent de Paul, golf togs are a matter of course in Augusta, GA, turquoise jewelry shines in Santa Fe. If a locale is wealthy, resorty, or otherwise chic, the area thrifts will reflect it. Residents are not going to schlep all the way to another town to unload the contents of their closets. Even organizations that distribute to a wide network of stores may send the cream of their crop to better areas. Goodwill Industries of Western Connecticut, for example, directs higher-priced items to its boutique store in the wealthy town of Westport, where items like $2,000 Oscar de la Renta gowns sell at a quarter of their original price.

By the same token, the least appealing goods are liable to be found in the poorest neighborhoods. Does this mean you should give such stores a wide berth? Not if you're a gambling gal. Downscale thrifts make up for their mostly lackluster merchandise with rare flashes of brilliance, pieces left untouched because the quasi-professional "pickers" who haunt the better outlets don't bother coming to such stores. It's a long shot, but if you've got the time and the patience, could be worth it.

Rise of the Boutique Rail   In recent years thrifts have adopted the boutique concept in a major way. At the store itself or at central distribution, workers section out top-name labels for display on "designer" rails. These goods are priced higher, reflecting their greater allure. The trend has its positive and its negative aspects. It does give shoppers a precise target, eliminating a lot of slogging through the racks. On the minus side, the prices can be outlandish (particularly for diffusion goods). Also, given that some very busy centers process 3,000 pieces per day, excellent quality is often missed, slipping onto the regular rails.

Priced to Sell   Stores take one of two approaches when it comes to fixing prices. Garments are either tagged individually according to quality and condition, or all items of a single type (coats, skirts) are ticketed at the same figure. The method shouldn't affect whether you shop at a given store—great bargains can be had either way. In terms of payment method, play it safe and assume they'll only take cash.

Markdown   Most thrifts routinely mark items down, and this is where the prices
Mania   really get good. *Rummaging Through Northern California,* a bimonthly newspaper covering resale in the San Francisco Bay area, describes the policies of the North Bay Salvation Army outlets: "In each store,

women's clothing is discounted 50% every Monday and Tuesday, men's is discounted 50% on Wednesdays and children's 50% off on Thursdays. Varying half-off sales occur on Fridays and Saturdays." Wizdom Thrift in Reno, NV, offers another example of price reduction on a regular basis. They mark down "by half if something does not sell in a month or so. We also place stuff on the dollar rack or the quarter table that has not sold for more than three months or that is not good enough for general merchandising. We also have half-price sales on selected items frequently to reduce inventory, which tends to grow rapidly unless constantly purged."

Not Many   At one of the upmarket thrift stores on Manhattan's East Side, if a
Happy   customer finds a flaw within five days, she can return the item (with
Returns   receipt and tags attached), for credit. But this kind of leeway is extremely unusual in the thrift store world, indeed in resale in general. To be safe, always ask about returns before you buy, and if you forget to, assume that you can't take it back.

Service   Expecting great service in a thrift store is like expecting to sniff the cork at Taco Bell—if you want deluxe treatment, you're in the wrong place. Customer relations in thrifts can be as spotty as the bargain-bin merchandise. Unlike retail clothes stores, which attract

commission-motivated "people persons" as sales help, and unlike consignment stores, whose owners have a huge stake in treating customers well, thrifts rely almost exclusively on volunteers or individuals in job-training programs—people doing hard work for little reward, people unaccustomed to sugar-coating their opinions and attitudes. All of which contributes to the inimitable thrift-store atmosphere. Which is not to say that the staffers can't be a real help. There are usually one or two who have been on site forever and *really* know their stuff about clothes. Getting to know them is all part of...

Making the Most of the Thrift Store Experience

Whether you love or loathe thrifting has less to do with a store's qualities than it does with your own approach. If you expect to strike gold in fifteen minutes or less, you are sitting up and begging for disappointment. Instead, slow down, flex your fingers, and clear your mind to a Zen state of calm, expecting nothing but the sensual pleasure inherent in clothing's texture, color, line, and detail. This state won't last, of course, but at least you'll get started in the right frame of mind. Once you've been at it for a while and the going starts to get heavy, try to keep your sense of humor at the fore. When you stop seeing the lighter side of the goods and the characters, it's time to go home. More advice:

Give yourself enough time. Ah, the frenzy of playing beat the clock when you're only halfway through the stonewashed jeans. Thrifting requires double or even triple the time needed per square yard in other stores, thanks to merchandise volume, merchandise disarray, insufficient dressing rooms/mirrors, crummy lighting, heavy flaw potential and consequent need for careful checks. To keep a grip on sanity, give yourself as much time as you'll need.

Shop frequently. Your odds of finding excellent buys increase if you are a frequent visitor to the store. Also, as you become familiar to and friendly with the employees, they may provide tips that would otherwise be withheld from unknowns.

Apply your quality detection abilities. Hand sensitivity is key on jammed thrift-store rails. Move deliberately, feel everything. Pull pieces that seem worthwhile, check out the size, hallmarks, and condition, and then look at the price. Your goal is to move down a rack once and once only, so be thorough the first time around. Try to avoid glomming onto a label, or at least try to avoid letting it cloud your opinion—quality always comes first.

Know your labels. Watch out for overpriced diffusion labels (often seen on boutique rails); keep a close eye out for potential counterfeits. If you let quality be your guide, brilliant pieces by a little-known name will occasionally leap out. I recently came across a lovely tweed suit piped with thin strips of real leather, and thought aha! Sure enough, it was a Per Spook, priced at $35—couture quality merchandise that went unrecognized and unsold.

Show some class. Treat the staff with respect, both to their faces and in how you handle and rehang the merchandise. They're there because they're volunteering to be, or because they're trying to turn their life around. In short, they're motivated by finer principles than yours. Do them the courtesy of suppressing any urge to razz the goods within earshot—some might take your disdain personally. Likewise, shoppers whose financial situation is grim bitterly resent the loud opinions of smart-alec slummers. Finally, make a point of

✳ **Common Thrift Store Pests** ✳

And then there's the less lovable quotient of thrift-store shoppers. Again, Zen-like calm is the best line of defense, but if somebody's really pushing your buttons, a bit of decisive action is called for.

The rail hog: You know the type. Forget moving for you, she wouldn't budge for General George Patton bearing down the aisle in a Sherman tank. There is only one effective way, short of a blunt instrument, to deal with her. Go around, saying very clearly, "Pardon me." If she continues to guard a portion of the rack with her body, feel free to bump (careful if she's ancient), this time saying "Oh, excuse me, I moved out of your way because I thought you were done with this section." (P.S.—whenever someone is gracious enough to move for you, it's nice to acknowledge it.)

The mirror hog: One time I couldn't get a look in a mirror because a woman was hunched right up to it, engaged in some obscure business with her face. As it happens, she was plucking her eyebrows. With absurd situations like these, feel free to use the old "pardon me" and loom very close, invading their personal space. But, if someone at the mirror has a pile of clothes to consider (especially if the store doesn't have a dressing room), the polite thing to do is to give her some breathing room and recommence searching, returning when the mirror is free.

The flinger: If, out of laziness or the impulse to hide desired items, somebody drapes a piece of clothing over the rail on your path, say "Pardon me, did you want this?" and hand it right back. For your part, try to rehang clothes as neatly as possible.

The crazy: Be gentle. Give her a smile, then ignore her. Do not interact in any further way. She'll soon find a more responsive victim to pester.

being open and generous rather than competitive with fellow shoppers. It makes for a happier environment, and you may get some great advice in return.

Dress appropriately. This means two things:

1. Dress down—nondescript clothing and minimal jewelry. You'll feel more at ease if the store's grimy. You'll feel less stressed about tossing no-big-deal-wear onto the dressing room floor (hooks are not a given in the dressing rooms). Finally, people are more likely to be pleasant if you don't look like a society deb hazarding a trip to the wrong side of town.
2. Ideally, your outfit should be form-fitting enough so that you can pull other garments on top of it and still get a reasonable idea of fit. For me, this means leggings and T-shirts under an easy-off jacket or sweater (if you drove, you may want to leave this in the car). Also, a pocketbook with a shoulder strap or a belly bag leaves both hands free to touch, speeding your progress along.

Pack appropriate supplies. This includes a small flashlight for checking mothholes, a pocket mirror for assessing the hind view, and a white travel soap to check stains. Also, raisins will keep you going once blood sugar starts to drop, and unlike chocolate, don't leave smears.

Stay focused. Save visits to the record stash or old lunchboxes until after you've finished up with clothes and accessories. It's amazing how distracting (and time-consuming) nostalgic junk can be.

Don't forget price add-ons. "It is always a good idea to clean whatever you buy from a secondhand store, as you never know where it has been."—Robert, Wizdom Thrift, Reno, NV. There's also mending and, possibly, alteration. Be sure to keep all of these figures in mind when tallying the true cost of an item.

Be realistic in your goals. Face it—the really spectacular, high-quality items are more likely to be found at consignment or vintage, and you're going to have to shell out more than $5 to get them. Amazing treasures do crop up, but you're bound to be disappointed if you expect them. Where thrift stores shine are for basics: a pair of jeans or khakis, a navy blazer, a toasty sweater.

Drag your sister along, go with a friend, or make one while shopping. Even the worst thrift store in the world (*especially* the worst thrift store in the world) can make for a splendid day out if you take the right approach, which is a lot easier to do with a like-minded pal.

✳ Where the True Treasures Hide ✳
(if they're there at all)

1. The boutique section.
2. Toward either end of a long rail (where staffers put fresh merchandise), or on the end of a rail closest to a mirror (the easiest drop-off point for others' no-gos).
3. In the store window (most thrifts will *not* tear apart a display until a given date—see if you can get your name on a list for a desired item).
4. Behind the register. Thrifts very often hang valuable clothes here to keep them away from shoplifters. Ask to see.
5. Under the counter. Valuable smaller items and accessories live here, for the same reason.
6. On the belt rack. People don't know from great belts.
7. In the coat section. Dollar for dollar, coats are often the best value at thrift.
8. Buried within 50 feet of worthless *schmatte*. Remember, it's not supposed to be easy.

WHERE TO FIND THRIFT STORES/
FURTHER INFORMATION

First, see pages 253–55 in Chapter 13, as many of the books, news-letters, and Internet sites mentioned there also cover thrift stores. Also keep in mind that directories go out of date, so do remember to call before making a trip.

One book of special interest to thrifters is Elizabeth Mason's *The Rag Street Journal* (Henry Holt, 1995). While this fine how-to-shop-and-sell guide is filled with useful information about shopping at con-signment stores, rummage sales, flea markets, and more, the author devotes most of her attention to thrift stores. The book contains an appendix with state-by-state and Canadian listings of 3,000 stores, most of them associated with the major nonprofit charitable organizations.

Another title that is a must for any thrifter's shelf is Al Hoff's *Thrift Score* (HarperPerennial, 1998). While Hoff's tastes lean more toward the kitschy than the quality end of the scale, her insights are hilarious and lovingly document a great American subculture. *Thrift Score* first came on the scene as a special interest 'zine and Hoff continues to publish regular issues. A subscription and/or back issues are available at $1 an issue via: Thrift SCORE, P.O. Box 90282, Pittsburgh, PA 15224. Finally, Hoff has a Web site offering info on thrifts

---

❋ The Never-ending Treasure Hunt ❋

I believe that everything can end up in a thrift store, from originals of the Declaration of Independence tucked behind a bad watercolor, to brand new 1930s men's shoes, to that one weird-sized screwdriver you've been looking for. Of course, it's pure chance where these items end up—whether it's at a thrift near you and on the day you choose to go—but thrifters are *ever* hopeful. It's like the lottery—somebody's gotta win.

—Al Hoff, *Thrift Score,* 1997

and other arcana, found at: www.members.tripod.com/~Al_Hoff. You can also contact her directly through hoffo@drycas.club.cmu.edu.

For more Internet information on thrifting as well as networking opportunities with like-minded souls, the "Secondhand Shopping Pod," accessed through the Lycos search engine, is top-rate. The address is www.tripod.com/pod_central/pods/secondhand/.

Finally, two of the major nonprofits now have Web pages listing the locations of their stores:

Goodwill: www.goodwill.org
The Salvation Army: www.redshield.org/index.shtml

Check them out to find the shops nearest you.

Chapter Fifteen

❖

The Vintage Advantage

"Vintage clothing to me is much more than fabric and stitches. Each garment represents the woman who originally owned each piece. I often wonder where she wore the garment, what her life was like, what her thoughts were, what her family was like, and who she was as a real person…"
— Donna Barr, Victorian Elegance

*O*f the three major modes of resale shopping, I find vintage the most fascinating—and challenging. Added to the usual issues of quality, fit, and suitability are historical significance, kitsch quotient, rarity, and wearability, making for a delightful multiplicity of purchase factors. What's more, the garments' past lends them a mystique that fresh-off-the-factory-floor clothes lack.

Two kinds of people pursue vintage clothing. The first is the collector. She wouldn't dream of exposing her antique treasures to excess handling or, worse, actual wear. Instead, she seeks to preserve her rare and fragile specimens under museum-quality conditions, as though they were works of fine art. The approach of the other type of vintage aficionado is, in contrast, more hands-, arms-, and thighs-on. Her tastes may be as refined and her knowledge as keen as her preservationist sisters, but she feels a garment doesn't come into its own until it's worn on a living, breathing human being. This chapter is in tune with her way of thinking.

OLD BEGINNINGS

In recent years, countless women who once snoozed their way through history class have become fascinated with past-era clothing. Why? It offers originality, exceptional construction, and drop-dead style. In keeping with the new popular interest, costume history, once the rather dusty realm of a handful of specialists, is now a glamour field. Sotheby's auction house recently opened a division dedicated to the sale of couture pieces, joining old-line New York auctioneer William Doyle and the Parisian house of Drouot, who have been in the business for decades. According to *Vogue* editor Hamish Bowles, such sales not only draw museum curators and the preservationist wing of the vintage crowd, but also "extremely well-heeled fashion-conscious Upper East Side girls" looking to pump up their wardrobe. And no wonder, with stars like Ashley Judd looking smashing at award shows in a succession of vintage gowns, and the press attention lavished on stores such as Lily et Cie in Los Angeles, some of whose treasures cost more than a new luxury car.

Items like these are beyond the grasp of most of us. Thankfully, the vast majority of vintage garments cost a lot less—somewhere in the double or triple figures. At this price point, you don't need a degree in costume history to shop successfully. Women who don't know a bustle from a barn door can browse purely for the pleasure of the clothes' visual punch, and find themselves wonderful buys.

Still, familiarity with broad strokes of fashion history—as well as with specific styles, designers, and periods—maximizes the thrill of the hunt. It's also easier to get better deals, since you have a more solid basis for comparison shopping. Vintage newcomers can either dip shallow or plunge deep into costume history—an enormous amount of information awaits at libraries, bookstores, and local museums and historical societies. However, practical information on how to shop vintage is harder to come by. Ironically, some of the best advice on finding old clothes is located on that newest of technologies, the Internet. The resources section at the end of this chapter will guide interested novices to the best sources. In the meantime, the following overview will give you a jump start.

BEYOND GRANDMA'S ATTIC

Where are the best places to find vintage clothes? While it's still possible to unearth them in thrift stores, pieces of true quality are increasingly scarce there. This is because thrifts are routinely plucked clean by "pickers," clothes spotters who buy up the very best and then sell them to wholesale or retail dealers. (Now that you're a connoisseur you can beat them at their own game, but only if you're willing to devote the time and drudge work it takes). Vintage clothing also features at flea markets, specialist exhibitions, rummage sales, auctions, and even on the Web (described in greater detail on pages 285–89). But you'll find the largest and most varied selections concentrated in dedicated vintage (also known as "retro") clothing stores.

Most vintage stores don't focus on a particular era—instead they offer a selection from roughly the past hundred years of fashion history. Clothes made before 1900 usually reside in specialist antique clothing shops. Clothing postdating the 1970s is also somewhat rare. That hot-pink power suit still reeking of Giorgio typically needs about a decade of downtime (and disrespect) before buyers rediscover its charms. Alongside the general vintage stores are those devoted to a particular type of merchandise or era: Victorian frillery, Hawaiiana, 1970s boogie togs. For hard-core aficionados these are not so much stores as they are ways of life, one-stop shopping outlets for the wardrobe, home furnishings, and personality.

Apart from a few exceptions in major cities, vintage stores don't open in the best parts of town—the profits just aren't high enough to support top-dollar rents. Instead, they cluster in the more raffish antique/café/student-centric districts. Ironically, the resulting bohemian vibe is a magnet for wealthy seekers of "authenticity," who often bring gentrification and impossible rents in their wake.

WHAT AWAITS IN VINTAGE STORES

Above all, expect volume. The square footage runneth over with clothes, accessories, and assorted bric-a-brac, making for an environment in which abundance often triumphs over shopping ease. It's hard to fault the poor owner, who's aiming to satisfy a century's worth of tastes. Besides, she probably started the business to offset her own collector's passions, so naturally the stock piles up. As it begins to encroach on every corner, dressing rooms and lighting may suffer. The funky attic atmosphere is definitely part of the vintage experience, and is best accepted with a cheerful shrug. Every so often, you may come across a gallery-like store, with a great deal of light and air between the objects. While merchandising of this sort makes shopping easier, it also cuts into sales volume, so the prices will generally be a bit higher.

As for the store owners, they tend to be delightfully offbeat, and are happy to share knowledge with enthusiastic novices. Get them talking about their favorite periods, and you'll come away with a trove of insider lore.

The Lay of the Land Some stores arrange clothing by period, with prominent designers showcased on their own rack. Other stores array it by type, with all pants, skirts, and shirts on communal rails, no matter what their age or style. The labels in vintage stores are usually quite helpful, providing details on size, era, designer (if known), flaws (sometimes), and last but not least, the price.

Making sense of the welter of styles and periods is one of the biggest challenges of vintage shopping. If you don't have time to immerse yourself in a full course of fashion history, this introductory timeline will help clarify the periods and predominant styles.

ERA/DATES	STANDOUT CLOTHING MOTIFS	BIG-NAME DESIGNERS
Victorian/ Edwardian late 1800s– 1914	High-collared blouses of cotton, linen, or silk, often embellished with embroidery or lace; lacy petticoats; ankle-length skirts, usually dark in color, possibly with tucks; linen car coats; boned undergarments; "Fortuny" pleats	Jacques Doucet, Emile Pingat, Redfern, House of Worth, Fortuny (note that these and subsequent designers often span later decades as well).
WWI Era 1914–20	"I" shaped silhouette; high waist, sometimes with cummerbund; "lampshade" silhouettes; tunics over hobble skirts; harem pants; Asian or Middle Eastern ethnic influence; trains on skirts and dresses; intense colors and richly decorated materials	Paul Poiret, Mme. Paquin, Callot Soeurs, Jeanne Lanvin
Jazz Age 1920–29	Skirts ranging from knee to midcalf; columnar silhouette; dropped waist; sleeveless dresses; beaded dresses with plunging necklines and/or backs; raccoon coats; knit Chanel-influenced suits; hand-knitted sweaters	Chanel, Jean Patou, Doucet, Vionnet, Sally Miligram
The Great Depression 1929–39	Bias-cut silk dresses; sarongs; silk pajamas; double-breasted suits; knee-length silk chiffon dresses with small floral patterns; handkerchief hemlines; large collars and cuffs; novelty buttons; self-belted waists	Balenciaga, Mainbocher, Molyneux, Schiaparelli, Vionnet, A. Beller, Hattie Carnegie, Davidow, Elizabeth Hawes, Germaine Monteil, B. H. Wragge
World War II Era 1939–45	Suits with prominent shoulder pads (early '40s) and tight waists; trouser suits; pencil skirts; "popover" wrap dresses; peplums; sloping shoulders (late 40s); three-quarter sleeves; side-closing zippers	Adrian, Tom Brigance, Pauline Trigère, Christian Dior, Eisenberg & Sons, Charles James, Alix Gres, Lilli Ann, Vera Maxwell, Norman Norell, Mollie Parnis, Clare Potter, Nettie Rosenstein, Carolyn Schnurer

New Look 1946–60	Extravagantly full skirts; constructed jackets; sweater sets; beaded and fur-collared cardigans; princess and A-line dresses; Capri pants; circle skirts; Hawaiian shirts; formal dresses of taffeta, tulle, and net; "chemise" waistless dresses; trapeze dresses; Peter Pan collars	Adolfo, Christian Dior, Bonnie Cashin, Oleg Cassini, Lily Daché, Tina Leser, Clare McCardell, Jacques Fath
Mini to Flower Power 1960–70	Jackie O–style sheaths and short jackets (early '60s); miniskirts; hotpants; bellbottoms; hiphugger waistlines; fringed suede; op & pop patterns; citrus-color "Palm Beach" prints, paisley and psychedelic prints; tie-dye looks	Courrèges, Pierre Cardin, Pucci, Rudi Gernreich, Geoffrey Beene, Bill Blass, Yves Saint Laurent, Halston, Pierre Cardin, Givenchy, Lily Pulitzer, Biba, Mary Quant
Disco 1970s	Granny dresses; pantsuits; wide collars and lapels; synthetic shirts; loud prints; wrap dresses; designer jeans; "prairie" influence; "le smoking" tuxedo jackets; leotards; wrap skirts; halter necklines; Fair Isle sweaters; "Qiana" fabric; punk styles	Laura Ashley, Gucci, Perry Ellis, Calvin Klein, Willie Smith, Zandra Rhodes, Betsey Johnson, Norma Kamali, Stephen Burrows, Mary McFadden, Giorgio di Sant' Angelo, Diane von Furstenberg

Off and On   When dressing to shop vintage, the goal is to get in and out of streetwear as quickly as possible. This means slip-on shoes, tops, and pants—clothes you won't mind getting a bit dusty if the try-on conditions are less than ideal. Also keep in mind the following special considerations (applicable to all secondhand try-ons but *especially* important at vintage):

✤ This is another instance where knowing your exact bust, waist, and hip measurements pays

> ✳ **Dimensions through the Decades** ✳
>
> If your body doesn't fall in with the modernist credo "less is more," take heart. Retro fashions accommodate all kinds of figures. According to the Internet-based expert Vintage Vixen, "because vintage clothing encompasses practically any style you can think of, there is always a silhouette to flatter your figure." Here is her roundup of each era's special characteristics.
>
> *1900s:* full, rounded bust/very small waist/flat stomach with full backside/legs not visible
>
> *1910s A:* high, smaller bust/small but emphasized waist/flattish stomach with full hips/legs not visible
>
> *1910s B:* solid, but soft bust/medium to large waist/vague, unoutlined hips/ankles only visible
>
> *1920s:* no outline of bust, waist, or hips/thin breadth/legs visible to knee
>
> *1930s:* high, small to medium bust/trim waist/little hips/legs visible to calves
>
> *1940s:* large, broad shoulders/soft, medium to large bust/severe, trim waist/medium hips/legs visible to knee
>
> *1950s A:* voluptuous, medium to large bust/small, cinched waist/full hips/flounced skirt/legs visible to knee
>
> *1950s B:* small to medium bust/trim waist/rounded hips
>
> *1960s:* small shoulders and bust/A-line from bust or hip/lots of leg
>
> *1970s:* no particular shape, but a generally natural silhouette
>
> —reprinted with kind permission of Vintage Vixen Clothing Co. from their Web site, www.vintagevixen.com

off. Older clothing—especially that made before the 1940s—often carries no indication of size. If you have your measurements at hand, inform the store owner, who will happily direct you to appropriate pieces.

✧ Be sure to do all try-ons at half speed, and don't ever force a piece that doesn't want to budge. Call for help instead.

- Think twice about trying on delicate pieces you're not really interested in or can't afford to buy. The less this stuff is handled, the longer it lasts.
- Your own jewelry, hair ornaments, belts, and other jagged items may snag and tear delicate fabrics. If you damage a piece, you are obliged to let the owner know, and if she's a toughie, she may insist that you pay for it. Better to avoid the whole unpleasant scene by leaving the snaggly accessories at home.
- Keep your makeup to a smudge-free minimum, for the same reason.
- Perfumes and, especially, scented oils are another no-no.

Short-circuiting Shortcomings

Careful flaw-checks (see Chapter 9) are imperative at vintage. A good once- or twice-over not only determines whether a piece is immediately wearable, it also indicates whether it will endure. Most of these garments have spent much of their life packed in storage, and are susceptible to mothholes, long-ignored stains, damaged material, and a host of other faults. The "shattering" of silk and satiny fabrics is a particular problem with older clothes (see page 181). If you're unsure of your flaw-spotting abilities, by all means ask the owner what, if anything, is wrong with the garment. It's in her best interests to be honest, and she's probably factored any flaws into the price. If problems exist, she can advise on the surest means of repair. On most occasions, by the way, there will be *something* wrong—given the age of the clothing, imperfections are a matter of course.

Wearability Issues

Before laying down any cash, give a few moments' thought to how you intend to wear the item. Vintage pieces are frequently less comfortable than modern garb. Take 1920s flapper dresses—the weight of the beading may quash any notions of dancing the Charleston till dawn. Fabrics from midcentury often feel stiffer and scratchier than today's sophisticated blends. There's a hot, sweaty reason why 1970s leisure suits hit the skids. All these factors need to be carefully weighed when considering a piece's overall appeal. You'll also need to factor in the general soundness of the garment and how it will withstand intended wear. A cobweb-light Victorian lawn blouse may

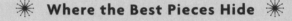

> ✳ **Where the Best Pieces Hide** ✳
>
> ✿ The out-and-out treasures are usually within sight of the register.
> ✿ Vintage stores often decorate with the clothing itself. Look around on the walls, see what's displayed. These are the showpieces the owner is proud of.
> ✿ On the no-name racks, pay particular attention to the quality of construction. Most vintage-store owners are incredibly savvy when it comes to workmanship and will price pieces accordingly, but a few may use less reliable criteria. You may find extraordinarily made pieces at low price simply because the origin is unknown.
> ✿ Ask if there's anything awaiting repair in the back that might be of special interest.

be perfect for a brunch outing, but exposing it to the slings and arrows of a full day in the office is probably more risk than the fabric should bear.

How Prices are Set Vintage stores generally purchase items outright from individuals and dealers. When the owners set prices, many variables come into play (rarity, condition, size, current trends, and what they paid the supplier). This makes it difficult to pin down exactly what a given item "should" cost. In the end, it comes down to the owner's judgment and experience. Two things to count on: haute couture and well-known designer names will be much pricier than mass-manufactured pieces, and stores in larger cities, especially on the two coasts, will be more expensive than their small-town counterparts. One way to get a notion of average and/or estimated prices is to refer to price guides and auction house catalogues (see pages 286, 288).

Is It Better to Barter? Yes and no. *Yes* if you can justify it—you know your stuff and the item seems pegged too high, or if there are serious flaws, or if you are making a sizable purchase. *No* if you're a stranger to the store, don't really know the market, and are just doing it to knock a couple bucks off. Remember, most vintage store owners are in the game for love rather than money and price the merchandise just high enough to stay afloat.

CARING FOR VINTAGE CLOTHES

First, see the basic clothes-care guidelines laid out in Chapters 11 and 12. The following do's and don'ts, which apply especially to vintage pieces, are courtesy of the experts at the Vintage Vixen Web site (www.vintagevixen.com):

- *Do* keep items with thin or fragile shoulder areas folded over by the waist or shelved. Gravity pulls on hung items, eventually causing hanger humps.
- *Don't* hang knits, because they're stretchy. Gravity has a greater effect on them. Fold them and place them on shelves.
- *Do* stay alert to fabric pests. If you see an unknown pest in your house (especially in closets or carpets and other warm, dark areas), find out what it is. Silverfish, clothes moths, and carpet beetles are likely culprits. Pests are best deterred by cleanliness of garments and their environment.
- *Don't* ever store vintage items in plastic bags or containers. Fibers naturally expand and contract with the changing temperatures, and if they are trapped in plastic, they can't breathe.
- *Do* be careful when wearing any type of vintage item. Unconsciously, people wipe their hands on their clothes, drop food on them, and brush garments against cars and walls that cause damage.
- *Do* keep clothes away from light if they're not being worn. Ultraviolet light deteriorates fabric over time.
- *Don't* let worn clothes sit unwashed. Even invisible stains (like perspiration) will show up after many years. If you don't allow the stain to set, it won't leave any trace.
- *Don't* wear a vintage item that is too fragile. Chances are, if it's that fragile, it is pretty rare and not worth the risk of damaging. If you

have an item that isn't as rare and could be worn for an important event, think about the activity you will be doing while wearing the item first and be prepared for accidents.

* *Do* monitor storage temperature and humidity and keep it steady
* *Don't* stack piece upon piece; folds will crease faster from the weight. Remember to put lightest items on top.
* *Do* put mothballs in a close-by location. You can place them between folds of muslin in the storage box, but they should not touch the clothes themselves.
* *Don't* use any mothball product except paradichlorobenzene. This type repels other insects besides moths.
* *Don't* store fragile collectibles in regular cardboard boxes. Regular paper products have acid in them, which deteriorates most fabrics. A cheap alternative is unbleached muslin (a cotton fabric); just softly fold items into the muslin. You can use a cardboard box if it is well lined in muslin.
* *Don't* carpet the storage area if possible. Carpets harbor dirt and pests.
* *Do* check on storage every three to four months. Refold items because creases set and fabric will weaken along the crease. Inspect area for pests; fabric holes, insect parts, fecal matter, and webs or cases.
* *Do* keep the storage area tight and inaccessible to pests.

NOT FOUND IN ANY STORE

Some vintage fans swear by outlets more transient than the traditional store, namely flea markets, vintage expositions, rummage sales, and auctions (how to locate these sources is described in the Resources section beginning on page 285).

Flea markets/fairs

While increasingly littered with fourth-rate new clothes and counterfeit gear, some flea markets still harbor sellers of lovely vintage garb. Expect to pay a moderate admission cost. When shopping at markets and fairs, rule number one is to get there early, before the merchandise is picked over and the stallholder burned out. Avoid trying on pieces for the sport of it, which increases the risk of damage with no benefit to the stallholder. Expect nothing more than a flap of canvas to serve as the dressing room. Also, count on paying in cash—many dealers are not equipped to handle credit cards, and don't like the rebound potential of checks. If you find a dealer and merchandise you like, get their card and some directions so you can find your way back the next time you visit the market, and do try to do so on a regular basis. Always make a point of speaking with the owner about the kinds of clothes she specializes in, what else she may have to your liking (the stock might not all be present on a given day), and where else she exhibits. If you're shopping with a friend, don't disrespect the goods in the owner's presence, even if her attention seems elsewhere. Above all, keep that fried dough away from the clothes.

Rummage sales

Though they may conjure visions of sweet old committee ladies proudly displaying chipped china and worn slippers, no less a glamourhound than Judith Krantz praised rummage sales in this memorable passage from *Princess Daisy:*

> When she first started spending weekends with the Horse People, Daisy had been forced to carve out a unique style for herself. She couldn't possibly buy fashionable dinner clothes so she became an old-clothes aficionado, avoiding the antique clothing boutiques with their exquisite garments which only a Bette Midler or a Streisand could afford; avoiding the almost-new shops which were crammed with last year's couture clothes, already dated; and avoiding as well the flea markets at which only a miracle could uncover a garment in good condition.
>
> Her buys all came from London jumble sales in church halls that she found time to go to each time she visited Dani. There she specialized in unearthing English and French couture originals, preferably over forty years old, clothes that had been

made in the great dressmaking decades of the twenties and thirties. She researched them after she had brought them back in triumph, for nothing she owned had cost over thirty five dollars.

This is a starry-eyed take on the possibility of rummages, which in fact are the secondhand equivalent of potluck suppers. To increase your chances of finding choice goods, keep these factors in mind:

- Location. Wealthier neighborhoods tend to have better-quality merchandise.
- Membership. If the sponsoring organization boasts well-dressed women, the goods will reflect it.
- Regularity. When church and charity organizations hold regular rummage sales, participants save their closet cleanouts for those dates, boosting the likelihood of high volume and good quality.
- Early bird = worm. You'll have plenty of rival shoppers who *live* for rummage and tag sales. Their expertise quickly wins them the best buys. Get there early, bring plenty of cash, and don't let the competitive buzz override good manners and sense of humor. If you do get there after the clothes have been fairly well picked over, don't give up—there's always accessories, where marvelous treasures often linger.

Expositions

Regularly occurring events like the Vintage Fashion Expo in California and the Sturbridge Textile show in Massachusetts give vintage dealers the opportunity to turn convention centers into vast bazaars of past-era clothes. The abundance of merchandise can overwhelm even the most diehard of shoppers, so it's best to go armed with a wish list. Again, these events tend to charge admission. Once inside, do a quick case of all the booths first, noting down enticing items, then try to narrow your search. If you find something you like, ask the exhibitor if they can hold it for an hour or two—she may turn you down but it's worth a shot. Otherwise, follow the suggestions for shopping at flea markets, above. One last note: stop at the information booth before you leave and see if you can get on the mailing list for announcements of forthcoming shows.

Auctions

If you're deeply serious about studying and collecting vintage clothing, here is where you'll find the ultimate goods—the haute-couture marvels, the pieces every fashion museum in the country hopes to add to their collections. As these garments are valued as art objects, trying-on is emphatically not allowed. Indeed, in some cases the garments cannot be removed from the rails. Auction houses issue catalogues that detail the "provenance" of each piece, meaning the history of the garment, including its designer, season, construction details, and its previous owner. Catalogues also provide estimates of the selling price, enabling you to determine whether a given piece is within your range. In order to bid, you need to supply credit information to most houses beforehand. It is usually possible to bid in person, over the phone, or by "reserve," that is, putting in your top figure and hoping for the best. Fast, furious, and a true social phenomenon, couture auctions offer a wonderful education in crème de la crème clothes.

WHAT THE EXPERTS RECOMMEND

Experience is the best teacher. Shop around until you know how much something should go for. Again, vintage shows are a great place for learning. The other good idea is to find a good, reputable dealer you like and shop there often.
A good dealer will not rip you off. There are certain dealers at the vintage clothing shows I shop that I seek out. I make a beeline to their dealer booth as soon as the show opens.
—Nancy Eaton, editor and publisher,
RETRO magazine, www.retroactive.com

Condition is relative, and not every dealer knows
everything about what they have. I would shop with someone
who has been around a while, someone with experience.
—Miss Kitty, The Cat's Pyjamas,
Millville, PA, catspjs@sunlink.net

I would recommend buying what appeals to you, and what would
blend with your current wardrobe. A beautiful black gabardine 1940s
jacket, nicely tailored, will compliment anyone's wardrobe. Or a slinky
satin 1930s gown for special occasions. This piece is a classic and will
come in handy when you need something formal. It will never go out of style!
Also, a nice piece of clothing to get might be a vintage 1930s–40s tailored
wool coat, a fraction of the cost of something similar today, and
will add timeless style to your outfit.
—Wendy Radick, Kitty Girl Vintage,
http://host.fptoday.com/kittygirl_vintage

We suggest judging a vintage item in the following ways to best insure
value for your money: fabric, cut/style, and wearability. This is why we
sell ten times more 1940s rayon dresses than we do 1900s dresses at the
same price. If you can't wear it, why buy it?
—Trashy Diva Vintage Clothing, New Orleans, LA,
www2.linknet/trashy/us/

People not familiar with vintage clothing sometimes are bewildered by the
price. To these people, vintage clothing is just "used clothing." Nothing could
be further from the truth. Vintage clothing is high fashion. Even if it is not a
couture or designer piece, most vintage was manufactured with better fabrics
and an excellent attention to detail... simply look through any fashion maga-
zine or stroll through a local mall and it is easy to see how current trends are
influenced... I like to believe that if the shopper has a fair sense of style, when
she shops at 5 and Dime Vintage she is likely to find the finest, most unique
items at a fraction of what it would cost for something comparable at the mall.
—Richard Paradis, 5 and Dime Vintage, Fort Collins, CO,
www.510vintage.com

Buy from a reputable dealer. Talk to them about the item you are interested
in purchasing. Ask questions as to why an item is dated as it is. Always
try to gain some knowledge when you are purchasing items. Know the
dealer's return policy. The last bit of advice I would give is to LOVE the
items you purchase! Whether you are purchasing an early Civil War gown
for your collection or a 1940s swing dress to wear, make sure the item
makes you happy—regardless of its value.
—Donna Barr, Victorian Elegance,
www.victorianelegance.com

RESOURCES

Finding
Vintage Stores
Vintage stores in your area can be found by looking in the Yellow
Pages under:

Vintage
Secondhand
Retro
Women's Apparel, used

While there are no dedicated guidebooks to vintage stores in the U.S.,
Pamela Smith's *Vintage Fashions and Fabrics* (Alliance Publishers, 1995)
offers an appendix with state-by-state listings of selected stores.

Books on
Costume and
Clothing
Hundreds of books cover the subject of general costume history. The
best, to my mind, is Lynn Schurnberger's *Let There Be Clothes* (Workman, 1991). The tongue-in-cheek style and zippy graphics counterbalance the extraordinarily detailed and comprehensive information
she provides. Unfortunately, fewer books exist on the subject of buying vintage clothing. Those in print are particularly helpful for dating
clothes and pinpointing prices. Most are published by smaller houses
and so may be unavailable at your local bookstore. You can ask
your store to special-order you a copy, or obtain it through an online
bookseller or visit your local library. Some of the more recent titles
include:

Antique & Vintage Clothing: A Guide to Dating & Valuation of Women's Clothing 1850–1940. Diane Snyder-Haug, 1996 (Collector Books)
Vintage Clothing 1880–1980: Identification and Value Guide. Maryanne Dolan, 1995 (Books Americana)
Vintage Style 1920–1960. Desire Smith, 1997 (Schiffer Publishing Ltd.)
Vintage Fashion & Fabrics. Pamela Smith, 1995 (Alliance Publishers)

Magazines and Newsletters

Check the listings for consignment (pages 253–55), and thrift (pages 268–69), which may also feature information on vintage stores.

Victoria is a general-interest magazine devoted to enthusiasts of the late 19th/early 20th century period. It is available at most larger magazine outlets and newsstands.

The Vintage Gazette is a quarterly newsletter with articles and listings of events around the country. The annual subscription rate is $12. *Vintage Gazette,* 194 Amity Street, Amherst, MA 01002.

The Federation of Vintage Fashion puts out a quarterly newsletter entitled *Vintage!* It is available to members of the Federation (annual dues fee $10). It features reviews of vintage stores as well as articles covering all eras. For more information, write: John Maxwell, Federation of Vintage Fashion, 401 San Gabriel, Vallejo, CA 94590.

Finding Expositions, Flea Markets, Rummage Sales, and Auctions

The following organizations promote *vintage clothing expos* in various regions of the country. Call or write to obtain the show schedules:

The Maven Company, Inc. & the Young Management Company
PO Box 1538
Waterbury, CT 06721
(914) 248-4646
This organization holds semiannual vintage shows in Stratford, CT.

Cat's Pyjamas Productions
125 W. Main Street
West Dundee, IL 60118
(847) 428-8368
Semiannual shows in Elgin, IL.

Brimfield Associates
PO Box 1800
Ocean City, NJ 08226
(609) 926-1800
Brimfield holds regular shows in Atlantic City, NJ.

Stella Show Management
163 Terrace Street
Haworth, NJ 07641
(201) 384-0010
Regular shows in Somerset, NJ, and at the NY Coliseum and the
Manhattan Piers.

Metropolitan Arts and Antiques Pavilion
110 West 19th Street
New York, NY 10011
(212) 463-0200
Seasonal shows in New York, NY.

Renningers Promotions
27 Bensinger Drive
Schuylkill Haven, PA 17972
(717) 385-0104
Regular shows in King of Prussia, PA.

David M. & Peter J. Mancuso, Inc.
Professional Show Management
PO Box 667
New Hope, PA 18938
Annual show in Williamsburg, VA.

For *flea market hounds,* the quarterly *Clark's Flea Market USA* provides listings of great outdoor sales around the country. Contact them at:
Clark's Flea Market USA
419 Garcon Point Road
Milton, Fl 32583
(904) 623-0794

Rummage sales are most easily found via notices in church and charity bulletins and listings in your local newspaper. Also keep your eyes peeled for signs. Usually posted a few days before the sale, these may be the only indication that it's taking place.

Auction houses are an excellent source of top-quality, designer-name vintage clothing. To find out about events in your area, call local auction houses and ask if they ever hold sales of clothing. If you live near or travel frequently to New York City, these houses offer regular sales of breathtaking goods:

William Doyle Galleries
175 East 87th Street
New York, NY 10128
(212) 427-2730
A recorded announcement of upcoming auctions is at (212) 427-4885

Christie's East
219 East 67th Street
New York, NY 10021
(212) 606-0400

Sotheby's
1334 York Avenue
New York, NY 10021
(212) 774-5304
fax: (212) 774-5393

On the Web   The Internet is a tremendous resource for women who love vintage fashion. You can use Yahoo's Yellow Pages function to find the location of stores in given parts of the country, or you can go virtual shopping. Quite a few stores have set up shop online, offering images, detailed descriptions, and a regularly rotating line of merchandise. To access these outlets, simply plug "vintage clothes" into Yahoo or another good search engine.

Also online are specialist 'zines and interest groups. If you take advantage of websites' links, you'll open up entire worlds of past-era garments. Two sites of particular interest for their how-to, historical, and other information:

Vintage Vixen Clothing: www.vintagevixen.com. In addition to her mail-order clothing business, the Vixen offers a splendidly comprehensive array of information on the subject of vintage clothing.

RETRO: The magazine of classic 20th Century popular culture: www.retroactive.com. Pure pleasure to read, this 'zine features articles on everything from how-to-shop vintage fashion expos to "How to live like you're rich, even if you're not." A must-visit for those with a hankering for the past.

Chapter Sixteen

◆

*Re-resale:
How to Profit
off Your Purchases*

You've put together a delightful collection of high-quality clothing. The pieces have served you well, and in return, you've given them the care they deserve. Now you want to get rid of a few, not out of dislike—who could dislike clothes like these—but because you need more closet space, your style direction has changed, or simply because you want something new. Once again, resale is your best option—this time as the taker (with any luck, a *paying* taker) of your unwanted goods.

There are all kinds of reasons to feel good about what I call re-resale—channeling clothes back into the secondhand flow. For starters, it's environmentally and socially sound. It always astounds me that people can throw away perfectly wearable clothing without a second thought, when the slightest additional effort would help lessen the solid waste filling our landfills, lighten the environmental impact/utility ratio of the garments' manufacture, and, most important of all, help clothe less fortunate individuals. These are reasons enough to keep good clothes in circulation, but then there's that other one...

Re-resale is nearly always a gainful venture. Whether the payback takes the form of a check from a consignment store or a tax write-off from a charitable thrift, your bank account benefits as well as your soul. The trick lies in playing the game sensibly. If you buy second-hand clothing at a great price, in new or almost-new condition, and care for it meticulously, it's theoretically possible to break even or *even make money* reselling it.

These are a lot of ifs. It's more likely that you'll simply recoup some of your initial investment, in one of a number of ways. If the goods are showing signs of wear, most consignment stores probably won't take them on, in which case you'll need to turn to a clothing reseller such as Buffalo Exchange (for more information on this type of business, see page 298). This will gain you slightly less return, but it's return all the same. If the clothes are quite broken in, donating to charity may be the best way to go.

This chapter provides the rules on how to play the re-resale game—how to sucessfully consign clothes, when resale may be the best option, the ins and outs of getting a tax write-off at thrift. Once this information is under your belt, you will be able to negotiate the entire secondhand cycle—from purchase to active duty to retirement—knowing that you're making the most out of your clothes.

HOW NOT TO CONSIGN CLOTHING— A PERSONAL TALE

About ten years ago, working in a low-paying "glamour" job and desperate for cash, I came up with what seemed a daring plan to earn a few dollars: sell off some recently cleaned garments via one of the best consignment stores on Manhattan's Upper East Side. Approaching the store, I was very nervous, as though I were doing something wrong (boy was I ever). I meekly approached one of the saleswomen, who led me into the back room and took a few seconds to look over my garments. A few seconds! She looked up, and in the kindest possible way said there was no way they could sell them. She was very gracious (to the store's eternal credit), but all the same I left feeling terrible. To avoid further embarrassment, I dumped the stuff off at a thrift store, not bothering to get a receipt. More mistakes. Had I persisted, I could have made a sale at consignment, or at least gotten a small tax write-off. Back then, I didn't understand even the simplest principles of how to make re-resale a success. Today, after a decade's experience dealing with all kinds of owners, it's a different story. Here's what I've learned:

*The Three
Golden Rules
of Consigning*

The label (or the quality) must fit the store's image. My Talbot's, Ann Taylor, and Liz Claiborne items—while desirable in other places—were no match for this particular shop's Escada, Donna Karan, and Valentino. The label or the quality has to be up to snuff or else it will look like a poor relation.

The finer the store, the less tolerant they'll be of wear and flaws. Despite the recent cleaning, my sweater was bobbly, and, on one of the skirts, the seam above the slit was starting to gap. While perfectly acceptable in day-to-day wear, these were definite demerits when it came to making a sale.

In better stores, the clothing's age really counts. All of my pieces, while classic in style, still looked a few years out of date. In fact, compared with the store's offerings, they looked outright frumpy. Why hadn't I noticed that before?

The answer is simple: on my previous visits to the store, I had been looking at the merchandise as a buyer rather than a seller. Now I know better. When consigning clothes, you work as a team with the store owner, and it's important to craft an approach that meshes with her own.

*Putting On a
Selling Hat*

The skills required to sell at consignment are similar to, but distinct from, the buying skills outlined in the first ten chapters. In short, you must:

1. Accurately analyze the type of merchandise sold in the target store
2. Know the store's consignment policies
3. Present yourself as a valuable present and future consignor

4. Sell your garment's merits convincingly
5. Provide a clear idea of the piece's retail value
6. Negotiate intelligently
7. Avoid walking away with regrets

Now let's take a closer look at the how-tos that drive these skills:

Analyze the Type of Merchandise the Store Sells

❖ Look carefully around the store first—never consign any garment "cold." You want to be sure it fits with the rest of the merchandise—that is, the quality is on a par, neither much better nor much worse than what's currently on the rails.

❖ "Fashion-forward" clothes from "downtown" designers sell quicker in their native habitat, while classics do better in the more conservative parts of town.

❖ A shop won't take a winter coat in April because they won't want to store it until fall. Consign seasonal clothes just before the season begins.

❖ Don't set your sights too high with once-trendy pieces. Consignment-store owners and customers dislike garments that look blatantly "last year."

❖ Likewise, unusual garments can be a hard sell. I once tried to consign a beautifully made, brand-new pair of designer city shorts, only to have three stores turn me down flat. Why? Because few customers see themselves as city-shorts kinds of girls. The same

---

☀ Consigning Accessories—A Tip ☀

If you are consigning high-caliber scarves and jewelry, your chances of making a sale are greatly increased if you can bring in the original boxes as well. Why? Because people craftily buy such items as gifts, and it's far more convincing to present them as new if they come in the original packaging.

goes for jumpsuits, microminis, unusually colored suede and leather items, extremely long sweaters, fur (these days at least), silk suits, and a host of other offbeat styles that appeal only to a limited audience.

Present Yourself as a Valuable Present and Future Consignor

* Many owners say it doesn't matter, but I *always* dress up when consigning garments—great outfit, accessories, full makeup. A classy appearance simply lends more luster to your goods.
* It's also good to imply you have a closetful of similar stuff at home (which is true, right?). Do this by bringing a casual air to the proceedings, letting the owner see your fine labels (rather than pointing them out), and being neither a snob nor a quivering wreck—simply a woman with great taste in clothes.
* Consigning clothes that show a bit of wear is often easier when the owner doesn't know you. Here's why—if you're a regular shopper in somebody's store, she may conclude that any pieces you present are also secondhand, meaning she has to sell *thirdhand* goods. Ironic as it may be, many owners find the idea loathsome. If your garments are in fantastic shape this shouldn't be an issue, but again, if they're not, you may gain a slight advantage by taking them to less familiar surroundings.

Know the Store's Policies

* *Always* call ahead to inquire about the store's clothes-viewing policy—some only consider consignments on specific days. Find out if there's a minimum—some stores don't like to take single items. Also, if there's any doubt, ask about the timetable for seasonal goods. If the store has a written consignment policy, ask them to send it to you. Then go ahead and set up an appointment. Even if they say "come in whenever," try to pin down a time during a calmer part of the day—you're less likely to wait should the owner or manager get tied up.
* Always assume the merchandise must be freshly dry cleaned. If you can bring it in in the plastic, all the better.

❖ Before negotiations begin, ask to see the consignment contract (if the store has one in writing), and question any points you don't understand. If they don't have a contract, be sure you:

—Understand the markdown system. You will make less money if your garment hasn't sold within a set period of time and the price is lowered. Better to know this sooner rather than later.
—Are aware of any hidden costs for paperwork or other administrative matters.
—Are clear on how you get paid. By check at the end of the month? Or some other method?
—Know whether it is your responsibility to check on the status of consigned items (it usually is). Beware that if you don't, you might lose the piece altogether (more on this below).

Provide a Clear Idea of the Piece's Retail Value

❖ Back when you *buy* a secondhand piece, try to obtain its original retail price from a knowledgeable person at the store. If it's unknown, perhaps some retail research will shed light. Once you get the figure, jot it down, preferably in your resale notebook. Besides reinforcing your shopping smarts, it will be invaluable when it's time to resell.

❖ Most stores won't ask how old a garment is unless the wear is obvious (in which case they're looking for excuses to say no). Replying "I've had it for two years" is acceptable; outright lying ("I bought it at the mall six months ago") is not. If you're going to be shot down, do it with your integrity intact.

✳ **Rumor Has It** ✳

Following the lead of a world-famous trophy wife, some well-kept women with a clothing allowance on their husbands' charge accounts convert the credit into hard cash by maxing out the cards at retail, then instantly reselling the clothes.

✳ **The Golden Names** ✳

Certain brand names have achieved a near-mythical status at resale—so classic that even older or slightly worn pieces are accepted without a blink. If it's near-new, better yet—you can reasonably expect that its consignment price will edge toward three-quarters of retail, with consequent added profits for you...

Hermès

Chanel

Yves Saint Laurent

Versace

Ferragamo

Armani

Sell your Garment's Merits Convincingly

❖ If the store owner doesn't appear to see the value of your item (perhaps it's a foreign or otherwise unfamiliar make), gently point out the quality details. When she starts nodding, you've not only convinced her of the piece, but of your own savvy regarding fine clothes.

Negotiate Intelligently

❖ Check out the prices of garments similar to yours on the store's racks. Figure on making about half the ticket prices.

❖ As paradoxical as it may sound, point out any flaw before the subject of money comes up. Why? So that the store takes it into account on the ticket price, and can't cave in to a customer's demands that the price be lowered—which would be a rude surprise for you later on.

❖ Try to get the owner to name a price first. If she seems interested in your garment, ask "how much do you think you could sell it for?" If her response sounds good, next ask "and would I get half?" If either answer surprises you, be sure to ask (nicely) why it's so.

❖ If you're asked for your selling price, you have one of two options.

Either name a quarter of the original retail price, or half of the ticket price of a comparable garment in the store, whichever is higher. Either way, you'll be able to defend your position. Remember that the age and the condition of your piece are critical factors. The better these are, the higher you can reasonably go.

Avoid Walking Away with Regrets

✥ There will be occasions when you don't see eye to eye with a store on price. Make every effort to find out why they feel as they do (this will arm you for future encounters), decline graciously, and leave on a pleasant note. Remember—it's business, not personal, and you don't want to burn any bridges. Then, try your luck with another store.

Once You've Made a Consignment Agreement

Keep track of your consigned garments. Most stores stock items for a given period only. I once had the very bracing experience of eavesdropping on a store owner and manager as they decided how to clear out their unsold stock. It soon became evident that the highly valued and/or famous consignors would get a courtesy phone call before

---

✳ The Gotta-haves ✳

Only time will tell if these names will become classics—and in a way, who cares, because they're so red-hot right now. If you present them in great condition to a consignment store owner, watch her eyes glitter...

Gucci (the Tom Ford version)

Prada

Donna Karan

Calvin Klein

Dolce & Gabbana

Chloe

Dries van Noten (ultra-hip urban stores)

Badgley Mischka

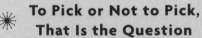

To Pick or Not to Pick, That Is the Question

Now that you have a connoisseur's savvy, a light bulb may suddenly pop on in your head. Why not make some money off this resale scenario? Why not comb thrifts for underpriced goods, then sell them higher up the secondhand food chain? People called "pickers" actually do this for a living, and if you're a shopaholic, it's close to the ideal career. The problem is, the more people out there picking, the less rewarding thrifting is for people who can't afford to shop elsewhere. If you're doing it because you have to, good luck and go for it. But if you're doing it for sport, you're depleting a natural resource for the less fortunate.

their clothes were shipped off to charity; the "nobodies" got no warning at all. The lesson? Most stores don't have the time, inclination, or manpower to keep consignors posted on what's up with their clothes. It's up to *you* to check periodically on your garments' progress, and up to *you* to collect pieces that don't sell. If you don't, you risk losing your items. If the store does not have a written statement about their particular policy, be sure you know exactly what's expected; otherwise you may get burned.

Selling to Other Outlets None of the local consignment stores see the inner beauty of your cast-offs? Probably because it's hidden under some blatant wear and tear. Now what? You actually have a couple of options. If the piece is old-ish to start out with, and you have the patience and storage space, you may want to stash it for a couple of years until the retro cycle once again deems it cool. Or, for a more instantly gratifying result, you can take it to a clothing reseller or for-profit thrift, typified by the chain Buffalo Exchange. At their 17 stores in the Western states, buyers can bring in garments seven days a week, and sell or trade them in instantly. The take probably won't be as high as at consignment, but it *is* instant cash.

☀ Auctions: The Ultimate in Re-resale ☀

Called upon to clean out a departed relative's attic, all grumbling stops when you discover a tissue-wrapped trunkful of mint-condition couture ensembles from Christian Dior's "New Look" heyday. Who knew Aunt Millie was so chic? Too bad she was such a tiny thing—there's no hope of fitting into the clothes. So what to do with them? They're too old for consignment, too exquisite for thrift, and somehow the local vintage store, with its heavy 1970s focus, won't do them justice either. If the items are in truly impeccable shape, there is another option—rare and spectacular pieces are often most profitably sold at auction. What exactly is involved in selling clothing this way? Tiffany Dubin, director of Sotheby's Fashion Department, kindly provided these guidelines for potential consignors:

1. The number of pieces sold at auction tends to be quite small (Sotheby's sales feature about 200 items, generally taking place twice a year). The clothes exemplify the greatest names of fashion history, capture the spirit of their times, and are in perfect condition, with labels intact. The auction house views all items before agreeing to feature them in a sale. If you are uncertain of a garment's value, contact the American Society of Appraisers (1-800-272-8258) or the American Appraisal Association (212-889-5405) to see if an expert near you can give you a clear idea.

2. If Sotheby's accepts an item, it is given an estimated selling price, subject to your approval, which will be printed in the catalogue.

3. You will be asked to sign a contract with the auction house, spelling out the terms of the sale.

4. You will be charged a fee for the cost of illustrating the item in the catalogue, insurance, and handling, if the item does not sell.

5. The auction will take a percentage of the sale price as their fee, generally ranging from 10–20%.

Is it worth it? If you've got something very special on your hands, absolutely. To find out more, contact the premiere auctioneers listed on page 288. And even if your pieces aren't destined for the ultra-big leagues, regional or local auctioneers may nonetheless be delighted to hear from you.

DONATING TO THRIFTS

Nothing beats the convenience of packing up unwanted clothes and dropping them off at a deserving local thrift—the feel-good factor can brighten your whole day. The combined elements of ease and virtuous glow are why so many people bypass the consignment route altogether, taking fabulous merchandise in to replenish thrifts' bounty. Whatever your motivations for donating, be sure to take advantage of any potential tax write-off. If a thrift is deemed qualified by the IRS (as are those run by national charities, religious organizations, and many nonprofit groups) they can issue you a *receipt* for your goods. In most cases, it's up to you to fill the receipt out, noting the *fair market value* of the donated items. Fair market value is a bit of a slippery concept, but basically it works out to about 20 percent of the original retail cost, or the ticket price of the goods if sold secondhand. Since you may have to defend your estimate if you get audited at tax time, it's best to play it as straight as you can. To give some guidelines, the California Society of Enrolled Agents, an accounting organization, has developed the following figures:

Dresses $4–28　　　　　　　Blouses $4–20
Suits $6–96　　　　　　　　Sweaters $4–20
Coats $10–90　　　　　　　Shoes $4–14
Skirts $3–16

Still confused? Certified public accountant Bill Lewis's 60-page *Cash for Your Used Clothing* may prove an invaluable investment. Updated yearly since 1990, it provides tips on documenting donations and gives values for hundreds of frequently donated items, including household goods. The book is available at a tax-deductible $25 (plus shipping) by calling (800) 875-5927.

Before you set forth with a bag of goods, it's sensible to call ahead to find out if the thrift has a donation-day policy. Certain stores in major cities are so swamped they actually decline contributions unless made on specific days. Also, if you call ahead, you'll be able to ascertain whether you can get a receipt.

Chapter Seventeen

◇

International Secondhand

Once you've conquered the resale horizons in your local area, what next? Go west, young woman, and east, and north, and south. Whenever you find yourself in another part of the country, try to visit new stores—chances are, your resale horizons will be expanded along with your wardrobe. Do your travels ever take you overseas? There's no reason to limit yourself to American shops. Resale thrives around the world. Experiencing it in another country could be as rewarding as discovering a new cuisine, or seeing a world-famous postcard come to life. And, strange as it may seem, visiting a secondhand store overseas could be the *least* foreign aspect of being in a new land. For resale, like love, speaks a universal language. Smart ladies all over the world adore a bargain, and stores that cater to certain segments of the market are remarkably similar, be they in London, Amsterdam, or Hot Springs, AK.

There are, to be sure, important differences as well. Some countries have not yet caught secondhand fever. As a rule, Italian and Spanish women still balk at buying previously owned clothes, and those countries are woefully short on good stores. On the brighter side, England has a secondhand sensibility that's even more avid than our own, with "charity shop" style acting as a major inspiration for that nation's booming fashion industry.

While top international consignment stores make much of their profit off the usual designer suspects (Prada and Gucci are beloved from Abu Dhabi to Zermatt), other big sellers vary widely from place to place. German designers such as Kurt Steilmann and Searle have a heavy representation in Frankfurt, whereas Paris favors home-grown favorites like Sonia Rykiel and Tehen. Meanwhile, the New-York-centric Daryl K and Cynthia Rowley are rarely found outside the U.S.

With thrift stores, the quality of the clothing and even the existence of shops differs greatly from country to country. The practical French know that they can make money off finer merchandise, and so tend to consign rather than give it away. Also, shoppers there are quite demanding about service and store atmosphere. All of this means thrift shops as you and I know them are rare in central Paris. In Copenhagen, thrifts are more common but the merchandise they offer tends to be lackluster—possibly reflecting the more relaxed dress style of this easygoing capital. In Madrid, where secondhand is a recent and scattershot phenomenon, thrifts are oriented toward students and clubgoers, whose interests lie less in finding great quality than in purchasing platform sneakers and rave T-shirts for hard-partying nights on the town.

Most foreign countries have a place for vintage clothing, especially in its antique or culturally specific "costume" guise. While dedicated vintage stores are not always a given, vendors are common fixtures of the open markets that are weekend attractions in most larger cities. At London's Portobello, Paris's Marché aux Puces, Dublin's Iveagh, and the rest, native costume or even military garb may mingle with the retro styles, making for a tantalizingly different shopping experience.

I'M ON VACATION. SHOULDN'T I BE GETTING REAL CULTURE INSTEAD?

Forsaking great museums, cathedrals, plazas, and cafés for extended binges in the local thrift stores is, admittedly, not the wisest use of vacation time. Still, there's only so much museum-going and café-sitting a body can take. There's no reason to feel guilty about spending a couple of hours exploring the local resale scene on a week-long vacation, if that's what you *really* want to do. You can even come up with some very plausible rationales:

✧ It gets you off the tourist track and into the soul of a foreign city. Secondhand stores tend to cluster in neighborhoods ignored by the package-tour crowd, and so offer a fascinating way of seeing how the locals really live.
✧ Finding these places develops your ability to read maps and use local transportation. Get somewhere successfully and you get that wonderful feeling of being a *traveler,* someone who can go anywhere and find anything you choose.
✧ You'll be visiting a place where English is probably not a given, and discover that it doesn't matter. Enthusiasm (and cash) speak volumes for you.
✧ You'll be exposed to labels and styles that are deeply unfamiliar, and therefore an excellent challenge for your quality-detection skills.

A Word on Sizes   In other countries, the size designations will be foreign too. The British and continental European versions translate (more or less) as follows:

American & Canadian	4	6	8	10	12	14	16	18	20
European	32	34	36	38	40	42	44	46	48
United Kingdom	8	10	12	14	16	18	20	22	24

As for shoe size, add 31 to your current size to get the continental European equivalent. For the UK equivalent, subtract 1½ from your size.

MY LITTLE BLACK BOOK

Here is a roundup of some of my resale favorites in selected cities around the world.

London   It may be hard to imagine a thrift store culture better developed than that in major American cities, but the so-called "charity shops" of London give ours a great run for their money. Multiple stores are operated by organizations such as the Notting Hill Housing Trust, Sue Ryder, the British Red Cross, and Oxfam, and they are frequented by everyone from impoverished art students to the occasional baroness. Oxfam has recently launched a chain of boutiques called "O," which present the very best top-label and vintage merchandise from their donations. Consignment stores (called "dress agencies" there) tend to stock marvelous merchandise, but beware— the prices will seem quite high compared with those in the States. If you only have a few hours to experience London stores, consider starting your day with a late breakfast at Terence Conran's Bluebird Cafe on the King's Road, walking westward just past World's End to hit a cluster of worthy thrifts, then drifting eastward again into Chelsea, with its posh dress agencies on Elystan Street just off the Chelsea Green.

Chelsea Oxfam
432 King's Road, SW10
(0171) 351-6863

Imperial Cancer Research Fund
393 King's Road, SW10
(0171) 352-4769

Trinity Hospice Charity Shop
389 King's Road, SW10
(0171) 352-8507

British Red Cross Charity Shop
70 Old Church Street, SW3
(0171) 351-3206
Just off the King's Road.

Steinberg & Tolkien
193 King's Road, SW3
(0171) 376-3660
One of the top vintage-clothing stores in London. It's possible to spend hours in its packed basement (many world-famous designers and models do just that), examining everything from 1920s Vionnet gowns to 1970s College Town corduroy blazers. On the ground floor are more clothes and an amazing collection of vintage jewelry.

These neighboring dress agencies, found north of Chelsea Green a few blocks away from the King's Road, routinely boast exquisite, top-name garments in beautiful condition:

Sign of the Times
17 Elystan Street
(0171) 589-4774

La Scala
39 Elystan Street
(0171) 589-2784

Another street famous for its fine dress agencies is Cheval Place, a few blocks north of Harrod's in Knightsbridge. Pandora, at #16, and Stelios, at #10, are particularly recommended for their warm welcome and exquisite-quality clothes.

Paris   If you're seeking big bargains, you will be disappointed with Paris, for the residents' exquisite calibration of price/value ratios means you usually get exactly what you pay for. What's more, secondhand garments from Paris-based designers such as Kenzo, Hermès, Saint Laurent, and the rest actually command *more* money here than elsewhere, simply because they have such high cachet. Nonetheless, the consignment stores (*depot-ventes*) make amends for the high prices with a bounty of riches, from last season's Chanel suits to the hottest looks from APC. There are a large number of consignment stores to choose from, including Réciproque, one of the biggest in the world, and Chercheminippes, which runs a close second. Both are easily accessible by metro from the heart of town and are a worthy destination for a few hours' break from the Louvre and patisseries. Another potential stop is Didier Loudot, one of the world's greatest vintage stores, practically a museum of haute couture from 1925–75. Les Trois Marchés de Catherine B, a jewelbox of a store in the Saint Germain de Prés neighborhood, stocks only Hermès and Chanel. Kiliwatch is a buzzing new shop commingling contemporary club gear and the highly flammable variety of 1960s and 1970s vintage clothes (*fripes*). I've never been, but word is the Guerrisold chain is not to be missed by fans of similarly latter-day, cheap-'n'-cheesy retro gear. Finally, don't miss the Marché aux Puces for more gently priced retro items.

Réciproque
88–123 rue de la Pompe
16th arrondissement
metro: Pompe
tel: 01 47 04 82 24

Chercheminippes
102–111 rue du Cherche-Midi
6th arrondissement
metro: Duroc
tel: 01 45 44 97 96

Les 3 Marchés de Catherine B
1, rue Ruisarde
6th arrondissement
metro: Mabillon
tel: 01 43 54 74 18
Web site: www.catherine-b.com

Didier Loudot
20/24 Galerie Montpensier (in the Palais Royal)
1st arrondissement
metro: Palais Royal
tel: 01 42 96 06 56

Kiliwatch
64, rue Tiquetonne
2nd arrondissement
metro: Étienne Marcel
tel: 01 42 41 17 37

Guerrisold
19–33 avenue de Clichy
17th arrondissement
metro: Place Clichy
tel: 01 53 42 31 31

Marché aux Puces
metro: Porte de Clignancourt
Open Saturday–Monday

Geneva Home to the International Red Cross, famed for its hush-hush bank accounts, watchmakers, and chocolate, this city is a discreet east-west crossroads of wealth and propriety. Little surprise, then, that it is host to some exquisite small consignment stores, proudly offering everything from Ungaro suits to "dotted Swiss" cotton voile blouses unlikely to show up anywhere else. In contrast to Geneva's consignment stores, the thrifts are clearly attuned to truly disadvantaged customers in terms of the merchandise on offer and the bare-basics atmosphere of the stores.

Danoushka
6, rue du Prince, 1st (American 2nd) Floor
1204 Geneva
tel: 311 36 19
Monday–Friday 2–6 P.M., Saturday 10–12
Excellent consignment selection of top-quality names and recent styles.

Audace
4, rue des Barrières
1204 Geneva
tel: 311 60 41
One of the most beautiful consignment stores I've ever seen, filled with delightful items.

La Fontaine
22, rue Neuve-du-Molard
1204, Geneva
tel: 310 10 16

Vet'Shop des Grottes
18, rue des Grottes
1201 Geneva
tel: 734 88 53
Though the surroundings and interior are dispirited, this thrift may yield the occasional find.

Vet'Shop des Eaux-Vives
84, rue des Eaux-Vives
1207 Geneva
tel: 736 34 45
Another thrift operated by the International Red Cross.

Copenhagen   Young, vibrant, with a delightful café culture, Copenhagen's charms are considerable. Some noteworthy stop-ins on the local resale scene:

Genbrugsbutikken Rosengarden
Rosengarden 7
1174 Copenhagen K
tel: 33 93 27 85
Extensive selection of low to moderate-quality goods. Excellent for heavy woolen sweaters, suede jackets.

Kitsch Bitch
Laederstraede 30
Copenhagen
tel: 33 13 63 13
Despite the store's name, you'll find a friendly owner and a fine selection of 1950s–60s era clothing and goods.

Amsterdam   Perhaps the most romantic city in the world after Paris, Amsterdam is further enhanced by a number of worthy consignment stores. In between visits, have a cozy beer or hot chocolate in one of the hundreds of cafes that dot the canals.

Lucky Lina
Reestraat 26
tel: 020-6228748
Contemporary women's and children's wear at gentle prices.

Second Best
Wolvenstraat 18
1016 EP Amsterdam
tel: 020-4220274
Exclusive names in a lovely shop.

MAKING YOUR OWN DISCOVERIES IN FOREIGN LANDS

When visiting a new city, the last thing you want to do is to waste time trying to find resale outlets that may not exist in the first place. That's why it's important to do as much initial research as you can before you go. Regrettably, no single guidebook lists the second-hand stores in the world's major cities. However, the *individual city guides* that have cropped up in recent years—especially those dedicated to the student or younger traveler—often touch on the subject of secondhand shopping (Lonely Planet's and Time Out's city guides can be useful in this regard). Another source is *shopping guides* to countries and individual cities, for example Suzy Gershman's *Born to Shop* titles. An hour or so spent in a good library or bookstore should get you started on tracking down possibilities. While you're at it, find a dictionary of your destination country's language and write down their words for "secondhand," "clothing," "vintage," and anything else of special interest (note that the term "resale" won't translate easily).

Another at-home option is combing the Internet for information. A search engine like Yahoo may yield terrific information about foreign destinations, all for the price of a local call. Try typing the name of your city along with the word "shopping" (look especially for listings of antique and flea markets, which usually host at least a few sellers of vintage clothes). As with all Net-oriented research, results will vary widely depending on the general availability of the information you desire, the time you can devote, and how you go about tracking it down. Say you were planning on visiting Calgary, Alberta, in Canada. If you happened to type "consignment stores" into the www.SearchCanada search engine, you'd get a bumper crop of six-teen shops in that town (ranging from the Peacock Boutique, with its emphasis on designer labels—to Second Time Around, with its maternity labels—to Lollipop, oriented to kids and teens). Is it always that simple? Frustratingly, no—*especially* with overseas stores. But as the Internet expands, so do the possibilities of using this powerful tool to pinpoint possible stores before you arrive.

The next step takes place once you're at your destination. Have a word with the hotel's concierge (they are paid to hunt down this sort of information, and the unusual nature of the request may set their detective instincts blazing). If there's no concierge, or if he or she seems unhelpful, try asking a friendly young woman on the hotel staff. You may get a blank look, but there's an equal chance that she has some personal favorites to share. Whomever you speak with, avoid misunderstandings by:

Being as clear as possible about the kind of clothing you seek. In some countries, secondhand equals old unappealing castoffs, and you don't want to waste your time in stores selling low-quality merchandise. Explain that you want high-quality, good names, and you are willing to pay a good price.

Bearing in mind your self-presentation. It will be read closely by those trying to understand your desires. If you are dressed in stretchy casualwear and sneakers, the stores suggested are likely to be filled with similar goods. If you are dressed more formally, you will likely be sent to the better addresses.

Using terminology that will be readily understood. "Resale" doesn't translate in most countries, likewise "thrift." "Secondhand" is a better descriptive term. "Vintage" may be understood, but it may be even better to say "antique clothing."

Making sure you obtain the stores' hours. Many small shops do not open until the afternoon, or close for siesta, or close at 5, or aren't open at all on, say, Monday, or in August. Better to find out in the comfort of your hotel than on the street in front of a locked door.

Asking your helper to jot down the names and addresses. Better yet, circle the locations on a local map.

And then there are some firm *don'ts* you should also keep in mind:

Don't go anywhere without a good map. At best you'll get frustrated, at worst you'll get lost, and who needs that kind of hassle on vacation?

Don't go into any neighborhood inadvised by hotel staff. If you feel uncomfortable in a particular part of town, heed your instincts and turn back.

Don't go too far out of your way. Even if there's a great consignment store out in the suburbs somewhere, the travel time and aggravation are probably not worth it.

Don't go anywhere without checking the hours first. Again, this is not the occasion to waste time on closed stores.

Don't assume that you can pay with a card. Cash is always the safest bet. Especially at markets, count your change carefully.

A FEW FINAL WORDS

There's a term used in the employment industry to describe abilities that transfer easily from one job to another—such skills are said to be "portable." You'll find that that's exactly what your clothing connoisseurship will turn out to be. Once you've got quality detection, fit assessment, and personal style points down pat, you'll feel at home at any secondhand situation anywhere in the world. And, on a deeper level, developing your clothing connoisseurship touches upon other life areas as well.

For one, you'll find yourself increasingly willing to *trust your own skills.* Relying on your own senses to detect the best frees you from the marketing barrage so many others succumb to. Instead of jumping on a hot trend just because some fashion copywriter says so, you will actively weigh it against other options—ultimately choosing the smartest all-around buy. Sure, you'll still go for the occasional famous name or fashion fad, but because you *know,* rather than *hope,* it makes you look good.

Related to this, being a savvy resale shopper means routinely checking out the retail arena for prices, styles, and quality indicators. This kind of *research ability*—turning available information to your own advantage—doesn't have to stop short at clothes. When it's time to buy a new CD player, a car, an apartment, you will know how to survey the market. Decisions that are informed by facts rather than by feelings *always* result in better deals.

Another area that clothing connoisseurship actively develops is *self-knowledge and self-acceptance.* While some might argue that knowing your hip measurement and figure flaws has little to do with being a happy, well-centered person, I disagree. Knowing them, and more importantly, managing them though well-chosen garments, means you can stop worrying about how you look and refocus on more important stuff, like personal pursuits, social life, and family.

Finally, women who are expert in secondhand chic know this above all: just because you weren't born into money, don't have a high-paying job, or weren't blessed with trophy good looks *doesn't mean you have to settle for second-best.* Your wardrobe can be as exquisite, as up-to-date, as eye-catching as you choose. And if this gives you the confidence to take on the world in other ways, your accomplishments will go well beyond buying great clothes.

Selected Bibliography

Bartolomeo, Christina. *Cupid & Diana.* New York: Scribner, 1998.

Bloch, Phillip. *Elements of Style: From the Portfolio of Hollywood's Premiere Stylist.* New York: Warner Books, 1998.

Burns, Leslie Davis, and Nancy O. Bryant. *The Business of Fashion: Designing, Manufacturing, Marketing.* New York: Fairchild, 1997.

Farro, Rita. *Life Is Not A Dress Size: Rita Farro's Guide to Attitude, Style, and a New You.* Radnor, Pa.: Chilton, 1996.

Goldsmith, Olivia, and Amy Fine Collins. *Simple Isn't Easy.* New York: HarperPaperbacks, 1995.

Gross, Kim Johnson, Jeff Stone, and Rachel Urquhart. *Chic Simple Women's Wardrobe.* New York: Knopf, 1995.

Halbreich, Betty, Sally Wadyka, and Jeffrey Fulvimari. *Secrets of a Fashion Therapist: What You Can Learn Behind the Dressing Room Door.* New York: HarperCollins, 1998.

Hoff, Al. *Thrift Score.* New York: HarperPerennial, 1997.

Ludwig, Susan, Janice Steinberg, and Barbara Rhodes. *Petite Style: The Ultimate Guide for Women 5'4" and Under.* New York: Plume, 1989.

Mason, Elizabeth. *The Rag Street Journal.* New York: Henry Holt, 1995.

Nanfeldt, Suzan. *Plus Size: The Plus-size Guide to Looking Great.* New York: Plume, 1996.

Schneider, Carolyn. *The Ultimate Consignment & Thrift Store Guide.* Bedminster, N.J.: Consignment & Thrift Store Publishing, 1997.

Schnurnberger, Lynn. *Let There Be Clothes: 40,000 Years of Fashion.* New York: Workman, 1991.

Smith, Pamela. *Vintage Fashions and Fabrics.* Pittsburgh, Pa.: Alliance Publishers, 1995.

Acknowledgments

$\mathcal{T}$his book could not have been written without the aid of former employers—and they know who they are—whose Dickensian wages prompted my earliest ventures into the world of secondhand shopping.

And then there were those who were intentionally helpful. Consignment store owners Myrna Skoller, Veronica Lytle, Karen Ryan, Rita Code, Kevin Raymond, Alessandro Matrati, Odiana Dauman, and Carole Selig all gave generously of their time and insights in the early stages of this project. And to my many Internet correspondents, thanks for responding to rather than deleting the requests for information. Warm thanks are also due to Caramel Kelly, course director of the London College of Fashion, who provided what amounted to a graduate seminar in the technical aspects of the construction of beautiful clothes. Richard Montauk and Clare Linney understood that tip-offs to reference books and professional connections make all the difference between a minute's work and hours. I'm also grateful to Barbara Lorenzo, Kathy Zdunski, and most especially Cindy Winterhalter, friends and fashion experts whose support and advice were invaluable.

Many thanks as well to my agent, Christy Fletcher, for embracing this project with gratifying speed and enthusiasm; likewise to my editor at Pocket, Greer Kessel Hendricks, who, along with her assistant, Kristen Harris, made the long and complicated process of publication a great pleasure. I'm also thankful for the efforts of publicist

Amy Rogers and all the others at Pocket whose behind-the-scenes efforts put books on the shelves. Chloë March, your drawings are a delight, and I'm so glad we were able to collaborate.

To my families in Connecticut and Chicago, I sincerely appreciate your putting up with those long stretches when the door was closed and the laptop on, when I should have been hanging out with you instead. I'm particularly grateful to my sister, Claudia, for demonstrating the patience of a saint (and the feet of a trooper) during all the "just a couple more minutes!" resale expeditions up and down the Boston Post Road.

Above all, loving thanks to Dean, reader and husband extraordinaire, whose unwavering belief and support—and whose admiration for all things chic—make it possible to say so in print.

Index

absorbency, fabric, 30, 35
accessories, 184–205
    color-matching, 186–87
    handbags, 193–96
    hats, 198–201
    information on, 186
    jewelry, 201–05
    price of, 185–86
    resale of, 293
    scarves, 56, 57, 155, 196–98
    See also belts; shoes
acetate, 41, 58, 75, 222
Ackerman, Diane, 51
acrylic, 42–43, 222
Agnès B, 108
Alaïa, 105
alcohol stains, 227
alpaca, 33
alterations, 139–41, 150, 174–75, 176, 181
Alverado, Antonio, 109

Amsterdam, 309
André, Adeline, 101, 104
angora fur, 33
A.P.C., 108
Aquascutum, 107
Armani, 103, 106, 115, 190, 296
auctions, 283, 288, 299
Audermars, George, 40

Baday, Lida, 109
bags, 193–96
Balenciaga, 105
Balmain, Pierre, 99, 104
Barney's New York Collection, 110
Barr, Donna, 181, 270, 285
barter, 278–79
Bartlett, John, 107
Bartolomeo, Christina, 256
Basile, 109
Basler, 109

Beene, Geoffrey, 106, 115
Belgian labels, 109
Bellissimo, Dominic, 109
belt loops, 93, 94
belts, 191 92
    and figure issues, 153–54
    fit, 137, 193
    and proportion, 162
    quality checklist, 79, 192
    storage of, 216
Berardi, Antonio, 107
Bergdorf Goodman Collection, 110
Bertin, Rose, 102
Biagiotti, Laura, 109
bias-cut, 90
Bis, Dorothée, 108
black, wearing, 169
Blahnik, Manolo, 165, 189
Blass, Bill, 106, 114

319